Urban crisis: Culture and the sustainability of cities

Edited by M. Nadarajah and Ann Tomoko Yamamoto

United Nations University Press

TOKYO · NEW YORK · PARIS

The views expressed in this publication are those of the authors and do not necessarily reflect the views of the United Nations University.

United Nations University Press
United Nations University, 53-70, Jingumae 5-chome,
Shibuya-ku, Tokyo 150-8925, Japan
Tel: +81-3-3499-2811   Fax: +81-3-3406-7345
E-mail: sales@hq.unu.edu;   general enquiries: press@hq.unu.edu
www.unu.edu

United Nations University Office at the United Nations, New York
2 United Nations Plaza, Room DC2-2062, New York, NY 10017, USA
Tel: +1-212-963-6387   Fax: +1-212-371-9454
E-mail: unuona@ony.unu.edu

United Nations University Press is the publishing division of the United Nations University.

Cover design by Mea Rhee

Printed in Hong Kong

ISBN 978-92-808-1125-4

Library of Congress Cataloging-in-Publication Data

Urban crisis : culture and the sustainability of cities / edited by M. Nadarajah and Ann Tomoko Yamamoto.
    p.   cm.
  Includes index.
  ISBN 9789280811254 (pbk.)
  1. Urban ecology—Case studies. 2. Urbanization—Environmental aspects—Case studies. 3. Sociology, Urban. I. Nadarajah, M. II. Yamamoto, Ann Tomoko.

HT241.U695   2007
307.76—dc22   2006032567

Contents

List of tables and figures

List of contributors

Sang-Chuel Choe is professor of urban and regional planning in the Graduate School of Environmental Studies, Seoul National University, South Korea. He holds a PhD in urban affairs from the University of Pittsburgh. Formerly he was dean of the Graduate School of Environmental Studies at Seoul National University. He has also served as the president of the Seoul Development Institute, the Korea Section of Regional Science Association, and the Korean Society for Environmental Education. He has contributed many papers for the UN Center for Regional Development, United Nations University, and the East-West Center. His research interests include urban and regional development studies, land-use planning, and urban planning history. His publications include *Seoul: The Making of a Metropolis* (John Wiley, 1997) and *Culture and the City in East Asia* (Oxford University Press, 1997).

Shigekazu Kusune graduated from Kyoto Prefectural University and went on to study at the University of Bonn in Germany. He completed his master's at Osaka University of Foreign Studies Graduate School, Faculty of Foreign Languages. After working as a visiting researcher at the University of Konstantz and a visiting lecturer at Lueneburg University, Germany, he now serves as professor of international communications theory in the Faculty of Law, Kanazawa University. He specializes in international communication theory, mass communication, and comparative culture.

Peter J. Marcotullio is a professor in the Urban Planning Department, Research Center for Advanced Science and Technology (RCAST), University of Tokyo, and a visiting research fellow at the UNU Institute of Advanced Studies in Tokyo. He obtained his master's degree in ecology from the University of Pennsylvania, as well as a master's degree in geography and a PhD in urban planning from Columbia University, New York.

M. Nadarajah, an independent researcher, is based in Kuala Lumpur, Malaysia. He obtained his PhD in sociology from the Jawaharlal Nehru University, New Delhi, in 1995. Before pursuing his PhD he worked as an education officer with a consumer association in Kuala Lumpur. Since 1995 he has worked in a number of areas. He has been a consultant for a project on sustainable development with the Asia Pacific Regional Office of Consumers International, then based in Penang. While associated with this organization and project he was involved in studies on sustainable consumption/ development. He is a committee member in the Philanthropy Initiative of Malaysia and has contributed to a pioneering study on the status of philanthropy in Malaysia, carried out by University Science Malaysia, based in Penang. As part of a team of consultants, in 2002 he contributed to the Consumer Master Plan for the government of Malaysia, which emphasized the critical importance of sustainable consumption. He is presently the secretary/deputy coordinator of the Asian Communication Network, based in St John's University, Bangkok, and is involved in activities to democratize the media in the effort to create a sustainable society.

Awais L. Piracha, formerly a research associate with the Urban and Regional Development Programme at UNU/IAS, received a PhD in environmental planning from the Asian Institute of Technology (AIT) in Bangkok, Thailand. Earlier he received a master's degree in both environmental engineering from the University of New South Wales, Australia, and environmental planning, jointly offered by the University of Dortmund, Germany, and the AIT. Piracha has taught and undertaken research at the King Fahd University of Petroleum and Minerals, Saudi Arabia, and the AIT. He has also served with the National Engineering Service of Pakistan. Piracha is a member of number of professional associations: the Institution of Engineers Australia, the Pakistan Engineering Council, the SPRING Association of Development Planners, Germany, and the International Association of Urban and Regional Planners, Netherlands. His articles have appeared in a number of peer-reviewed journals. His research focuses on the analysis and solution of environmental problems faced by Asian cities and regions. The specific areas of his research interests include urban ecosystems, the role of culture and technology in sustainability, computer applications in environmental planning, and environmental planning and management for regions and cities in Asia.

Ratna S. J. B. Rana was previously a professor at the Center for Economic Development and Administration (CEDA), Tribhuvan University, Nepal. In 1969 he received his PhD in a multidisciplinary programme based in the Geography Department, University of Pittsburgh, USA. His education in the USA also included some time at the East-West Center, University of Hawaii. Professor Rana has held several important positions in Nepal. He was first deputy director and later director of CEDA, before becoming a full professor at Tribhuvan University in 1975. He has served the government of Nepal as member and vice-chair of the National Planning Commission. He was responsible for formulating the Sixth National Plan and the 1981 Population Census of Nepal. He is also the founding vice-chancellor of the Royal Nepal Academy of Science and Technology as well as being the founding chair of several other national bodies, including the National Council for Science and Technology and the National Committee for Man and the Biosphere. Professor Rana also has extensive international experience. He is the founding chair of the International Centre for Integrated Mountain Development and has served on the board of several international organizations, including the Asian Institute of Technology, Thailand, and the East-West Center Association.

Masayuki Sasaki is professor of urban and regional economy at Ritsumeikan University and Kyoto. He graduated from Kyoto University and obtained his doctorate in economics from the Graduate School, Kyoto University. He worked as a professor at Kanazawa University for 15 years. He joined the Ritsumeikan University and Kyoto University in 2000. He has published extensively.

Sudarshan Raj Tiwari obtained his master's in architecture at the University of Hawaii, USA, in 1977 and his PhD at Tribhuvan University, Nepal, in 1996. After working as an assistant architect at the Department of Housing and Physical Planning, Ministry of Works, Government of Nepal, he now serves as a professor at the Institute of Engineering at Tribhuvan University. He is also a member of the Nepal Engineers' Association, a life member of the Nepal Heritage Society, and a member of the Society of Nepalese Architects.

Ann Tomoko Yamamoto is a PhD candidate in the urban engineering department at the University of Tokyo, where she is writing her dissertation on local government cultural administration and policy in Japan. She holds a master's degree in urban planning from Columbia University. Her professional experience includes television and film production and producing art exhibitions and other culture-related projects, and her primary interest is utilizing culture toward community development.

Preface

The UNU-IAS has undertaken research on cities as part of the Institute's commitment to generating policy solutions to the most pressing global issues. The Institute's urban programme has taken a cross-disciplinary approach in addressing how information technology and globalized economies are transforming the dynamics of cities. Research has conceptualized urban issues both in terms of an international city system and within localized contexts. This present study expands upon the UNU-IAS's extensive work on the role of environmental issues in sustainability and urban development, tackling the broad theoretical issues of culture and sustainability and also contributing to our understanding of how these concepts operate within local settings.

Both culture and sustainable development are potentially powerful responses to the negative impacts of globalization, as they challenge us to create modes of living that consider the intergenerational consequences of our actions. Culture is the trickier and more slippery concept, and one of the primary aims of this study is to help forge a tool that can be useful in implementing sustainable development at the local level. This volume explores cultural indicators as a means for achieving the sustainable development goals laid out in Local Agenda 21 at the 1992 Earth Summit in Rio de Janeiro. The case studies also provide valuable clues to the many ways that local institutions use culture to mediate between present and future generations through such diverse forms as local policy, festivals, or networks of non-governmental organizations.

Three international conferences on "Culture in Sustainability of Cities" held in Kanazawa, Japan, and Cheongju, Korea, form the basis of this book. The deliberations during these conferences, the intense side-arguments and discussions of experienced persons coming from many disciplines and cultures, and the post-conference meetings have all gone into writing/editing this book. This volume serves as a collection of ideas, or actually starting points, for a cultural theory of sustainable urbanization. The aim is to engage the reader through the ideas articulated within, and foster debate and serve as a catalyst for further exploration. If, in the end, the importance of culture in the sustainability of cities as conceived in this volume is drawn into one's thoughts and work in some form or the another, an important aim of the book will have been met.

I would like to take this opportunity to thank all of the contributors to this volume. While engaged with their own busy schedules they have made significant contributions. I would also like to give special thanks to Professor Ratna Rana, who guided this project in his capacity as director of the Ishikawa International Cooperation Research Centre (IICRC), and UNU-IAS research fellow Peter Marcotullio, who made critical and substantial contributions to every phase of this project. Needless to say, a project of this scope is a collaborative effort reflecting the efforts and goodwill of numerous individuals and organizations, and it is my greatest hope that everyone involved can share in the satisfaction of seeing this volume through to publication.

A. H. Zakri
Director
UNU-IAS

List of acronyms

ADB	Asian Development Bank
CAGIN	Canada-ASEAN Governance Innovations Network Program
CAP	Consumers Association of Penang
CBO	citizen body organization
CCN	Cultural Cities' Network
CHT	cultural heritage tourism
CIDA	Canadian International Development Agency
CSD	UN Commission on Sustainable Development
DEP	Department of Statistical and Prospective Studies (France)
DSR	driving-force-state response
EMR	extended metropolitan region
EU	European Union
FAR	floor area ratio
GNP	gross national product
GUO	Global Urban Observatory programme
HABITAT	UN Centre for Human Settlements
HDI	Human Development Index
ICCROM	International Centre for the Study of the Preservation and Restoration of Cultural Property
ICOMOS	International Council on Monuments and Sites
IICRC	Ishikawa International Cooperation Research Centre (Japan)
ILO	International Labour Organization
IMT-GT	Indonesia-Malaysia-Thailand Growth Triangle
IOG	Institute on Governance (Canada)
ITIP	integrated neighbourhood (*toles*) improvement programme (Nepal)

xiv

IUCN	International Union for Conservation of Nature (World Conservation Union)
KR	Kanazawa Resolutions
LEG	Leadership Group on Cultural Statistics of the European Union
MCA	Malaysian Chinese Association
MIC	Malaysian Indian Congress
NGO	non-governmental organization
NIE	newly industrialized economy
NPO	non-profit organization
PCDP	Patan Conservation and Development Program
PHT	Penang Heritage Trust
PPCK	Patan, Penang, Cheongju, and Kanazawa
PSDP	Penang Strategic Development Plan
PSR	pressure-state response
PTDO	Patan Tourism Development Organization
RCA	Rent Control Act (Malaysia)
SAM	Sahabat Alam Malaysia (Friends of the Earth Malaysia)
SCP	UNCHS Sustainable Cities Programme
SERI	Socio-economic and Environmental Research Institute (Malaysia)
SILA	Sustainable Independent Living and Access (Malaysia)
SMR	Seoul metropolitan region (Korea)
SOS	Save Our Selves (Malaysia)
SPI	Sustainable Penang Initiative
STEP	Sustainable Transport Environment Penang
TDR	transfer of development rights
TUGI	UNDP Urban Governance Initiative
TWN	Third World Network
UNCED	UN Conference on Environment and Development
UNCHS	UN Centre for Human Settlements
UNDP	UN Development Programme
UNEP	UN Environment Programme
UNESCAP	UN Economic and Social Commission for Asia and the Pacific
UNESCO	UN Economic, Social, and Cultural Organization
UNICEF	UN Children's Fund
UNMO	United Malay National Organization
UNRISD	UN Research Institute for Social Development
UNU-IAS	United Nations University Institute of Advanced Studies
USM	Universiti Sains Malaysia
WCCD	World Commission on Culture and Development
WCED	World Commission on Environment and Development
WHO	World Health Organization
WMF	World Monuments Fund
WWP	WaterWatch Penang

Part I

Culture in sustainability of cities I

1

Introduction

M. Nadarajah and Ann Tomoko Yamamoto

Our world is becoming more urbanized, and as the World Summit on Sustainable Development underscored, we must make sure that this urbanization is sustainable. Indeed, the success of our collective efforts for economic growth, social justice, biodiversity and climate protection depends in large measure on how well we protect and manage our urban environments.[1]

This volume is an enquiry into the nature of urbanization in general and Asian urbanization in particular, not so much to philosophize as to align its course in the direction set by the global agenda of sustainable development, as articulated by the United Nations and observed by Kofi Annan above. It is an effort to make deeper sense of the growing urban crisis in Asia and to address it comprehensively. The effort is animated by the complex vision of a sustainable city, which compellingly proposes a future in which the urban problems confronting us today can be effectively overcome. It is the aim here to explore this complex vision from the perspective of (local) culture, transcending both the economic and environmental viewpoints that dominate popular constructs of sustainability. This volume seeks to build a plausible "narrative order" which captures conceptual schemes, case studies, community participation, and cultural indicators that contribute to and shape a cultural theory of the sustainable city, moving beyond purely techno-economic (or techno-scientific), market-driven urbanization strategies based on Euclidian planning and top-down decision-making.

Table 1.1 Mega-cities and population, in millions

1950		2000		2015	
1. New York, USA	12.3	1. Tokyo, Japan	26.4	1. Tokyo, Japan	26.4
2. London, England	8.7	2. Mexico City, Mexico	18.4	2. Bombay, India	26.1
3. Tokyo, Japan	6.9	3. Bombay, India	18.0	3. Lagos, Nigeria	23.2
4. Paris, France	5.4	4. São Paulo, Brazil	17.8	4. Dhaka, Bangladesh	21.1
5. Moscow, Russia	5.4	5. New York, USA	16.6	5. São Paulo, Brazil	20.4
6. Shanghai, China	5.3	6. Lagos, Nigeria	13.4	6. Karachi, Pakistan	19.2
7. Essen, Germany	5.3	7. Los Angeles, USA	13.1	7. Mexico City, Mexico	19.2
8. Buenos Aires, Argentina	5.0	8. Calcutta, India	12.9	8. New York, USA	17.4
9. Chicago, USA	4.9	9. Shanghai, China	12.9	9. Jakarta, Indonesia	17.3
10. Calcutta, India	4.4	10. Buenos Aires, Argentina	12.6	10. Calcutta, India	17.3

Source: Population Reference Bureau, 2005

Urbanizing Asia

The World Bank predicts that over "the next three decades the urban population of developing countries will grow (from natural increase, migration, and reclassification of rural areas) by 60 million people a year".[2] This transformation is fuelled by urban growth in the Asia-Pacific region, which included only eight cities of more than 5 million inhabitants in 1970; today there are more than 30. In 1990 the population of Asia's cities totalled 1 billion; by 2020 the urban population of Asia will have more than doubled to nearly 2.5 billion, about half of the total population. More than half the urban areas of the planet will by then be located in Asia, and they will hold more than a third of the world's population.[3]

A large number of these urban areas will become mega-cities – a city with more than 10 million inhabitants. Mega-cities within Asia include Tokyo, Osaka, Seoul, Beijing, Tianjin, Shanghai, Jakarta, Calcutta, and Bombay (Table 1.1[4]), and projections predict their ranks will be joined by Lahore, New Delhi, Karachi, Dhaka, Manila, Bangkok, and Hyderabad by 2015.[5] It is clear that the twenty-first century is witnessing the birth of an urban Asia that is more complete and comprehensive (Figure 1.1[6]).

Though similar in many respects to urbanization in general, there are some distinctive features that mark urbanizing Asia.
- *Immense urban growth.* The sheer size of urban populations forces governments to cope with tremendous growth in a very short period of

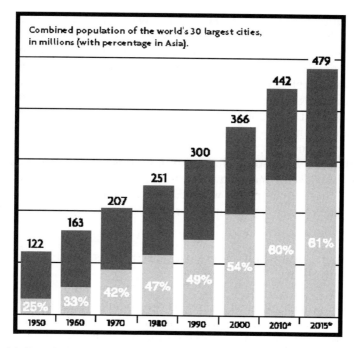

Figure 1.1 Populations of world's 30 largest cities, in millions and with percentage in Asia (*Source:* UNESCO, 2002)

time. The urban populations of both China and India, for example, will grow by more than 340 million by 2030, creating tremendous challenges in the provision of infrastructure, environmental management, and employment. Even a small country such as Laos (5.3 million inhabitants in 2000), one of the poorest countries in the world, will add 3.2 million to its urban population while moving to a level of only 43 per cent urbanization in 2030. This will account for more than 60 per cent of the country's total population growth in that period. Given its very low national income and the continuing high proportion of people in rural areas, it will be very difficult to give strategic priority to urban development, even in the capital city of Vientiane.

- *The prominence of mega-cities.* By 2015, 16 of the world's 24 mega-cities (cities with more than 10 million people) will be located in Asia. While most urban residents in both Asia and elsewhere will continue to live in smaller towns and cities, the urban hierarchy of Asia will be dominated by the emergence of these larger cities. Urban development will often stretch in corridors between the main city core and secondary cities, much like the megalopolises of the eastern USA.

• *Uneven globalization.* For the past two decades Asia has surpassed the rest of the less-developed world in terms of integration into the global economy, creating greater opportunities for urban development. This development has proceeded unevenly, however, and a two-tier urban system is likely to emerge in Asia as a result. Some urban areas will be increasingly integrated into the global economy and become more international in character. These cities – such as Seoul, Singapore, Taipei, and Shanghai – will have to manage the challenges and opportunities that come with rapid economic growth and change. On the other hand, there will also be cities with more domestically oriented economies that develop more slowly, such as Dhaka, Phnom Penh, and Vientiane. These urban places will face greater challenges in terms of poverty and creating opportunities for economic growth.[7]

Urbanization and city formation: Features, issues, and unsustainability

While the growth of urban centres has given millions of people access to what we call "progress", social, demographic, economic, and political problems result when cities "become too big to be socially manageable and when such large cities distort the development of the surrounding countryside or even the whole society itself by drawing to themselves resources that are needed for more balanced growth nationwide".[8] As argued by Ernest Callenbach, this situation can be attributed to the rules of market-driven society: on waste – goods are cheap and disposable; on costs – trust the market, everything has its monetary price; on population – go forth and multiply; on energy – always do the cheapest thing, no matter what the consequences; on happiness – focus on accumulating material possessions; on relationships with other species – only humans matter; and on the future – let the future worry about the future.[9] Such rules guiding people's behaviour have led to a number of systemic problems.

John Clammer groups urban problems into 14 categories: extent, speed, and intensity of world urbanization; primate cities and their effects; rural depopulation and effects on hinterlands; poverty and labour issues, including problems of women and children; urban lifestyles and economy; physical infrastructure, such as roads, schools, health, water, power, and sewage; housing; pollution; land use and values; crime; stress and psychological problems; ethnic conflict; inequality and class issues; and social patterns and family instability.[10] While some of these problems are specific to cities in either the developed or developing world, there is also a "convergence" – "declining infrastructure, deteriorating urban environment, growing unemployment, fraying social cohesion, and institutional weakness".[11] These issues have led to critical challenges to the sustainability of urban growth.

Imagining sustainable urbanization

The questions raised by urban growth are simple. Will cities be able to provide a suitable environment for the present and future human generations[12] to satisfy their basic, social, and cultural needs in a sustained manner across "earth time"[13]? Will natural resources be available and equitably distributed to achieve equity and equality across groups, space, and time?[14] Will goods and services be adequately mobilized to provide for the high population concentration in the population giants? Will a vibrant, enabling local culture, which is actively engaged with globalization, be available to offer the inhabitants a distinct cultural identity,[15] the basis for creativity and for developing the tools for cultural survival?

Such concerns have resulted in the transformation of discussion on urbanization to discussion on sustainable urbanization. While a more elaborate and useful discussion on the notion and history of the concept of sustainable development is presented by Rana and Piracha in Chapter 2, here we will pay attention to some key concerns of sustainable urbanization.[16]

- *Limits to urbanization.* Are there limits to urbanization? Will the complexity of the urban phenomena and the ensuing problems outweigh the initial advantages of sheer size? If our future is increasingly and inevitably urban, where do we and future generations live if cities become both physically and psychologically unhealthy places? What does this mean for planning?
- *Endangering local culture and heritage.* Urbanization has been a major threat to local and distinct cultures. Both material and non-material heritages are in danger of oblivion. Globalization and commercialization/commodification driven by hegemonic pressures of the global market move forward in the absence of community deliberation and endogenously agreed-upon cultural transformation. A loss of distinct urban culture is a loss of "place identity" and "people identity". It confines culture to passivity and adaptation and puts into jeopardy the heart of culture, i.e. creativity and dynamic and active transformation.
- *Urban planning.* Solutions proposed by urban planners often exacerbate existing problems, and almost all Asian cities are testament to this situation. This reality of governance points to a fundamental question in politics and decision-making: should urban planning be expert-

directed and top-down, or decentralized, bottom-up, and directed by people in the community? When critical decision-making processes are globalized, how does one deal with and protect local path(s) of development? How can urban planning address the problems of sheer size, provision of goods and services, and loss of culture, location, and identity when sustaining urban population growth?

While this volume is sensitive to these problems and issues, it directly focuses on the second aspect and seeks to explore the role of culture in the sustainability of cities, thus going against the current of studies on urbanization and cities and their planning. The focus is not exclusively on cultural sustainability but also ecological,[17] economic,[18] and political sustainability, as these aspects are essential to achieving a "sustainable cultural city".[19] Exploring culture (and its core, creativity) in the context of urbanization and city formation is a critical step towards creating both sustainable cultural cities and a sustainable urban future.

Studies on city, culture, and planning

While there are a growing number of works on sustainability and Asian cities, studies tend to approach sustainability from an economic point of view. In this discourse, culture has no value if it makes no economic contribution. While there are studies on culture in an urban context, including those representing postmodern concerns, it is important to note here that a serious, sustained consideration of culture in sustainability of cities is almost entirely absent.

An overview of selected studies illustrates this situation. *Five Cities: Modelling Asian Urban Population-Environment Dynamics*[20] covers Faisalabad (Pakistan), Khon Kaen (Thailand), Cebu City (the Philippines), Pusan (South Korea), and Kobe (Japan), asking two basic questions: how do population and environmental conditions interact in specific urban areas; and how does that dynamic interaction produce a distinctive quality of life? The study is built on a simple model of population-environment dynamics. The four sectors of water, air, energy, and land use, which represent the environment, and three institutional sectors – production, transportation, and social services – interact to produce a "quality of life" in urban Asia. While attention to culture comes with the observation that the specific outcome of quality of life is affected by the social-political-economic-cultural system that governs the city, it is a secondary concern. *Culture and the City in East Asia* examines national capitals in late-industrializing countries, defending themselves against Western capitalism while trying to catch up with it.[21] *Theorizing the Southeast Asian City as Text* looks at "the way in which culture, ethnicity, languages, traditions, governance, policies and histories interplay in the creation of the urban experiences", and while culture is dealt with in all its complexity, sustainable urbanization is neglected.[22] Similarly, Clammer's classification outlined in the above section neglects the continued destruction or threat of destruction of local, distinctive material and non-material cultures, communities, and heritage of a city.[23] Major textbooks on the sociology and social geography of contemporary Asian cities are also insensitive to culture in sustainable development, and are dominated by four main issues: migration and its effects; the informal sector and its ramifications; cities, the state, and the new international division of labour; and the impact of structural adjustment policies of such agencies as the World Bank, International Monetary Fund, and Asian Development Bank. There is a dearth of studies and writing that articulate a cultural theory of a sustainable city in which (local) culture becomes a value of its own, not something merely seen as opposite to globalization and responding it, or something of economic value, or treated as postmodern reading of a text.

While the mainstream academic community has been developing its discourse on sustainable urbanization, culture, and cities, a different and alternative gathering of (Asian) NGOs, academics, and local authorities have been developing their own understanding and perspectives of the same. Three such efforts particularly relevant to this volume are the Yokohama Statement on Urban Cultural Individuality,[24] Our Cities, Our Homes: The People's Agenda,[25] and Architecture: Future in Cities Declaration of Calcutta.[26] These three declarations offer a sustainable view of urbanization and city, and recognize the importance of (local) culture as well other issues that are of little concern in the mainstream, more often than not academic, discussion, such as gender or disability issues in urban/city areas.

The Kanazawa Initiative

The Kanazawa Initiative goes a step further in fully exploring a cultural theory of sustainable urbanization through culture, creativity, and sustainable governance. This three-year project was developed and managed from 2000 to 2002 by the Ishikawa International Cooperation and Research Centre (IICRC), based in Kanazawa, Ishikawa prefecture, Japan, in collaboration with the United Nations University Institute of Advanced Studies (UNU-IAS), based in Tokyo. The initiative focuses on *culture in sustainability of cities*, and was developed in three international conferences, the first two in Kanazawa and the last in Cheongju, Korea. The first conference focused on the cultural framework, and the second conference held in late 2000 focused on the creativity and adaptability of culture and presented case studies of Patan (Nepal), Penang

(Malaysia), Cheongju (Korea), and Kanazawa (Japan). The last conference in 2001 addressed the creation of cultural indicators as a critical tool to identify, record, and promote aspects of (local) culture in sustainability of cities.

About the content of this book

Chapter 2 on "Cultural frameworks" addresses the primary focus of the First International Conference on Culture in Sustainability of Cities, namely articulating a framework for understanding the role of culture in the sustainability of cities. The authors give a comprehensive background to sustainable development, sustainable urbanization, and cultural issues. The next chapter, "Voices I", includes portions of papers presented at the first conference.

Chapters 5–9 cover the four case studies. The case study on Kanazawa, Japan, is concerned with a culturally sensitive *new production model*. The case study on Cheongju, Korea, explores the importance of creating and sustaining *a distinctive cultural identity*. The case study from South Asia, based in Patan, Nepal, explores the theme in terms of culture's *internal transformation*. The case study of Penang, Malaysia, examines the various "discourses on sustainability" and attempts to capture the growing importance of *multiculturalism and localism*. The case studies present four approaches to modes of engagement with culture, enlisting culture in the broader effort for sustainable urbanization.

Chapter 11 focuses on cultural indicators, the theme of the third conference held in the historical-cultural city of Cheongju, Korea. This chapter covers the need to examine cultural indicators in order to assist cities to incorporate cultural aspects into overall and urban sectoral development policies and strategies. This chapter is followed by another entitled "Voices II", which as before includes critical portions of papers that provide a more comprehensive and in-depth understanding of cultural indicators. The concluding chapter reconsiders the major themes of the Kanazawa Initiative, opening theoretical and empirical areas that need further enquiry and research, and ends with a proposal for the promotion of an intellectual enterprise with policy and practical implications in the form of a "Kanazawa School of Sustainable Urbanization".

Conclusion

This book takes a stand on the central importance of culture in achieving sustainability of cities. This is not just a scientific endeavour but also a political one, consistent with the global recognition of the critical importance of sustainable cities, sustainable urbanization, and (local) cultures. As a minimum, it is hoped that this volume provides some approaches to responding to the Asian urban crisis by further consolidation and strengthening of the movement for culturally oriented sustainable urbanization and gives some starting points for initiating discussions and debates on an alternative urban theory and future: a "cultural theory of sustainable urbanization" and an achievable sustainable cultural city. The maximum is of course the development of a coherent cultural theory of sustainable urbanization that can influence university curricula and the action strategies of civil society organizations and policy-makers.

Notes

1. Opening lines of Kofi Annan's message to the Global Meeting of the Sustainable Cities Programme and the Localising Agenda 21, Havana, Cuba, July 2005.
2. World Bank. 2003. *World Development Report 2003: Sustainable Development in a Dynamic World*. New York: Oxford University Press/World Bank, p. 108.
3. UNESCO. 2002. *Cities of Asia*, available at http://whc.unesco.org/events/asiaciti.htm.
4. Population Reference Bureau. 2005. *Human Population: Fundamentals of Growth Patterns of World Population*, available at www.prb.org/Content/NavigationMenu/PRB/ Educators/Human_Population/Urbanization2/Patterns_of_World_Urbanization1.htm.
5. Roberts, Brian. 1999. "Urban management in Asia: Issues, priorities and opportunities", paper presented at Asia Pacific Summit, Brisbane, 28 February–3 March, available at http://hds.canberra.edu.au/cities/policy.html.
6. UNESCO, note 3 above.
7. McGee, Terry. 2005. "Urbanisation takes on new dimensions in Asia's population giants", available at www.prb.org/Template.cfm?Section=PRB&template=/ ContentManagement/ContentDisplay.cfm&ContentID=3931.
8. Clammer, John. 1996. *Values and Development in Southeast Asia*. Kelana Jaya, Malaysia: Pelanduk Publications, p. 139.
9. Callenbach, Ernest. 1999. "Ecological 'rules' of a sustainable society", in Takashi Inoguchi, Edward Newman, and Glen Paoletto (eds) *Cities and the Environment: New Approaches for Eco-Societies*. Tokyo: United Nations University Press, pp. 19–22.
10. Clammer, note 8 above, p. 140.
11. Cohen, Michael. 1997. "Convergence, marginalisation and inequality: Directions for the urban future", in Ismail Serageldin (ed.) *The Architecture of Empowerment: People, Shelter and Livable Cities*. London: Academy Editions, pp. 38–39. Cohen also observes that there is today a convergence of "resurgent localism", a theme which is articulated in this volume.
12. Inherent in the notion of sustainability is a temporal order linking the future to the present and the past. This has been addressed by Sudarshan Raj Tiwari in the present volume.
13. The duration the planet Earth survives before it is destroyed by natural causes over which humanity has no control.
14. Consider the city of Tokyo, which may have resolved its density problem. Its ecological footprint is way beyond any notion of sustainability: "This means that for sustainable

living, the people in Tokyo alone need an area of 45,220,000 ha – which is 1.2 times the land area of the whole of Japan. If mountains and other regions are discarded and only habitable land is included, then this becomes 3.6 times the land area of Japan." See *Ecological Footprint of Tokyo*, available at www.gdrc.org/uem/observatory/jp-tokyo.html, June 2005.

15. A good exploration of these realities is found in Oncu, Ayse and Petra Weyland (eds). 1997. *Space, Culture and Power: New Identities in Globalising Cities.* London and New Jersey: Zed Books.

16. Based on a discussion in Clammer, note 8 above, pp. 155–156.

17. Used interchangeably with "environmental sustainability".

18. See King, Ross. 1999. "Sustainable urban design", in A. F. Foo and Belinda Yuen (eds) *Sustainable Cities in the 21st Century.* Singapore: NUS, pp. 82–84.

19. This is also something that came out strongly during a post-conference meeting after the First International Conference on Culture in Sustainability of Cities in Kanazawa, 18–19 January 2000. This meeting was attended by a small team of those who participated in the first conference, organizers, and those involved in the case studies. It was clear at this meeting that sustainable development went beyond mere concern for the environment to concern for the social context that makes possible environmental/ecological sustainability.

20. Ness, Gayl D. and Michael M. Low (eds). 2000. *Five Cities: Modelling Asian Urban Population-Environment Dynamics.* Singapore: Oxford University Press.

21. Won, Bae Kin, Mike Douglass, Sang-Chuel Choe, and Kong Chon On. 1997. *Culture and the City in East Asia.* New York: Oxford University Press. Reviewed by Richard Child Hill. 2002. *Journal of Asian Studies*, February.

22. Goh, Robbie B. H. and Brenda S. A. Yeoh (eds). 2003. *Theorizing the Southeast Asian City as Text.* Singapore: WSPC, available at www.wspc.com.sg/books/eastasianstudies/5205.html.

23. Clammer, note 8 above, p. 150.

24. Sofjan, Sri Husnaini and Eugene Raj Arokiasamy (compilers). 2000. *Our Cities, Our Homes: A to Z Guide on Human Settlement Issues.* Penang and Kuala Lumpur: Southbound and Asia Pacific, pp. 168–169.

25. *Our Cities, Our Homes.* "Meeting at the Asia Pacific Regional NGO Consultation on *Our Cities, Our Homes* held in Kuantan, Malaysia in April 1995 as members of citizen organizations and networks – representing a diverse range of interests including the environment, health, media and communications, youth, children, women's development, housing, consumers, human rights, and development – we find that we share a common vision of a world of socially just, ecologically sustainable, politically participatory, economically productive, and culturally vibrant communities in which all people, women and men, people with disabilities, children, youth, adults, and the elderly live productive lives and prosper in peace and harmony. During the consultation, we have affirmed our shared commitment, forged new friendships and alliances, and built an agenda towards the realization of our vision." Available at www.southbound.org.sg/2000/2000ch1.htm, August 2002.

26. Sofjan and Arokiasamy, note 24 above, pp. 166–167. The declaration is the result of the International Workshop on Architecture and the Futures in Cities, Calcutta, 17–19 November 1995, organized by the Centre for Built Environment, Calcutta.

2

Cultural frameworks

Ratna S. J. B. Rana and Awais L. Piracha

Introduction

Every epoch seems to be characterized by a world view of what is good and desirable for society, and the present pursuit of development, and more recently sustainable development, reflects this world view. Consequently, despite the vast expansion in the world's capacity to produce material goods and services over the past two centuries, further expansion of this capacity within a sustainable development framework remains an urgent imperative today. Yet the terms "sustainable development" and "sustainability" seem to have become so hackneyed that they have often been a source of confusion. Daly observes that the notion of sustainable development continues to be used for pursuing economic growth, and criticizes its "growth ideology". He argues that the present levels of per capita resource consumption in the USA and Western Europe, generally accepted as being developed nations, cannot be followed by all nations without destroying the ecological sources on which economic activities depend. He has argued that the concept of sustainable development is being used in ways that are vacuous, wrong, and probably dangerous.[1]

Emergence of a sustainable development paradigm

What development implies

While "development" can be loosely defined as improving people's lives in some "definite" way, it is not merely increasing production and con-

13

sumption levels. In the final analysis, it may be said to involve building mutually supportive human relations to uplift all humanity, not just a select few.[2] In short, it is increasing the capabilities of people to lead the sorts of life they desire.[3]

Considering that development involves the continuous improvement of the human condition, can a continuous process like this be anything other than sustained and sustainable – even as we should be careful not to confuse sustainability with continuity? If so, why use this superficial adjective at all? It seems that this is not necessarily due to the strength of the concept, but rather the ease with which all things can be encompassed by "sustainable development".

Early industrialization pattern

The term "sustainable" entered the development lexicon after industrialized countries became more aware of the environmental consequences of development, which had been conceived of narrowly as economic growth. This paradigm is the product of the experiences of the industrialized countries in the West with a voracious appetite for natural resources. In the course of tremendous economic growth over the years, these countries remained blissfully unconcerned with the dynamic relations between natural resources, production, and consumption and, more generally, living organisms and their habitat and the impact of "development" on these relationships.

The optimism of capitalistic growth obscured the issues of equity in general and of intergenerational equity in particular – an equity of critical importance to sustainability and continuity. Thus, policy interventions were seen as unnecessary, and the adverse environmental effects were the logical conclusion of the economic regime and associated values they subscribed to.

Former colonizers (or neo-colonizers) had the benefit of accessing vast resources at a price that suited them, obscuring the issue of environmental damage for a long time. Development of the New World in North America followed a similar approach to resources. As colonies and other underdeveloped countries were neither free nor able to use their natural resources to develop their own economies, the present industrialized countries were able to use these resources in a most disproportionate manner. They were insensitive to the enormous exploitation central to their relationship with the colonized world and the environmental damage both there and in their own countries.

Dawning of awareness

Perceptions of the environment started to change from the early 1970s with the growing literature on population growth and regard to environmental degradation. *The Limits to Growth*, sponsored by the Club of Rome in 1972,[4] suddenly told world leaders that ecological disaster was imminent if steps were not taken to contain population growth and check the growth of industrial production. The report's basic premise was that infinite growth based on the use of finite resources was not possible. Schumacher's *Small is Beautiful*, published in 1973, was another important book espousing many of the same ideas.[5]

Although the degree of pessimism was unwarranted, *The Limits to Growth* drew wide attention to the environment and unfolded a paradoxical condition affecting developing countries. In the process of trying to accelerate development through rapid industrialization, developing countries also contributed to overexploitation of natural resources and environmental degradation, although this was mostly said to be due to their fight against poverty.

Environmental concerns go global

Concern for the environment first emerged as a critical global issue in the UN Conference on Human Environment in Stockholm in 1972. Barbara Ward and Rene Dubos's book *Only One Earth*, written for the conference, reflects the growing global concern for the environment and its relationship with development.[6] Subsequently, the UN Environment Programme (UNEP) was established in Nairobi, Kenya, with the mission "to provide leadership and encourage partnership in caring for the environment by inspiring, informing and enabling nations and peoples to improve their quality of life without compromising that of future generations".[7]

As environmental degradation worsened even as awareness was growing, UNEP established the World Commission on Environment and Development, headed by Gro Harlem Brundtland, the former prime minister of Norway.[8] The Brundtland Commission was asked to formulate a "global agenda for change" proposing realistic solutions to critical environmental and development issues.

The commission's report, *Our Common Future*, published in April 1987,[9] significantly begins with a view of the earth as finite space. *The Limits to Growth* was apparently the paradigm of this vision, and "sustainable development" was proposed to solve the problems of environment and development. It was defined as "development that meets the needs of the present without compromising the ability of the future generations to meet their own needs". The term "sustainable development" has since emerged as a key concept in development literature and policy initiatives.[10]

The importance of the concept was highlighted at the 1992 UN Conference on Environment and Development (UNCED, also called the Earth

Summit) in Rio de Janeiro, which issued the Rio Accord, known as Agenda 21, an action plan for sustainable development. The UN Commission on Sustainable Development (CSD) was then created to ensure effective follow-up and implementation of the Rio Accord.

Basic characteristics of the sustainable development paradigm

Sustainable development has been heavily debated[11] and has many meanings associated with it.[12] The concept's multidimensionality makes it appealing to virtually all groups interested in development and the environment, and in practice it serves as a kind of guiding principle to almost all international development establishments. Its appeal arises because it seeks to build bridges between environmentalists and proponents of economic growth, and offers comforting assurance that the drive towards well-being and economic security is not being brought to heel by ecological collapse. In industrialized countries, where people may be afraid of losing their standard of living due to ecological disaster, sustainable development also comes across as capable of preserving what has been achieved in a lasting way.[13]

Much literature, especially from the North, focuses on how present environmental constraints might be overcome and the standard of living maintained.[14] Some have even argued that the whole notion of "sustainability" is simply the ideological fiction of industrial society – sparing it from potential ecological disaster and sustaining the privileges of the rich and the powerful.[15] The assertion that the notion of sustainability is purely ideological and fictional and therefore not real is debatable. Resource depletion and the dangers of unresolved inequitable distribution are genuine fears underpinning the need for sustainability, and the pursuit of sustainable development should be a concern of industrialized and developing countries alike.

While it is generally accepted that sustainable development implies a better integration of economic, environmental, and social goals, there are widely differing views on how to "meet the needs of the present without compromising the ability of the future generations to meet their own needs".[16] Several major elements which are useful in defining the term are briefly described below.

View of the environment

This view stresses the continued functioning of the ecosystem as essential to sustaining the survival of human beings and other species. Two components are ecosystem degradation, seen as a major cause of the current development crisis, and ecosystem protection, viewed as an integral part of the development process. The basic idea is that the magnitude of environmental damage suffered can itself cause major harm to development, and this is strongly reflected in the Brundtland Report. The impact of development on the environment and the need to safeguard it remain at the heart of the sustainable development debate. This also means a critical role for non-environmental factors.

Limits of the planet

Clearly, the earth is a finite space with finite resources, leading to the concept of "limit" as a variable. Nature as a resource has led economists to introduce the notion of weak and strong sustainability concepts, referring to the degree that natural resources can be replaced with other resources in the face of growing populations and human impacts.[17] "Weak" sustainability assumes natural resources can be substituted. In contrast, sustainability is "stronger" in, for example, a good natural heritage site, where natural resources are preserved without allowing substitution.

Multisectoral dimension

Sustainable development is essentially a multidimensional concept involving complex interactions and trade-offs with economic, technological, environmental, political, and social aspects. Economic aspects focus on resource use that preserves productive capacity while equitably meeting present and future "needs". Social aspects include equity considerations, employment, and adjusting to demographic changes.[18] Even when the term is applied to the social dimension, it is still often used in an ecological sense to focus on maintaining the stability of biological and physical systems, thus preserving access to a healthy environment.

Technology as key

Technology is viewed as a major instrument for implementing sustainable development and reducing the pressure of human activity on the environment. Some argue that sustainability rests on whether human ingenuity can find new technologies so as not to consume natural resources more rapidly than they can be replaced. Eco-efficiency – the environmental impact per unit of consumption – is a concept that provides a convenient common denominator to designate the improvements expected from technologies. But caution is needed in considering whether a particular technology relates well to local needs and conditions.

Concern for equity

Equitable pursuit of the developmental and environmental needs of present and future generations implies the objectives of fairness and alleviation of poverty intra- and intergenerationally. Sustainability can be viewed as leaving behind for future generations as many opportunities as we ourselves have had, if not more. This aspect is fundamental for broad acceptance of the concept of sustainable development beyond the realm of nature conservation. While the idea of intergenerational equity may seem novel, the perpetuation of peoples and the objective of steady or growing prosperity are part of ancient and modern traditions alike. Intergenerational equity is important because of the magnitude and fast pace of the changes that mankind has experienced and produced.

Long-term perspective

Sustainable development draws attention to the long-term perspective alongside short-term intra- and intergenerational equity considerations. In other words, it moves away from exclusively economic considerations towards broader social and environmental concerns. Thus, present and future needs are integrated into development considerations within this framework. The planning of time-frames for sustainable development cannot be established from a traditional point of view.[19]

Global approach and partnership at all levels

Sustainable development issues such as climate change, desertification, and ocean pollution are global in nature and must be addressed with a common consensus among all countries, particularly between the North and the South.

In addition, the pursuit of sustainable development calls for the involvement of public and private sectors, including business, introducing the notion of stakeholders' responsibility. Environmental issues can be best handled with the participation of concerned citizens and social groups at the relevant levels, because they are also the stakeholders. Such an approach will also be needed because of the growing strength of the private sector, NGOs, and citizens' groups.

Sustainable development indicators

As sustainable development is a broad, multidimensional concept, it is not easy to operationalize it in terms of a single model. It is not only an objective to pursue but also, in some way, an organizing principle and an analytical approach. Hence approaching the sustainable development paradigm for analysis raises a number of difficult issues. Some call for a total system view to begin with, dealing with different components separately by different disciplines. Others call for focus on subsystems that are changing over time. Still others suggest interdisciplinary case studies at different levels to add to better understanding.

In order to assess progress made in the pursuit of sustainable development, we need to understand and be able to measure the effects of policy initiatives on the economy, the environment, and people's well-being – hence the need for indicators which can help us to figure out whether we are charting the right course towards sustainable development. The Brundtland Report called for new ways to measure the degree to which present societies and practices are sustainable and the progress we are making towards greater sustainability. This call was repeated in Agenda 21, requesting countries and international organizations to develop the concept of such indicators.

Work on developing indicators has been under way in many international organizations, particularly at the UN Commission on Sustainable Development (CSD), the OECD, the World Bank, and various research institutes. For example, the CSD has developed some 130 indicators which are now being tested at the country level.[20] Such indicators have been classified in different ways, depending upon their specific purpose, but they have generally been grouped in the following categories: sectoral indicators; resource indicators; outcome indicators; and summary indicators.[21]

The interest in sustainable development has called for assigning appropriate values to natural resources and the environment. There are two separate considerations when assessing the value of environmental goods. First of these is to assess their value today and in the future; the second is to assess what these future values are worth to us today. The issue of how values change over time is also critical, as many of the issues dealing with sustainable development are about intergenerational equity. But "monetary reductionism", i.e. reducing all such components to terms of monetary value, poses problems and cannot be meaningfully applied in all cases.

Framework for sustainable development

How do we put together the different components of sustainable development into a systematic framework that captures their intuitive sense, signifies their importance, and illustrates their relationship? The choice of a framework depends upon our objectives. Existing frameworks include pressure-state response, driving-force-state response, capitals framework, genuine savings, and a system of environmental economic accounts.[22] It is not possible to review them all here, but a few are briefly mentioned for the purpose of illustrating the concept.

Pressure-state response (PSR) framework

The PSR framework, developed by the OECD, provides a useful way of organizing information to visualize sustainability. "Pressure" signifies impact exerted on various resources by different human activities, obviously some harmful (like release of pollutants) and others beneficial (like investment in tree planting). These pressures in turn cause responses in the "state" or level of sustainable development, and society then "responds" with policies or other actions. This framework highlights the relationships between different dimensions of sustainable development and helps us to see if we are moving in the right direction.

The CSD modified and enlarged this PSR framework in what it called the driving-force-state-response (DSR) framework. "Pressure" has been replaced by "driving force" to accommodate social, economic, and institutional indicators in which culture could be viewed as propelling the social aspects. "State" indicators refer to the level of sustainable development, while "response" indicators suggest policy choices in reaction to changes in the state of sustainable development.

Capitals framework

In economics the traditional concept of capital is based on human-produced assets that are assigned monetary value and can be consumed. While historically economic development has sought to maximize this kind of capital while ignoring non-monetary capitals such as human and natural capitals, a sustainable development framework expands the traditional definition of capital to include these factors. The central idea is at least to maintain, if not enhance, the total capital stock – usually comprising man-made, natural, and human capitals – passed on to future generations.[23] The condition for sustainability is that the total capital stock does not decline. Substitution and complementarity between different types of capital are important issues, and some natural capitals are considered irreplaceable. This framework is considered most relevant for the intergenerational perspective.

Genuine saving framework

The traditional measures of savings and investment in national accounts do not consider depletion of natural or environmental assets. The World

Bank has proposed the measure of "genuine saving" to remedy this, based upon a measurement of wealth that includes natural resources and the natural environment. This concept is a comprehensive measure of a country's rate of savings after accounting for investments in human capital, depreciation of produced assets, and depletion and degradation of the natural environment. Thus, a positive genuine saving would reflect better sustainability while a persistently negative genuine saving would indicate the opposite situation.

Culture in the sustainable development paradigm

Profound changes taking place in the cultural interpretation of the world include a shift from passive to active approaches to culture. Twenty years ago culture was treated passively and almost ignored; today almost all countries are involved in many measures to promote culture.[24] How does culture figure in the sustainable development paradigm? While the Brundtland Report reflected the contemporary preoccupation with the environment and development, culture nonetheless entered indirectly in terms of meeting "needs", defined in large part socially and culturally.

As the concept of sustainable development gradually evolved, cultural elements also began to be considered in the sustainable development paradigm, albeit as a sideline. Though there is no universally acceptable practical definition of sustainable development, the concept has evolved to encompass three major points of view – economic, environmental, and socio-cultural – which are depicted in Figure 2.1.[25]

As indicated in Figure 2.1, each viewpoint corresponds to a domain or system with a distinct driving force. The economy is geared towards improving human welfare mainly through increases in the consumption and production of goods and services. The environmental domain mainly focuses on protecting the integrity of ecological systems. The socio-cultural system seeks to enrich the human dimension by harmonizing social relations and cultural pluralism.

Culture may be viewed as the glue that binds together all other concerns and becomes one of the main issues of sustainability in this century. Thus, Gao Xian's view helps us to elaborate the notion of sustainability: "A sustainable world is a world developed with political, economic, social, cultural, as well as ecological, sustainability. And in all these aspects, culture is the key link."[26] The main reason for this is that culture provides the building blocks of identity and ethnic allegiances and moulds attitudes to work. It underlies political and economic behaviour. Most importantly, it builds the values that can drive collective action for a sustainable future in the new global context.[27]

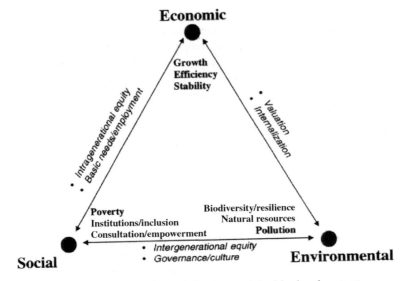

Figure 2.1 Three points of view on sustainable development

Sorting out some conceptual and definitional issues

Culture has become one of the most popular and contested words in our global vocabulary. When Kroeber and Kluckhohn, two distinguished American anthropologists, set out to clarify the nature and meaning of culture several decades ago, they ended up writing an entire book on the subject. Entitled *Culture: A Critical Review of Concepts and Definitions*, it reported as many as 150 definitions.[28] As this term has many meanings and involves much ambiguity, let us first clarify our understanding and the way it is used here. It should be seen neither as a "prestige commodity" reserved for the élite nor a folkloric phenomenon. It is born out of formalization of practices by individuals and/or communities as they adjust to, survive, and prosper in special contexts. As Nadarajah points out, culture is born wherever humans had to work out a relationship with nature and themselves.[29]

Several factors fashion the development of culture. First, it is about a *sense of place*, i.e. perceptions about adjustment to ensure survival in a physical place. The second is the *state of knowledge*, i.e. skills and practices that have proven viable to adjust to the place and ensure survival, and which are transmitted to future generations. The third is the *state of mind*, i.e. judgements about ways and means of adjustments and spiritual quests beyond the fulfilment of basic needs. And finally there is the *state of external contacts*, i.e. sharing of perception and knowledge from outside the group, which modifies existing cultures over time.

The constituent elements of culture may be divided into the following categories:[30] those relating to human beings' relationship with nature, such as technology, crafts, popular medicine, cooking recipes, divination, etc.; those governing relationships between human beings, for example language, communication, education systems, festivals, arts (folklore, music, dancing), games, conflicts, etc.; those concerning human beings' relationship both with nature and with other men, such as social and economic organization, production relations, family links, etc.; and those governing the links between man and the supranatural environment, such as religious doctrines and popular beliefs and practices.

"Culture" is often used in an everyday sense in two ways: as a "way of life" and to refer to the "expressive arts". These uses are also combined by suggesting that culture (in the sense of art, music, etc.) both draws from and participates in the construction of culture as a way of life, as a system of values and beliefs which, in turn, continues to affect culture as a creative, representational practice.[31] Thus, culture is increasingly being seen as way of life and a way of living together rather than just being a shared pattern.[32]

Evolution of culture as a concept

Etymologically "culture" means "to till", or "tillage of soil". Here, culture is seen as a process that requires constant tending and nurturing. Hence terms like agriculture, horticulture, silviculture, etc. are found in the lexicon of culture.

Later on the literal meaning was extended to the cultivation of mind and intellect, and hence the acquisition of knowledge, wisdom, and understanding. As such, many people think of culture in personal terms and a "cultured person" has the connotation of being someone who is intelligent, knowledgeable, and well-behaved. What is to be noted is that if emphasis on culture as *cultivation* is important, so is the emphasis on culture as a *process*.[33]

Another concept of culture, which is centuries old, is associated with literature and arts. It is generally believed to embrace the performing arts (music, drama, opera, dance, puppetry, etc.), the literary arts (poetry, literature, etc.), the visual arts (painting, sculpting, etc.), the material arts or crafts (weaving, pottery, engraving, and the like), and often the environmental arts (landscaping, architecture, etc.). While there is broad agreement in most parts of the world on what is included in the artistic concept of culture, there are some exceptions as well.[34]

It was not until the nineteenth century that interest in culture started to intensify and take shape. While culture was still very much associated with the arts, philosophy, and education, and while the "cultured person" was very much seen as the person conversant with the finer things in life and the legacy from the past, a number of scholars wanted to visualize culture in much more expansive terms. The process whereby this came about is elucidated by Raymond Williams in his book *Culture and Society 1790–1950*:

> Before this period, it [culture] had meant, primarily, the "tending of natural growth", and then, by analogy, a process of human training. But this latter use, which had been a culture of something, was changed, in the eighteenth and early nineteenth century, to culture as such, a thing in itself. It came to mean, first, "a general state of habit of the mind", having close relations with the idea of human perfection. Second, it came to mean "the general body of arts" ... Fourth, later in the century, it came to mean "a whole way of life, material, intellectual and spiritual".[35]

The broadest concept of culture, and that which has had the most influence on contemporary thinking, came from anthropologists. It was originally put forward by Sir Edward Tylor in his *Origins of Culture*, first published in 1871, which has since become the classic definition of the anthropological concept of culture:

> Culture or civilization, taken in its wide ethnographic sense, is that complex whole which includes knowledge, belief, art, moral, law, customs, and any other capabilities and habits acquired by man as a member of society.[36]

Ever since Sir Edward propounded his version of "culture" it has had a profound influence on academic and popular thinking in terms of culture's nature, meaning, and scope. This may be regarded as a watershed in the historical evolution of concepts of culture. Previously, all concepts of culture were in a sense partial; Sir Edward's concept was deemed to be total. Virtually all well-known anthropologists since his time, for example Benedict, Mead, Kroeber, Malionowsky, etc., have tended to share the view of Sir Edward of culture being that complex whole representing the sum total of all activities in a society.

The anthropological concept of culture reveals a great deal about the nature and meaning of culture. By focusing on the total sum of human activity, or for that matter human experience, this concept provides a much broader and all-encompassing way of looking at culture. This has several implications. First, it makes culture the product of all and not just certain classes of society. From this perspective, culture becomes an egalitarian and populist affair. Second, it focuses attention on culture as a whole and the relationship that exists between and among the component parts of this whole. Finally, it emphasizes the relative and absolute nature of culture, indicating that its nature will vary from one part of the world to another, and from one period of time to another.

Whereas anthropologists conceptualized culture in terms of "the complex whole", sociologists were weaving the idea of culture as "shared values, symbols, beliefs, and behavioural characteristics". Their definitions have coalesced over time, with difference in emphasis on certain aspects – which is reflected in the following:

Culture, a word of varied meanings, is used here in the more inclusive sociological sense, that is to designate the artifacts, goods, technical processes, ideas, habits and values which are the sociological heritage of people. Thus, culture includes all learned behavior, intellectual knowledge, social organization and language, systems of value – economic, moral or spiritual. Fundamental to a particular culture are its law, economic structure, magic, religion, art, knowledge and education.[37]

A number of elements embedded in the sociological sense of culture are significant. First and foremost is the idea of values, value systems, patterns, and themes, which is pertinent to overall understanding of culture. Viewed from this perspective, not only is the totality of activities in itself important, but also the way in which these activities are combined. Cultural experiences are largely based on different perceptions, preferences, and possibilities, so they are configured and organized differently in different parts of the world.[38]

Another important aspect is the emphasis on shared symbols, beliefs, and behavioural characteristics. Clearly, membership of any group, be it a family, a community, an ethnic group, a class, a society, or a race, is inconceivable without sharing certain values, symbols, and beliefs in common, and acquiring certain ways of acting and behaving.[39] Thus race, ethnicity, class, gender, and identity are very much germane in the sociological sense of culture, which has assumed great importance in the modern world. Language and communication are also very important, for through them bonds are developed (or not developed) which bind people and societies together.[40]

In recent years interest in even broader concepts of culture has appeared, extending the concept to other species and the entire domain of nature. From a biological perspective all species have a culture – as, for example, the bee possessing a highly complex and intricately designed system of economic and social arrangements.[41] This view is clear from the following:

We can now give the word, culture, its exact significance. There are vital functions, which obey objective laws, though they are, inasmuch as they are vital, subjective facts, within the organisms; they exist, too, on condition of complying with the dictates of a regime independent of life itself. These are culture. The term, therefore, be allowed to retain any vagueness of content. Culture consists of certain biological activities, neither more or less biological than digestion or locomotion. Culture is merely a special direction which we give to the cultivation of our animal potencies.[42]

Culture is also viewed as a symbiotic relationship between human beings and the natural environment rather than as the sum total of human creations. From this perspective culture is an interactive process involving human beings and nature. Clearly, this concept is an outgrowth of the environmental movement.

It is also viewed as a process of community identification, a particular way of living and producing, of being and willing to be; it is a comprehensive interpretation of nature, a whole system of understanding and changing the world. Culture comprises all the productive expressions of man – technological, economic, artistic, and domestic. It implies a systematic relationship between every aspect of life as it is lived. Science and technology may provide material well-being, but culture enables society to maintain its cohesion through a feeling of identity and belonging, and enables mankind to preserve its mental balance. It provides a particular framework, specific structures, and symbolic values which make social and economic transactions and human relations feasible and meaningful.[43]

In some way this movement has made people aware of the fact that technology, which is often regarded as the crowning achievement of human creation, has not liberated humanity from its traditional dependency on nature. As a result there is much greater appreciation of nature's role in shaping culture, as well as the incredible dependency that human beings have on all forms of life. So the concepts of culture are very broad, opening doors to all kinds of ramifications. This adds up to what was said earlier: culture is not only a *product*, but also a *process*.

When viewed as a process, culture is understood to be constantly evolving in response to new conditions. Information about the organization and conduct of all forms of plant and animal life may yield valuable insights for sustainability. It is clear that many animal species – ants, bees, insects, and the like – have developed modes of social organization and collective behaviour which manifest an intimate understanding of the way large populations are organized and regulated when resources are scarce. Viewed from the sustainability perspective, the biological concept of culture may offer important insights.

By depicting culture as an evolutionary process, the biological concept offers an opportunity to understand the complexities and intricacies of

Leaves, flowers, fruits

art, music, literature, objects, spiritual and

moral practices etc.

Trunk, branches

economic system, technology, political system,

social structures, educational system etc.

Roots

religion, myth, philosophy, beliefs, ethics,

aesthetics etc.

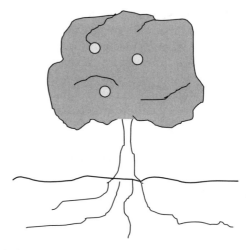

Figure 2.2 Culture as a tree

other species. It will be of much interest to learn from their continuous adaptation in terms of their general systems and structures, as well as their specific functions, characteristics, and interrelationships. This may prove useful for anticipating and preventing unfavourable events, reversing certain trends, and forecasting potential problems. Careful study of the reasons for the survival, extinction, and transformation of non-human cultures, for example, may provide valuable clues for dealing with sustainability issues including overpopulation, environmental degradation, and resource depletion.

Drawing an analogy from cosmology, this holistic definition visualizes culture as a gigantic tree with different parts corresponding to aspects of culture, as shown in Figure 2.2.[44] Culture in this sense addresses the perception of "world views" against which to consider other needs. It emphasizes the fundamental importance of how people perceive and interpret the world as a prerequisite to the way they act in the world. It further emphasizes the need to create world views that are more appropriate to the future, suggesting that such world views may well come from Afro-Asian, Latin American, and aboriginal groups and ethnic minorities whose ways of looking at and interpreting the world have been marginalized and suppressed.

When we consider culture as a process, questions arise about who makes it and how, who decides how it is used, etc., as well as issues of power relations between different groups. From this comes the notion of a dominant culture imposed by an élite or strong group on minority groups.

While these many different concepts of culture may have drawn on experiences, theories, or practices prevalent in other parts of the world, they are from a Western intellectual tradition. This is to be borne in mind, since how culture is conceived and defined has a powerful impact on how it is applied and practised as a reality. Clearly, there is a pressing need for concepts of culture that originate in non-Western societies, particularly when culture is becoming an important force in human affairs.

Given this background, what conclusions can be drawn to consider sustainability in terms of a culture? When there exists such a broad conceptualization of culture, how then are we to approach a cultural framework in a manner that is analytically and operationally useful from the point of view of sustainability?

Let us look at how culture is generally approached by governments, educational institutions, foundations, and business organizations. Clearly, their perspective would be for administrative, policy, planning, and trade purposes.

Several years ago a group of researchers analysed the way in which member states of UNESCO employed the term "culture" for their contributions to UNESCO's series of studies on cultural policies.[45] Their findings indicated that while some member states included science, education, broadcasting, mass media, religion, and other activities, all included the arts in their definition of culture. This would appear to be consistent with the way many educational institutions, foundations, corporations, and governments define culture. The emerging trend is to define culture as "the arts, heritage, and the cultural industries of publishing, radio, television, film, video, and sound recording".

The institutional approach is straightforward and logical, but clearly it is too narrow, and is usually used for operationalizing, managing, and controlling.[46] It would be difficult to conceive of sustainability in this narrow framework. However, if we try to use a broader definition of culture, it is so exhaustive that almost everything is included and it would be like trying to imprison the air. Despite these difficulties, let us make an attempt by first looking at the relationship between culture and economy, since the idea of sustainability is intimately interlinked with economic development and how the cultural dimension has emerged in the development paradigm.

Culture and economy

Culture and economy are the two important aspects of our social landscape, alongside politics. The new cultural activists would argue that there is no example in history where people first create economic and commercial relations and then establish a culture. Commerce and government are secondary, not primary, institutions. They are derivative of the culture, not the progenitors of it. People first establish a common language, agreed-upon codes of behaviour, and a shared sense of purpose – to wit, social capital. Only when social cultures are well developed is there enough social trust to support commercial and governmental institutions.

However, cultural relationships and processes also exist within an economy and can be interpreted in economic terms. If culture is seen as a system of values, customs, beliefs, etc. shared by a group, then cultural interactions among members of the group or between them and members of other groups can be viewed as transactions or exchanges of symbolic or material goods within an economic framework. The notion that all cultures are adapted to, and explicable through, their material environment has been built around this context.[47]

The following statement by Mark Casson, quoted by Throsby, reflects the fact that economists are increasingly recognizing the influence of culture:

Just a few years ago an economic theorist would typically claim that culture simply does not matter so far as economic performance is concerned; everything that matters is explained by prices – real prices in external prices and shadow prices in internal ones. Today the theorist is more likely to admit that culture matters . . .[48]

Throsby suggests that culture may affect economic outcomes in three broad directions.[49] First, culture will affect economic efficiency via the promotion of shared values within the group, which condition how group members respond to the economic processes of production. Secondly, culture may affect equity by inculcating shared moral principles of concern for others. Thirdly, culture may be seen as influencing or even determining the economic and social objectives that the group decides to pursue.

An emerging viewpoint on what makes economic and social gains sustainable emphasizes that cultural imperatives are intrinsic to development imperatives. Sustainable development and the flourishing of culture are thus considered interdependent. Culture is also seen as emphasizing an alternative set of priorities from the markets, stressing the humane and inspiring in life and caring for others.[50] By investing in culture, we are also investing in the capacity of people to participate in decision-making for their own development. In this sense, an improved knowledge base and human development are fundamental to bringing about other developments.

It is clear that failure to take cultural factors into account can lead to social conflicts and exclusion, particularly in multi-ethnic societies where different groups have multiple claims to resources which are often a source of misunderstandings and interethnic conflicts. From this angle, sustainable development would not be possible without inclusion of culture in terms of respect for cultural pluralism, ethnic diversity, and religious tolerance and gender equality.

Emergence of cultural emphasis in the development paradigm

In industrialized countries the role of culture in influencing economic performance may scarcely be recognized.[51] In developing countries, however, the role of culture is being increasingly appreciated. The UN World Commission on Culture and Development (WCCD) has made it abundantly clear that the concepts of culture and development are inextricably intertwined.[52] Rethinking development from a uniform commodity-centred notion to a pluralistic people-centred notion brings culture in from the margin of development thinking and places it at centre stage, which seems to be more evident in the world of development assistance than in the theoretical world of academicians.

As the concept of "development" remained Western, the non-Western traditions, institutions, and values, or simply cultures, of developing countries were perceived as "obstacles to development". Economists were primarily concerned with economic variables, and they tended to look at non-economic factors as their partial determinants.[53] Interest in non-economic or cultural factors grew because empirical evidence necessitated it; economic logic and reasoning were not always working in the developing countries as economists tried to fire the engine of economic growth there. Other social scientists, notably anthropologists and sociologists, began to take creative interest in the subject of development, and the role of culture began to be recognized over time.

UNESCO's lead

The cultural dimension of development was initially looked upon as subsidiary or even as ornamental, and during the 1960s and 1970s was usually restricted to cultural products, particularly works of art and literature and cultural heritage in the form of both objects and buildings. This view was progressively extended to the notion of cultural development.[54] However, this notion was partial and ambiguous, implying that development is first and foremost a matter of economics, and that culture is just something added to the economic process. The "cultural dimension of development" thus distorts the real meaning of "culture" as well as that of "development". Even if the importance of culture is recognized, an oversimplified approach to culture is often applied, by advocating its "aesthetic" dimensions and confining it to the spheres of the mind, the fine arts, and literature. In order to achieve a cultural dimension, planners have often adopted a compartmentalized approach to the various dimensions of "cultural" affairs: protection of cultural heritage, archeological excavations, drama, dance, folklore, artistic creations, etc.

The World Conference on Cultural Policies held by UNESCO in 1982 in Mexico City decided to launch the World Decade for Cultural Development (1988–1997), formally adopting a definition of culture to reflect its newly recognized role in development. The World Decade was reasonably successful in promoting the importance of culture at national and international levels, and interest in culture and development has burgeoned since the publication of UNESCO's *Our Creative Diversity* (the report of the WCCD) in 1995[55] and the *World Culture Report* in 1998.[56] In addition, UNESCO's Intergovernmental Conference on Cultural Policies for Development convened in March/April 1998 in Stockholm adopted the Action Plan on Cultural Policies for Development, which clearly indicated wide acceptance of cultures as promoters of development and recognition of the need to pursue this goal.[59] Policy objectives recommended to member states include "[d]esign and establish cultural policies or review existing ones in such a way that they become one of the key components of endogenous and sustainable development" and "[p]romote the idea that cultural goods and services should be fully recognized and treated as being not like other forms of merchandise".

Whatever the reason for the increased interest in culture in development, the WCCD report looks at the subject in a different light. It attempts to set "cultural diversity" as the goal of development. The meaning of "culture" is defined as "ways of living together", and that of "development" to the "widening of human opportunities and choices".[60] The report does not confine culture to the role of an instrument that "sustains" some other objective, but suggests that "culture is the fountain of our progress and creativity". It further states that "once we shift our attention from the purely instrumental view of culture to awarding it a constructive, constitutive and creative role, we have to see development in terms that include cultural growth". In order to achieve this goal, the WCCD proposes to create a set of global ethics that guarantees cultural plurality. This proposal reflects upon the concern of the body politics of the West as how to combine multiculturalism and/or pluralism with governability.

Some researchers believe that the WCCD proposal is inherently contradictory.[61] They point out that, according to the scheme of the WCCD, cultural diversity is guaranteed by a superior culture called "global ethics". Human vulnerability and suffering, which are said to form the central and recurrent theme of all cultural traditions, could provide the basis for global ethics.[62] However, it is not clear whose values define this "global ethics". Besides, the boundary of a culture does not necessarily coincide with a national boundary. Moreover, recent studies emphasize multi-local and emerging cultural processes rather than a bounded culture as such.[63]

UNESCO's monolithic cultural diversity appears fundamentally different from earlier growth theories. Marx's idea of progress and civilization and Rostow's stages of economic growth implied modernization and Westernization. From their viewpoint, cultural differences were merely a question of economic backwardness. Development or modernization would bring about the universalization of the culture peculiar to modern industrial society. Evolution theorists, implying that societies would acquire cultural homogeneity in the process of evolution in order to survive, also deny any idea of cultural difference.

But these ideas had already changed due to political emancipation and awareness of human civilization as a mosaic of different cultures. The notion that the Western system of values alone generated universal rules was challenged. It led peoples to assert the value of their own culture and forge new ways towards their own versions of modernization. However, the idea of a universal "global ethics" in the name of preserving cultural diversity seems to suggest some sort of a homogenization of culture at a global level with diversity at the local level. Or perhaps the idea was simply to inspire a process: to do for "culture and development" what the Brundtland Report had done for "environment and development" in leading to the Rio Earth Summit, as mentioned in the President's Foreword to the WCCD report.

World Bank joins

Culture has also recently come within the purview of the World Bank. The World Bank approaches culture from the viewpoint of its drive for poverty reduction, empowerment, and social inclusion.[64] This is not to suggest that the Bank had not included culture in its policies before. Its earlier interest was primarily focused on cultural heritage issues, with the "do no harm" approach. Its current approach is to bring cultural issues into its mainstream policies while dealing with social issues, poverty, participation, empowerment, social capital, and so on. But in the final analysis the World Bank is understandably looking at culture from an "economic" point of view, that is employment and income generation, so that it can justifiably finance investments in cultural projects in developing countries.

While the Bank recognizes the uniqueness and specifics of different cultures in enriching our lives, it rejects the use of traditional culture to legitimize the unjust division of labour, oppression and perpetuation of intolerance, and obscurantism. So the Bank's approach to culture is to encourage diversity and create a space for freedom in each society for minority expression and contrary views while promoting inclusion and social cohesion, in line with its people-centred development paradigm.[65]

The Bank espouses the same kind of economic and financial analyses for loans and investment in culture as in other areas. Here come the difficult task of attaching monetary values and the whole range of issues regarding measurements related to cultural issues. For example, how do we calculate the costs and benefits of managing cultural assets? How do we attach costs to irreplaceable cultural heritage, and assess the benefits of preserving it beyond the utilitarian commercial benefits of, say, tourism revenue?

Attaching economic values to cultural assets in conventional economic terms is obviously difficult. Work is going on regarding the issues of assigning economic values to cultural heritage from both conceptual and methodological perspectives. Drawing from the work in environmental economics regarding the valuation of environmental assets – including the intrinsic existence value of biodiversity – the Bank has come up with various methods to estimate the intangible benefits of cultural assets.

Culture and sustainable cities

How does culture relate to sustainable cities? Intuitively it seems apparent, because cities are where cultural forms are manifested, take root, and evolve over time. Culture is said to be the prism through which urban development should be viewed. Cultural resources are said to be the raw materials of the city and its value base, replacing assets like coal, steel, or gold.[66] But how does this actually relate to sustainability, and what do we actually understand by *sustainable cities*? This is where we run into problems, because a clear understanding of these concepts seems to be lacking.

Lacking clear conceptualization

Chapter 7 of UNCED Agenda 21 is entitled "Promoting Sustainable Settlement Development". However, it does not conceptualize "sustainable settlement" as much as it attempts to diagnose the settlement issues in developed and developing countries and suggest measures for their improvement. The overall human settlement objective is described as being "to improve the social, economic, and environmental quality of human settlements, and the living and working environments of all people, in particular the urban and the rural poor".[67]

The Habitat Agenda conceptualizes sustainable settlement thus: "Sustainable human settlements development ensures economic development, employment opportunities and social progress, in harmony with environment." While detailing the actions required, it goes on to state that "Sustainable urban development requires consideration of the carrying capacity of the entire ecosystem supporting such development, including the prevention and mitigation of adverse environmental impacts occurring outside urban areas."[68]

Diverse perspectives

A quick look at the literature indicates that the terms "sustainable" and "sustainability" are often used literally following their common dictionary meaning, but not necessarily in terms of the sustainable development framework as generally understood. Even when these terms are used in a sense other than their literal dictionary meaning, they are generally limited to the environmental aspects of sustainability – that is, how cities could overcome present environmental constraints while keeping up with various urban services, still stressing economic growth as an overriding goal.[69] In other words, sustainable cities are primarily viewed in terms of meeting their needs for urban services, reducing resource use, recycling, reclamation, and so forth.[70] The UN Centre for Human Settlements' Sustainable Cities Programme (SCP) visualizes such a city thus: a sustainable city has a lasting supply of the natural resources on which its development depends and a lasting security from environmental hazards which may threaten development achievements.[71]

Another approach suggests a conceptual framework for sustainable urban development in terms of urban, energy, environmental, and technological dimensions, shifting the focus away from short-term economic gain and environmental exploitation towards long-term social and economic viability and environmental integrity.[72] Still another approach considers sustainability in terms of meeting basic needs by utilizing local knowledge and institutions, stressing a better quality of life that does not depend upon high resource use but on health, participation, social interactions, and more freedom to choose satisfying lifestyles.[73]

Landry and Bianchini observe:

We know that more sustainable environments will not be created if we only look at the environmental dimension; we also have to address how people mix and connect, their motivations and whether they take responsibility and "own" where they live and change their lifestyles appropriately. To make cities respond to change we need to assess how "feel", ambience, atmosphere and "soft" infra-structures are created, something which requires different skills from those of planners brought up to think in terms of physical solutions.[74]

Different perspectives are observed with regard to writings on cities of industrialized and developing countries. Whereas the literature on cities of industrialized countries seems to emphasize sustainability in terms of environmental dimensions, that on cities of developing countries clearly tends to focus on economic and social problems and governance.[75] Understandably, concerns for the urban poor and providing basic urban services figure higher in terms of sustainability in the cities of developing countries, where cities are often viewed as "basket cases", than environmental concerns.

From the above and the literature surveyed so far, certain general conclusions may be drawn. First, there does not seem to be any clear consensus in the understanding of "sustainable cities", although one common element is invariably the focus on environmental management. Indeed, environmental management and planning could be said to have been the prime concerns. Second, meeting the various needs indicates continued emphasis on economic growth. Third, differing perspectives of sustainability are observed for cities in industrialized and in developing countries. Finally, cultures come in only peripherally in terms of needs for social development.

This is not to suggest that cultures are totally left out; they come into the picture in a different way. "Cultural vibrancy" is often mentioned as one of the ways leading to sustainable cities and communities, but this is visualized more from the point of view of conservation and a "do no harm" approach rather than looking at cultures in their dynamic roles.[76] But this is only a new trend in so far as cities of developing countries are concerned.

Writing about East Asian cities, Choe observes that cities have been mostly a material expression of development, which has been largely devoid of cultural identity and has a benign neglect of the cultural heritage in the urban process.[77] He argues for the need to move away from the Western path of urbanization and for Asian cities to look for their own way of urban process based on the cultural roots of city formation. But how do we bring in cultures more prominently, from the margin to the centre, in sustainability of cities?

Culture-centred sustainability

A city would have a critical mass of cultural activity, from various festivals to organizations that regularly create works. For example, architecture would mix the old and new visually with its contrasts. Such an approach enriches identity, distinctiveness, and confidence in a place. This would reinforce and adapt for modern purposes the characteristics of a place or locality and its traditions, values, myths, and history.

Thus, fostering a strong local identity is important for culture-centred sustainability. This would have positive impacts in creating the preconditions for establishing civic pride, community spirit, and the necessary caring for the urban environment. Identity provides the anchor and the roots for a city to select what is central or peripheral for its development. It can provide a bond between people with different institutional interests cooperating for the common good of the city and those who live there.

A city, especially a large one, is often made up of diverse identities that express themselves in varied lifestyles. Tolerance is certainly a critical characteristic in harnessing identities so they contribute to overall vitality and do not cause disharmony and fragmentation. Making the specific symbols of the city and its neighbourhoods visible through cultural traits such as arts and crafts, food, music, dance, festivals, and other traditions is important in this process. Equally important is creating new traditions so the city's images are not frozen in the past. Obviously, cultural and historic cities have in-built advantages in projecting their unique identities. This is more difficult for newer cities, but they too must strive to create their own identities, which could be harnessed towards their sustainability.

A cultural approach to sustainability involves looking at each functional area from a cultural perspective. In the health sector, for example, it would be important to look at indigenous healthcare systems into which newer practices could be incorporated. Mutual aid systems would need to be examined in order to provide support structures for needy or handicapped groups like the elderly or drugs users. Old craft skills in a city could be attuned to the needs of the present. Even the enthusiasm of unemployed youth could be explored to see whether economically viable businesses might be created from their pastimes. The main point is that we must look into culture as a source of creativity for sustainability of cities.

Approaching a workable framework

Having surveyed the conceptual underpinnings of culture and how it has come to be used in the context of sustainable development, let us now try to see if it will be possible to come up with a workable cultural framework within which sustainability of cities might be cast. For our purpose, we shall understand culture as broadly defined in the Kanazawa Resolutions, which state that "culture should be viewed as a way of life and as a way of living together in dialogical coexistence, creatively adjusting to changes and encouraging them".[78] This definition attempts to catch the overall understanding and spirit in which culture has been variously used.

It brings out the sense in which culture is used broadly in anthropological and sociological frameworks to describe a set of attitudes, beliefs, mores, customs, values, and practices as a way of life which are common to, or shared by, groups of people living in a given place or city. In other words, this brings out all the distinctive spiritual, material, intellectual, and emotional features that characterize a society or social group.[79] In this sense, culture is viewed as a mass of interplaying stimuli, in contrast to the classical view, which posits culture as a self-contained whole made up of inherent patterns.

The above also helps conceive of culture as egalitarian rather than élitist. It is popular music as well as classical music; science as well as art; gardening as well as education; and blue- as well as white-collar workers. Viewed in this way culture is the business of all citizens; it includes all groups of people, institutions, and activities in society; it is a manifestation of group or collective behaviour. This interpretation of culture is important when we conceive of sustainable development as people-centred, something which has to be brought in and sustained by people themselves for their own progress.

As may be noted, this conceptualization has a more functional orientation in terms of not only activities but also indicating their purposes in a subtle way, i.e. creatively adjusting to changes and encouraging them. From this angle, culture is not only passively responding to external stimuli; it is also active in inducing change to accomplish a world view or vision of its own good society. And this conceptualization can be extended to include the products of activities undertaken by people which result in arts, crafts, music, heritage, etc.

For our purpose cultural heritage indicates those aspects of the past that people preserve, cultivate, study, and pass on to the next generation. It encompasses material culture in the form of objects, structures, sites, and landscapes as well as living (or expressive) culture as evidenced in forms such as music, crafts, performing arts, literature, oral tradition, and language. What is important is cultural continuity from the past through the present and into the future, recognizing culture as being dynamic or evolving.[80] Cultural heritage can provide people with opportunities to orient themselves with their past and in relation to one another.

Now let us briefly recapitulate the sustainability concept in the context of culture. Culture is essentially a long-term view; it is dynamic, evolutionary, intertemporal, and intergenerational. Sustainability as a concept also takes a long-term view, which basically means that whatever is under consideration will not slow down or wither away but will be self-perpetuating in some way. Culture may be viewed as a source of sustainability for both the present and the future. This implies that sustainability should be viewed as a process more than a concept, representing a set of conditions rather than trying to define the concept in a rigid term.

Cultural capital framework

Looking at the intersections of cultural and economic systems, Throsby has extended the theory of value in economics to culture and put forward the notion of "cultural capital" as assets, which gives rise to both economic value and cultural value.[81] It is distinguished from others by one important characteristic – the type of value which cultural capital creates. Cultural assets have value to people, so they want to look after them. But cultural value, unlike economic value, cannot be rendered easily in monetary terms.

From the perspective of "cultural capital", Throsby has identified six criteria which might be applied to judge sustainability. These criteria would identify whether sustainability can be achieved, might be achieved, or has been achieved.[82] Briefly, these are material and non-material well-being; intergenerational equity and dynamic efficiency; intragenerational equity; maintenance of diversity; the precautionary principle; and maintenance of cultural systems and recognition of interdependence.

Whether the goods and services produced from cultural capital provide both material and non-material benefits for people is the first criterion of sustainability. As cultural capital is what we have inherited from our ancestors we need to hand it on to future generations; intergenerational equity is regarded as another criterion. The intergenerational equity considers sustainability in terms of rights of the present generation to fairness in access to cultural resources and to the benefits flowing from cultural capital. This criterion might be pursued in several different ways, ranging from the economic approach of time preference and discount rate to the qualitative approach of ethical or moral dimensions of taking into account the interest of future generations.

The diversity criterion is significant for maintaining cultural systems in terms of diversity of ideas, beliefs, traditions, and values. The precautionary principle simply relates to avoiding decisions which may lead to irreversible changes. Throsby's final criterion of sustainability indicates that no part of any system exists independently of other parts. Neglect of cultural capital by allowing heritage to deteriorate, by failing to sustain the cultural values that provide people with a sense of identity, and by not undertaking investment needed to maintain heritage will place cultural systems in jeopardy and may cause them to break down, with a consequent loss of welfare and economic output.

Dialogical equilibrium framework

The fact that sustainability is not unidimensional also comes out from Tiwari's research in Patan city.[83] He considers sustainability from three different perspectives, viewing it as a dialogical equilibrium to be maintained in three sets of relationships across spaces, generations, and social strata. Culture is viewed as the mediator, seeking a balanced dialogical coexistence.

In this framework three different sets of relationships are conceptualized: those between man and economy (economic pursuits), between man and man (societal heterogeneity), and between man and nature (environment and ecology). Tiwari's idea of equilibrium is not just maintaining a balance, but extends to providing safety and equity across time (present and future generations), social strata (citizen groups), and space (city and hinterland). He thinks that the present planning frame is short and must extend to at least three generations from the viewpoint of sustainability.

Drawing examples from his study of Patan, Tiwari mentions how various cultural activities had sought to maintain this equilibrium over the years.[84] His study indicates how various cultural activities in the past helped in developing a culture of sustainability in Patan, and how the current economic and cultural activities have been able to help sustain Patan into the future.

Nadarajah's eight principles framework ("sustainable enlightened localism")

In his paper presented at the First International Conference on Culture in Sustainability of Cities, Nadarajah suggested a series of comprehensive criteria that might be applied to judge sustainability in particular cases.[85] In view of the fact that cities carry various connotations and meanings to different individuals and groups in terms of their experience and perception, the notion of sustainability must take into consideration multiple cultural factors. Nadarajah has put forward eight principles as a general framework to guide both sustainable and culturally informed urbanization and city-building. These are briefly described below.

The principle of symbolic universe

This principle refers to the physical world around us, which carries special meaning in terms of our own experience and perception, and the way we respond to this world. A city is viewed as a complex symbolic object with a distinct "meanings complex". The principle involves recognition of the fact that we are from a "physical location" that is wrapped with meanings, a condition that transforms three-dimensional physical space into a place. Being in a specific location, responding to the specific environmental context, we develop distinctive response patterns, produce distinctive meaning complexes, and consequently evolve different ethnic cultures.

The principle of wholeness

This principle refers to the interconnectedness of various elements which make up nature. This interconnectedness is across time as well as in space. What we did yesterday in rural Europe has an impact on us here in Asia today, and may continue into the future affecting the lives of future generations. There is another aspect of this principle. It is about our relationship with nature: how this relationship is mediated is of fundamental importance. Nadarajah contends that traditional cultures, guided by a non-materialistic value system usually sustained by a notion of the sacred or a clear idea of deep interconnection, are more characterized by wholeness and are more sustainable than a modern industrial society driven by materialist ethics and the orientation of profit maximization.

The principle of development

The idea here is that development should not be confined to economic growth and GNP, which are primarily concerned with the material expansion of human life and supposedly aimed at the satisfaction of human needs. Development should involve both material and non-material, or ethical, progress. Sustainable development is viewed as a kind of a moral project to create an intentional social world guided by a dematerialized value system and practices towards a decommodified economy.

The principle of democracy

This principle advocates a grassroots participatory approach *vis-à-vis* a representative democratic system. It calls for location of institutional power in the community, exercised through direct communal involvement, decision-making, and participation. Democracy should provide an environment that allows people the right and the ability to interpret events, behaviours, and texts and create alternative political narratives; the units involved in direct democratic activities are visualized to be small and not large, bureaucratized social entities. A need for strong media to encourage a participatory, self-conscious democracy built on the principle of social criticism and societal learning is also visualized, which will contribute to the achievement of equity and democratic governance. This is considered critical for sustaining sustainable development.

The principle of circularity

This principle considers the relationship of inputs to outputs in sustaining the urban system. The metabolism in a city needs to be shifted from one marked by "unilinearity" to "informed circularity". Unilinearity suggests a disconnection between past, present, and future in our contemporary production-to-consumption system. We produce without understanding the future implications to society and environment. We consume without understanding where the products come from or how they were produced and what kind of impact they are going to have on society and the environment. Circularity suggests a conscious understanding of the relationship between pre-consumption and consumption stages, and further to post-consumption, providing for feedback loops between the time-frames of the past, present, and future and therefore contributing to sustainability.

The principle of diversity

This principle counters the negative underside of globalization, which has a strong tendency to create regimes based on standardization, homogenization, or uniformity, forcing "monocultures" as a standard in place of diversity. The principle recognizes the intrinsic goodness of cultural diversity, as is the case with biodiversity.

The principle of localism

This principle recognizes that all life is embedded in a particular ecological context and is not free-floating. It is location-specific, which relates to the symbolic universe of people as they make sense of their social and natural environments. Localism is important for sustainability in several ways. Take the case of knowledge production, for example. Knowledge is produced at all levels as people build patterned responses to their ecological contexts within the natural and social worlds. It is produced in the context of specific situations, and such indigenous knowledge covers wide areas. Many of these local knowledge systems feature sustainability not as a concept of today but as a lived activity.

The principle of spatialization

Spatialization is viewed as a process whereby what we understand as physical, objective, three-dimensional space becomes a place endowed with meanings. This is how a "space" is transformed into a "place", a "place" into a "home", and a "home" into a "homeland". At present the socio-cultural process of spatialization takes place through the interest articulation of the various subgroups that constitute a human group inhabiting a city environment.

Focusing on culture

All of the above frameworks have culture in their centre, because one of its fundamental attributes is the ability to adjust and adapt. Chapters 5–10 offer more possibilities for the development of a coherent framework.[86] Thus focusing on culture essentially means developing a strategy of encouraging local people as the principal asset through which sustainability may be realized. In other words, this is to recognize the human potential of a community as its most important asset for wealth creation, social cohesion, and quality of life. So the cultural approach is to engage people's creativity to realize sustainable cities. Such an approach may lead to a cultural production/consumption system where consumers will demand goods and services with high cultural and artistic value, and help to strengthen the quality of the local consumption market and increase the demand for cultural production.[87]

Culture has always played important roles in the vitality and character of cities. When cities in Western countries underwent restructuring due to the decline in manufacturing activities, cultural projects were often initiated to revitalize them. Over the past two decades the potential of cultural activities to contribute to the prosperity of cities has been increasingly recognized. In post-industrial, service-oriented societies culture can become an important factor in influencing urban economies and enhancing their competitiveness.[88] As we move towards an economy based less on manufacturing and more on knowledge, creativity originating from different cultures will be at a premium.[89]

There has already been a progressive shift of urban economies from goods production to services and information handling. As in industrially advanced countries, the great majority of the workforce in cities no longer deal with material outputs. "With the disappearance of local manufacturing industries and periodic crises in government and finance, culture is more and more the business of cities – the basis of their tourist attractions and their unique, competitive edge."[90] Consequently, cultural imperatives are now being viewed as intrinsic to sustainable urban development.

Generally, a cultural approach to city revitalization may produce five kinds of impacts. First of all, it could provide economic benefits in terms of creating new jobs. Secondly, it may create physical and environmental benefits through enhancing aesthetics and healthy living conditions. Thirdly, it could bring about various social benefits like creating safer public spaces. Fourthly, this approach would bring about another important benefit – improving the image of the city and hence its attractiveness. And lastly, investment in culture and related industries, including tourism, promotes labour-intensive economic activities that generate not only wealth and income but also promote localism, or a sense of identity against homogenizing globalization. In short, investment in culture produces wealth, and wealth pays for cultural development, which in turn stimulates sustainable development of cities. Hence culture can be considered as a basis for an alternative approach to sustainable urban development.

As the economic importance of the cultural sector has grown in recent years, culture is also increasingly being viewed as a potential source of increasing consumption. This means taking an economic view of cultural activities and interpreting certain areas of culture as industries.[91] This sector is said to be one of the fastest growing in the world's developed economies after financial services, IT, and tourism.[92] Consequently, cultural policy-makers have begun to look at development of cultural attractions as magnets for tourism, retailing, and associated services.[93] It is no longer viewed in the conventional sense only as something to be valued and preserved for posterity.

Because of this changed view, culture is being increasingly considered as an active ingredient for job creation in the local economic development of cities. Such development may involve refurbishing historical buildings and heritage sites or encouraging a contemporary creative industrial sector.[94] This sector is now viewed more favourably as being sustainable and providing better-quality jobs than the often seasonal, low-paid jobs associated with tourism and retailing. As such, culture is now being increasingly integrated not only in urban renewal but also in urban sustainability. Unfortunately, it seems to be more appreciated as a money-making possibility rather than as enriching human experience and spirituality.

Besides contributing to the employment and revenue aspects of the "benefits" package, the cultural approach to the development of cities is a means to harness the potential of built heritage in terms of generating civic pride, identity, and distinctiveness. In Nadarajah's terminology, this is building the "cultural infrastructure" which will help articulate, develop, disseminate, and circulate cultural meaning to living in a city.[95] In a sense, this approach is basically a way of thinking through local development to respond to what is unique or special about a given city. Focusing on cultures helps bring out local distinctiveness – ever more important in a world where places are more and more looking the same.

Some balance, however, needs to be maintained in emphasizing culture as an instrument to drive the local economy. The usual argument that "what is good for business is good for the town" may lead to using culture only for economic or marketing purposes. For example, increasing emphasis on tourism development may diminish local quality of life and court resentment from people who might feel bypassed on social or economic grounds. It is also important to recognize that focusing on culture alone cannot solve every problem involved in sustainable cities. Cultural initiatives must integrate with others like training, education, and so on. The important issue is to assess realistically what culture can do for sustainable cities without underestimating its subtle impact.

Concluding remarks

It may be said that cities are formed primarily because many people choose to live in relatively small geographical areas because of actual or perceived benefits which they value. Some may be born in a place and continue to live there habitually, and do not move out because they are reasonably satisfied with the "benefits" they enjoy living there. Others may be drawn to a place from other areas because of the perceived "benefits". But the magnet that holds them down is that package of "benefits", which is not static but changing.

In the authors' view the issue of sustainability should hinge on this idea of long-term "benefit" fulfilment and how people work towards achieving this goal. The perception of benefits and the ways and means people adopt to gain them are essentially culture-driven. If the majority of the residents of a city derive this "benefit" to the extent that they feel satisfied living in that city, and if this condition can be maintained over a certain specified period, then such a city could be considered "sustainable". On the other hand, if people feel otherwise, and the overall "benefits" are declining over time, such cases would be considered unsustainable.

In between these, various scales of sustainability are conceivable. Indeed, such indicators could be new measures to judge the wealth and well-being of cities, as well as their sustainability indicators. Since these "benefits-related" indicators seem to be lacking presently, development of such measures would be desirable. A generally stable population in inner or core areas of cities over time could possibly be a rough indicator, but this again would fall far short of indicating the package of "benefits" enjoyed by the residents and their satisfaction or otherwise.

What do we understand by these "benefits"? Briefly, it may be said that this is the package of things that are supposed to make a better life. Looking at it from a materialistic point of view, we come to the same mundane matters – availability of and access to all those essentials like employment, health, education, housing, electricity, drinking water, transportation, communication, safety, recreation, and so forth that we think we need to make a decent living. Put differently, these are the never-satisfying fruits of what we call economic development.

It is well known that urbanization and economic development go together. Needless to say, cities have played a decisive role in economic development. Cities provide industry with easy modes of transportation and communication, good access to skilled labour, and plenty of consumers. In this way cities became centres of growth-promoting activities with accelerated use of natural resources for the relentless pursuit of growth and creation of wealth. The result is that cities have now become essentially commodity-based and consumption-driven.

For cities to grow, production and consumption should expand. In order to achieve this, production resources need to be intensively used and valued in terms of economic priorities. Thus economic costs, not the broader social costs, become the primary concern. This also calls for more energy use as a prerequisite to maintaining growth and urban infrastructures. Without this kind of growth process, the "benefits" package may not be available. However, this growth process cannot be continued forever because it is based on certain wrong premises: it views the natural environment as an inexhaustible source of raw materials and energy as well as the reservoir or sink for the absorption of industrial and urban wastes. We already know what this has led to – increasing pollution, resource depletion, and environmental degradation. As this kind of development cannot be sustainable, we should look for an alternative framework. It is against this background that a cultural framework becomes particularly important.

The Western model of techno-economic development was transferred to, or borrowed by, developing countries for various reasons with little or no adaptation.[96] This has not worked well and is certainly not going to be sustainable. Whatever development model is to be applied has to be culturally supported. It must reflect a self-conscious culture that actively perceives social problems and generates endogenously informed solutions, developed from the cultural resources of the society itself. In this way, people will be eager to take action and commit themselves, body and soul, to the sustainable development of their societies.

Notes

1. Daly, Herman E. 1996. *Beyond Growth: The Economics of Sustainable Development.* Boston, MA: Beacon Press, p. 9. Daly calculated that world resources must increase some sevenfold for all the world to enjoy the level of resource use currently enjoyed by the USA. He concludes that continued consumption growth is impossible, although development in a qualitative sense can continue.

2. After long debates and discussions as to what should constitute "development", some sort of consensus seems to have emerged among development professionals that the goals of development should be broad-based, consisting of the following components: economic development in terms of per capita income; human development, typically measured in terms of life expectancy and literacy rates; political development, in terms of freedom and democracy (although some emphasize good governance rather than basic liberties and freedoms); and sustainability. See Savitt, William and Paula Bottorf. 1995. *Global Development: A Reference Handbook.* Oxford: ABC-CLIO Contemporary World Issues Series, p. 69.

3. Amartya Sen has argued that although increase in output per person may enlarge such capabilities, the ultimate concern of development should not be output as such. See

Griffin, Keith and John Knight (eds). 1990. *Development as Capability Expansion: Human Development and International Development Strategy for the 1990s.* London: Macmillan, pp. 40–41.

4. Meadows, Donella H., Dennis L. Meadows, Jorgen Randers, and William W. Behrens III. 1972. *The Limits to Growth.* New York: Potomac Associates.

5. Schumacher, E. F. 1973. *Small is Beautiful: A Study of Economics if People Mattered.* London: Abacus.

6. Ward, Barbara and Rene Dubos. 1972. *Only One Earth – The Care and Maintenance of a Small Planet.* London and New York: Pelican.

7. United Nations. 1995. *A Guide to Information at the United Nations.* New York: UN Department of Public Information.

8. It is perhaps worth recognizing the fact that the leadership of the global environmental movement has remained and largely continues to remain in the hands of the Western/developed world. This situation presents certain problems.

9. World Commission on Environment and Development (WCED). 1987. *Our Common Future.* New York and Oxford: Oxford University Press.

10. It may be mentioned that the basic idea involved in sustainable development was first introduced in forest management by foresters. When the development of scientific forestry began in the late eighteenth and nineteenth centuries, foresters developed the concept of "sustainable yield", drawing upon concepts from growth biology. In simple terms, this referred to the amount of timber which can be extracted from a stand of forests on a regular basis in perpetuity. At a later stage, this was made more rigorous by complementary developments in economics, particularly the examination of the economic implications of a sustainable yield policy (for example, rates of time preference and the opportunity cost of capital). Agriculturists also had the notion of "sustainability" embodied in what they called "integrated crop management" – that is, utilizing land for producing maximum crop outputs over the longest period of time. It should be noted that early use of the term "sustainability" also focused on the specific nature of "projects" in developing countries: international development assistance establishments mostly used this term in regard to whether the projects will continue after their aid is ceased or terminated.

11. See, for example, Mitlin, Diana. 1992. "Sustainable development: A guide to the literature", *Environment and Urbanization*, Vol. 4, No. 1, pp. 111–124.

12. Daly, note 1 above; Zaccai, Edwin. 1999. "Sustainable development: Characteristics and interpretations", *Geographica Helvetica*, Vol. 2, No. 54, pp. 73–80.

13. It may be recalled that sustainable development has sometimes been described as "development that lasts". See Palanivel, T. 1999. "Towards sustainable development: An overview of concepts, indicators and framework", unpublished ms.

14. Mitlin, note 11 above, p. 111.

15. Shrestha, Nanda R. 1997. *In the Name of Development: A Reflection on Nepal.* Lanham, MD and New York: University Press of America, p. 23.

16. For instance, there exist theoretical and practical problems in defending the rights of beneficiaries who do not exist at the moment. Moreover, while taking into account the needs of future generations, a uniform approach would not be possible because of the considerable environmental, social, and cultural differences between different human groups at the local and regional levels.

17. Palanivel, note 13 above, p. 14.

18. It may be noted that the Brundtland Report introduced the idea of intergenerational equity, but did not explicitly focus on the social dimension as much as did the UNCED version.

19. See Tiwari's case study of the city of Patan in this volume.
20. UN Commission on Sustainable Development. 1998. *Measuring Changes in Consumption and Production Patterns: A Set of Indicators.* New York: United Nations.
21. Palanivel, note 13 above.
22. *Ibid.*
23. Daly, Herman E. and John J. Cobb. 1989. *For the Common Good: Redirecting the Economy Toward Community, the Environment and a Sustainable Future.* Boston, MA: Beacon Press, 1989.
24. Schafer, D. Paul. 1998. *Culture: Beacon of the Future.* Westport, CN: Praeger.
25. Munasinghe, Mohan. 2000. "The nexus of climate change and sustainable development: Applying the sustainomics transdisciplinary meta-framework", in Fu-chen Lo, Hiroyasu Tokuda, and N. S. Cooray (eds) *The Sustainable Future of the Global System III.* Tokyo: UNU Institute of Advanced Studies.
26. Xian, Gao. 2000. "Culture and development: A sustainable world in the twenty-first century", *Culturelink*, Special Issue, pp. 173–176.
27. Arizpe, Lourdes. 1996. "Introduction", in Lourdes Arizpe (ed.) *The Cultural Dimensions of Global Change.* Paris: UNESCO.
28. Kroeber, Alfred L. and Clyde Kluckhohn. 1963. *Culture: A Critical Review of Concepts and Definitions.* New York: Vintage Books.
29. Nadarajah, M. 2000. "City, culture and sustainable development: Towards a cultural framework for sustainable urbanization", in *Report of the International Conference on Culture in Sustainability of Cities I.* Kanazawa: IICRC, pp. 48–61.
30. Tri, Huynh Cao, Le Thanh Khoi, Roland Colin, and Luo Yuan-Zheng. 1986. *Strategies for Endogenous Development.* New Delhi, Bombay, and Calcutta: Oxford University Press and IBH Publishing, p. 8.
31. King, Anthony D. 1995. "Re-presenting world cities: Cultural theory/social practice", in Paul l. Knox and Peter J. Taylor (eds) *World Cities in a World-System.* New York and Cambridge: Cambridge University Press, pp. 215–231.
32. UNESCO. 1998. *World Culture Report 1998: Culture, Creativity and Markets.* Paris: UNESCO.
33. That culture is much more a process than a product is implied by the general distinction which is often made between culture and civilization. The former is viewed as the progressive movement towards an end product, while the latter (civilization) is viewed as the end product.
34. What is considered art in one country may not necessarily be considered as such in another country. For example, in Japan tree dwarfing and flower arranging are art forms. Tattooing is considered an art form in Tanzania but might not be elsewhere.
35. Williams, Raymond. 1966. *Culture and Society 1780–1950.* London: Penguin Books, p. 16.
36. Tylor, Edward B. 1958. *The Origins of Culture.* New York: Harper & Row, p. 1.
37. Braisted, Paul J. 1945. *Cultural Cooperation: Keynote of the Coming Age.* New Haven: Edward W. Haven Foundation, p. 6.
38. For instance, it is said that European cultures are organized around intellectual patterns and themes whereas African cultures are organized around emotional patterns and themes.
39. For example, T. S. Eliot identified a number of distinctive and shared symbols such as Derby Day, the dog races, the dart board, and so forth which comprise "English culture" and set it apart from other cultures.
40. In the modern world it is the mass media and the whole range of activities described as "cultural and communication industries", such as radio, TV, film, video, internet, etc.

41. Many people are reluctant to extend the concept of culture to other species. They contend that culture is the very thing which sets human beings apart from nature and other species.
42. Kroeber and Kluckhohn, note 28 above, p. 57.
43. Tri *et al.*, note 30 above, pp. 13–15.
44. Schafer, note 24 above, pp. 30–46.
45. UNESCO. 1976–1996. Studies and documents on cultural policies for member states. Paris: UNESCO.
46. It should be noted that history is filled with examples of the political and corporate use of culture for propagandistic, imperialistic, and commercial purposes.
47. The proponents of this view, identified as "cultural materialism", contend that cultures may differ but their evolution will be determined not by the ideas they embody but by their success in dealing with the challenges of the material world in which they are situated.
48. Quoted in Throsby, David. 2001. *Economics and Culture.* Cambridge: Cambridge University Press, p. 64.
49. *Ibid.*, pp. 63–64.
50. Borofsky, Robert. 1998. "Cultural possibilities", in *World Culture Report 1998*, note 32 above, pp. 64–73.
51. Throsby, note 48 above, pp. 61–62.
52. Perez de Cuellar, Javier. 1995. *Our Creative Diversity (Report of the World Commission on Culture and Development).* Paris: UNESCO.
53. Among the few exceptions, Hagen may be noted for his belief that the change from stagnation to growth was basically a cultural phenomenon in which economic variables played a "conditioning role". See Hagen, Everett. 1962. *On the Theory of Social Change.* Homewood, IL: Dorsey Press. Thus in developing countries a lower price of a product may not necessarily lead to an increase in its demand, as expected by economic theory, because of cultural factors governing consumption.
54. UNESCO. 1995. *The Cultural Dimension of Development.* Paris: UNESCO, pp. 21–23.
55. Perez de Cuellar, note 52 above.
56. UNESCO, note 32 above.
59. This action plan is too detailed to summarize here without losing its substance and focus.
60. Perez de Cuellar, note 52 above, p. 24.
61. Uchiyamada, Yasushi. 1998. "Culture and development: A quick review", in Kazuo Takahashi (ed.) *Agenda for International Development.* Tokyo: FASID, pp. 103–110.
62. The WCCD report proposes five principles as the core of a new global ethics: human rights and responsibilities; democracy and the elements of civil society; the protection of minorities; commitment to peaceful conflict resolution and fair negotiation; and equity within and between generations. See Perez de Cuellar, note 52 above, pp. 40–46.
63. Appadurai, Arjun. 1996. *Modernity at Large: Cultural Dimensions of Globalization.* Minneapolis and London: University of Minnesota Press.
64. Serageldin, Ismail. 1998. "Culture and development at the World Bank", in *Cultural Heritage (An Urban Age Special Issue)*, September. Washington, DC: World Bank, pp. 11–13.
65. *Ibid.*
66. Landry, Charles. 2000. *The Creative City: A Toolkit for Urban Innovators.* London: Earthscan Publications, pp. 7–9.
67. Cities in developed countries are portrayed as stressing the global ecosystem because of their consumption patterns, whereas settlements in the developing world are said to be in need of more raw materials, energy, and economic development simply to overcome

basic economic and social problems. Measures for improvement should be based on technical cooperation activities, partnership among the public, private, and community sectors, and participation in the decision-making process by community groups and special interest groups, such as women, indigenous people, the elderly, and the disabled. See Sofjan, Sri Husnaini and Eugene Raj Arokiasamy (compilers). 2000. *Our Cities, Our Homes: A to Z Guide on Human Settlement Issues.* Penang and Kuala Lumpur: Southbound and Asia Pacific, pp. 150–161.

68. *Ibid.*, pp. 99–149.

69. Tsenkova, Sasha. 1999. "Sustainable urban development in Europe: Myth or reality", *International Journal of Urban and Regional Research*, Vol. 23, No. 2, pp. 361–363.

70. This is how the issue on sustainable cities of *Environment and Urbanization* (Vol. 4, No. 2, 1992) is described, but the authors were unable to access this particular issue at the time of writing this chapter.

71. TUGI/UNDP. 1999. *Action for Better Cities*, draft dated 29 September. Kuala Lumpur: TUGI/UNDP.

72. Byrne, John, Young-Doo Wang, Bo Shen and Xiuguo Li. 1994. "Sustainable urban development strategies for China", *Environment and Urbanization*, Vol. 6, No. 1, pp. 175–187.

73. Meier, Richard L. 1993. "The way to sustainability for poor cities", *Environment and Urbanization*, Vol. 5, No. 2, pp. 174–185.

74. Landry, Charles and Franco Bianchini. 1995. *The Creative City*. London: Demos, p. 13.

75. See, for example, Mega, Voula. 1996. "Our city, our future: Towards sustainable development in European cities", *Environment and Urbanization*, Vol. 8, No. 1, pp. 133–154; World Bank. 1996. *Livable Cities for the 21st Century*. Washington, DC: World Bank, p. 47.

76. While describing various actions for better cities, "cultural vibrancy" is identified among 10 others such as social justice, economic productivity, ecological sustainability, and so forth. It is stated that "Cultural vibrancy may be achieved by conserving traditional communities, historic enclaves and structures of cultural, architectural, historical, political, economic, spiritual and religious significance. The creative development of new communities and the building of new structures and cities can be inspired by these efforts." See Sofjan and Arokiasamy, note 67 above, p. 6.

77. Choe, Sang-Chuel. 1998. "A search for a cultural paradigm of urbanization in East Asia", in Hemalata C. Dandekar (ed.) *City, Space and Globalization*. Ann Arbor, MI: College of Architecture & Urban Planning, University of Michigan, pp. 72–75.

78. UNU-IAS and IICRC. 2002. "Kanazawa Resolutions on culture in sustainability of cities", in *Report of the International Conference on Culture in Sustainability of Cities II*. Kanazawa: IICRC, p. 98.

79. Based on the final declaration adopted by the World Conference on Cultural Policies, entitled the Mexico City Declaration on Cultural Policies, UNESCO, 6 August 1982, which stressed that "in its widest sense, culture may now be said to be the whole complex of distinctive spiritual, material, intellectual and emotional features that characterize a society or social group. It includes not only the arts and letters, but also the modes of life, the fundamental rights of the human being, value systems, traditions and beliefs."

80. Since valuations and expectations change over time, what counts as cultural heritage may also change. Some aspects of cultural heritage that seem of little value to a community now may become of greater value later.

81. Throsby, David. 2002. "Cultural capital and revitalization of cities", in *Report of the International Conference on Culture in Sustainability of Cities II*. Kanazawa, Japan: IICRC, pp. 78–81; Throsby, note 48 above, Chapters 3 and 4.

82. Throsby, note 48 above, pp. 54–57.
83. Tiwari, Sudarshan R. 2001. "Preliminary thoughts on developing indicators for measuring sustained cultural urbanism: Suggestions from Patan case study", in *Report of the International Conference on Culture in Sustainability of Cities*. Cheongju: The Organizing Committee, pp. 192–201.
84. *Ibid*. For details, see Tiwari, Sudarshan R. 2000. "Transforming Patan's cultural heritage", in *Report of the International Conference on Culture in Sustainability of Cities I*. Kanazawa: IICRC, pp. 82–104.
85. Nadarajah, note 29 above.
86. It must be kept in mind that these frameworks are not the bases on which the case studies were carried out. The case studies provide other potential pathways for framework development.
87. Sasaki, Masayuki. 1998. "Redefining policy directives: A cultural economic view", in *Report of the International Conference on Towards a New Vision: Traditional Crafts for Sustainable Development*. Kanazawa: IICRC, pp. 58–62; Sasaki, Masayuki. 1997. *The Economics of Creative Cities* (in Japanese). Tokyo: Keiso-Shobo.
88. Dziembowska-Kowalska, Jolanta and Rolf H. Funk. 1999. "Cultural activities: Source of competitiveness and prosperity in urban regions", *Urban Studies*, Vol. 36, No. 8, pp. 1381–1398.
89. Landry, Charles. 1998. "Revitalizing cities through culture", in *Cultural Heritage (An Urban Age Special Issue)*, September. Washington, DC: World Bank.
90. Zukin, Sharon. 1998. *The Cultures of Cities*. Malden, MA and Oxford: Blackwell Publishers, pp. 1–2.
91. The term "cultural industries" includes the performing arts (theatre, dance, etc.); music (classical, popular, folk); the visual arts (painting, sculpture, decorative arts); the audiovisual and media sector (film, television, photography, video); and publishing and digital technology. It also includes those sectors where the creative input is a secondary but crucial means of enhancing the value of other products – design, fashion, and the graphic arts, including advertising. Also included are the craft sectors (both traditional and contemporary), whose skills, ideas, and methods of working are crucial in helping the cultural area to develop.
92. Landry, note 89 above.
93. Matarasso, Francois and Charles Landry. 1999. *Balancing Act: Twenty-one Strategic Dilemmas in Cultural Policy*. Strasborg Cedex: Council of Europe Publishing.
94. A wide range of activities from fashion, music, media, publishing, design, arts, and crafts to digital technological services have come to be collectively known as creative industries. See *ibid.*, p. 45.
95. Nadarajah, note 29 above.
96. Claxton, Mervyn. 2000. "Culture and development revisited", *Culturelink*, Special Issue, pp. 23–32.

3

Voices I

Archie Kleingartner: Active cultural policy

Archie Kleingartner is professor of management at UCLA, USA. At the first conference in Kanazawa he presented a paper on "Policy implications of culture and revitalization of cities".[1]

There are three main factors that are transforming culture and cultural policy from a somewhat passive element in the environment to something that can be actively and positively harnessed for change.

The first is culture as an *economic force*. It is widely accepted by now that culture and the associated cultural industries are themselves a formidable economic force at a national, regional, or city level. Once that fact is established, as is often the case, people stand up and take notice. Most importantly, policy-makers take notice ... When economic power speaks, people seem to listen. It seems to me that our job, as those associated with cultural industries and the policy process, is to make clear to policy-makers and others who matter this characteristic of culture so as to define it, to measure it, to quantify it, and to make it compelling.

The second reason is the definition of the *cultural industry*. This ranges from art museums to heritage to other aspects of culture as an industry. This industry is developing a lobby. And it advocates in the policy process and wherever decisions on cultural industry matters affect the future of cities. Other related items of interests are also addressed.

Thirdly is *affluence*, which is not evenly spread throughout the world. With affluence comes a search for an improvement in the quality of life.

People look to culture and things associated with culture, and they look for it in the cities ...

Sang-Chuel Choe: Reinstating cultural identity in local urban processes and built environment

Sang-Chuel Choe is a professor in the Graduate School of Environmental Studies, Seoul National University, South Korea. These are observations on a paper presented to the first conference in Kanazawa by Ratna S. J. B. Rana, entitled "Cultural and sustainable development paradigm: Sharing experience and building new perspectives".[2]

The collapse of socialist utopianism and the surge of globalization have suddenly awakened East Asian cities. A strong sentiment is on the rise to reinstate their cultural identity in search of their own urban processes and built environment. The rich urban traditions of the East Asian countries have been unfairly overlooked. Seen from the Western eyes of those who lived by geometrical purity, Euclidean land use, and stylized architectural design, the East Asian cities seem hazardous, confused, and devoid of planned development, although they also like to point out the virtues of the Oriental quiescent and adaptive approach towards nature in contrast to the aggressive masculinity of Western culture. A Western architectural critic who had spent some time in Japan gave his image of Japanese cities as follows.

The Japanese city is not design that had been done badly; it is the negation of design, an urban happening with its own special vitality ... I found a personal theory that the special circumstances of Japanese land use make the city the only place where an impetuous, anarchical, and instinctive life is possible ... The city has become the Japanese jungle.

Contemporary Chinese and Korean cities would be much more so when compared to the Japanese cities: confused and hazardous like a jungle ... East Asian cities are cities of humanity and convenience. Viewed from high above, East Asian cities are not greatly different from Western cities, with their sprawling highways, skyscrapers, and high-rise apartments, but upon closer examination one may find that even the smallest urban neighbourhoods offer a wide range of texture and colour, and there are marked differences in the way of life. Each section of the neighbourhood has various services, shops, and eateries, many of which are open until midnight, people waiting to serve customers. They do know how to live in a compact environment. Mixed land use is a part of their ordinary lifestyle. Spatial segregation in land use is largely a Western cultural habit and the accepted process of urban development, and is highly space and energy consumptive. Communal facilities like public baths and shrines are still a popular place to share information, grief, and joy in these neighbourhoods. It is a hidden dimension of urban life that is strongly embedded in culture.

Suddenly Westerners, especially Americans, are beginning to reflect on their way of life in the urban environment, especially after a century-long indulgence with automobile-oriented low-density suburban development, resulting in the loss of neighbourhoods, an unsustainable way of life in terms of the preservation of agricultural land and energy consumption, inner-city decline, and residential segregation by income and race. They are looking for new paradigms of urban development ... Sustainable development is becoming a catchword on a local as well as a global scale. If urbanized China, with some 600 million inhabitants, is motorized to the extent of America car ownership, the world cannot afford the necessary oil reserves and East Asia would be suffocated by air pollution and cross-border acid rain. East Asian cities are not able to afford Western lifestyles. Although this does not mean to say that the East Asian city is more environmentally and culturally sustainable than cities in other parts of the world, we should not underestimate the characteristics of East Asian cities that are deeply rooted in Confucian and Buddhist legacies, as they are better able to facilitate solving global environmental problems.

East Asian cities are very much in transition, and are struggling to find and keep their own identity. Japan and Korea are already highly urbanized and China will follow the same path, whether it wants to or not. The city is a crucial element in societal transformation, with efforts to construct new forms of societal guidance as an area for culturally enriched and environmentally sustainable development. After all, the city is a moral entity expressed through cultural characteristics. My comments do not pretend to say what East Asian cities should be, culturally, but are merely the beginning of a long journey to explore the East Asian ways of urban transformation.

David Throsby: Economics and cultural capital

David Throsby is professor of economics at Macquarie University, Australia. At the first conference in Kanazawa he presented a paper entitled "Cultural capital and revitalization of cities".[3]

Most economists do not pay much attention to culture and the way in which it affects economic life ... We are trying to build bridges between the two discourses.

The first theoretical concept to bring to your attention is the notion of cultural capital. The idea of culture as capital is not altogether a new one, because with greater or lesser degrees of rigour we have been thinking about culture as an asset for some time. Indeed, in Japan the Cultural Properties Protection Council in fact identifies certain practices and institutions as being tangible and intangible cultural assets. This has been going on for some time. This demonstrates that when you think about these phenomena, you think in terms of assets that have value to people ...

Of course, the word "asset" has a lot of resonance for an economist, and so does the idea of capital. So the notion that cultural assets can be seen as capital in the economic sense is something which can draw in a whole range of economic theories and assessment methods which are associated with the way in which economists view capital in general. Thus thinking about cultural capital is one very useful way in which we can draw the interest of economists to culture, because it is talking in a language which they understand, and is bringing to bear techniques and methods with which they are familiar. So cultural capital can be considered alongside the economic capital with which we are familiar, such as physical capital (building, equipments, machines, etc.), human capital (clearly recognized as existing in the brains of the people who make up the community), and natural capital (the stock of natural resources and ecosystems which nature has provided for us). Cultural capital is distinguished from the others by one very important characteristic, which has to do with the type of value that capital creates.

The second theoretical concept to put before you has to do with this notion of value ... The idea of value is something that has been absolutely fundamental to economics and economic thought. What we need to do when we start to think about culture is to broaden our notion of what we mean by value, to incorporate the fact that cultural value stands in some ways distinct from the notion that we all understand, namely money. Economists claim that this is a very powerful way of representing value in economic analysis, because money can be transformed into almost anything else. So a wide variety of phenomena can be reduced to monetary terms, because people can say how much they are prepared to pay ... If we live in a world that is governed by economics, then cultural value has no real part to play and would be seen as something that arises outside the economic system and is not relevant to economic decisions.

My proposition is that to try to segregate economics in that way is far too narrow a way of representing what is important in decision-making in human affairs, and that we need a wider system which is going to encompass both economic and cultural value in the way in which we do things. What this means in relation to cultural capital is that it makes the going quite a bit harder. This is because we have to go beyond thinking about evaluation of the rate of return on assets in pure monetary terms, which is what we do every day of the week in economics. We have to transform our thinking about this in relation to cultural capital. This requires us to broaden our analytical approach from one which simply says everything can be broken down into money to one that acknowledges that other sources of value may also be important.

Praful Pradhan: Nine principles of urban governance

Praful Pradhan is a programme manager at the UNDP. These are comments on a paper presented to the first conference in Kanazawa by M. Nadarajah, entitled "City, culture and sustainable development: Towards a cultural framework for sustainable urbanization".[4]
My own institution, the Urban Governance Initiative (TUGI), has some experience in regional programmes. Our project is about good governance. We think of good governance, we talk of good governance, and we try to advocate good governance. As was suggested in the paper presented by Nadarajah, we need the principle of democracy. This means that power needs to be located in the community and exercised through direct communal involvement, decision-making, and participation. The presentation also suggested that the gap between decision-makers, planners, and the person on the street needs to be bridged. The paper quotes part of the preamble of the Istanbul Declaration, which states that democracy, respect for human rights, transparent, representative, and accountable government and administration in all sectors of society, and effective participation by civil society are indispensable foundations for the realization of sustainable development. I think that it is vital to move forward with the recommended principles. However, in order to realize this, what do we need? Let me add some other principles ...

If Kanazawa is doing well in cultivating sustainability, then we can say that there is good governance behind it. Without good governance there cannot be sustainability in the city. These are the nine principles of governance.

- The first is *participation*. All men and women should have a vote in the decision-making process, either directly or indirectly through legitimate institutions.
- The second is *the rule of law*. This legal framework must be enforced impartially, particularly the laws of human rights.

- The third is *transparency*. This related to the free flow of information. Processes, institutions, and information must be made easily accessible to all concerned.
- The fourth is *responsiveness*. Institutions and processes try to serve all stakeholders. We say "cities for all". That does not mean all have to live in the cities, but it means making available the benefits of cities to the underprivileged and those otherwise excluded from these benefits.
- The fifth principle is *consensus orientation*. This means figuring out what is best for the group.
- The sixth is the *principle of equity*. All men and women have the opportunity to improve their well-being.
- Next is *effectiveness and efficiency*. Processes and institutions must give results, making the best use of resources.
- The eighth principle is *accountability*. Decision-makers in government, the private sector, and civil society organizations are accountable to the public and the stakeholders.
- Finally we have *strategic vision*. If we do not have vision, we cannot talk about culture in sustainability of cities. We also need a long-term strategic perspective on good governance and human development.

Paul Taylor: Civic culture

Paul Taylor is acting head of the Urban Development Branch, UN HABITAT, Nairobi, Kenya. He presented a paper at the first conference in Kanazawa entitled "Culture, governance, and civic capital".[5]

It is increasingly understood that the problem of management failure is not just a matter of technical or professional competence – it is also related to political and governance factors. Dealing with the problems of the excluded poor means that their needs have to be understood by decision-makers and responded to by them. In reality, the poor, even though they are often a majority, are frequently excluded from having a voice in processes of city government. The denial of a voice means that the poor are denied access to services (health, education, etc.) that will enable them to re-engage with society.

The failure of cities to integrate the poor in their decision-making is often a function of inertia and of bureaucratic and unresponsive forms of management. City governments act as if needs are the same now as they were in earlier times. In the globalized world, this is just not the case. Working practices must change to respond to new realities. This is true of cities in the North as well as the South.

But the failure of many city governments to meet the needs of the poor is sometimes due to other factors. Active discrimination to create exclusion has made matters worse. Some groups are discriminated against almost as a matter of course: women are rarely fully represented in city decision-making bodies and minority ethnic communities are often deprived of the basic protection of the law. Powerful groups have sometimes managed to gain and maintain control of the levers of authority and patronage within cities, and use these to further their own sectional interests. The pursuit of personal gain overrides any commitment to the improved welfare of the city as a whole, or to the improvement of the lot of the excluded.

Therefore, the contention is that one of most serious barriers to integration of the city poor is institutional. Constraints are often systemic in nature in that they concern a deficit of governance, more particularly a lack of democratic involvement of excluded groups, and a lack of accountability of city leaders to city residents. They can be ethical in that the values of public service and commitment to city residents' welfare by city leaders are often lacking. It is HABITAT's view that solutions to the divided city require strong local governments that are deliberately inclusive of all city groups, particularly the excluded, in the ways that they set policy, devise their plans and budgets, and implement their projects and programmes.

In essence, the position set out above is that the failure to engage with the poor is closely connected with issues of civic culture. The argument made here is that it is necessary to create a culture of social solidarity and positive civic values if any serious attempt is to be made to address the problem of the exclusion of the poor. HABITAT's argument is that there needs to be a dialogue between city administration and key stakeholders, particularly the excluded poor, if cities are to become successful and sustainable. HABITAT has devised specific new tools, particularly the city consultation approach, that are intended to increase cities' responsiveness to the publics they serve.

The city consultation approach is an embodiment of the tenet of partnership whereby all stakeholders involved in developing city government strategies interact with each other on the basis of response and equality. This bundle of values needs to be significant enough to constitute a culture that may be characterized as civic capital. Without civic capital, the views of the excluded are unlikely to given a space to be heard, and dialogue will not work. The city consultation approach both depends upon and creates the necessary culture of tolerance and respect between different stakeholder groups within the group. Cities will not work effectively without a strong civic culture, and this is particularly true in the increasingly polarized cities of the globalized world.

Notes

1. IICRC and UNU-IAS. 2000. *Culture in Sustainability of Cities 2000*. Kanazawa: IICRC, pp. 77–78.
2. *Ibid.*, pp. 41–42.
3. *Ibid.*, pp. 78–81.
4. *Ibid.*, p. 64.
5. *Ibid.*, pp. 15–16.

Part II

Four Asian case studies

4

Introduction

Sudarshan Raj Tiwari, M. Nadarajah, Sang-Chuel Choe, Masayuki Sasaki, and Shigekazu Kusune

The decision to carry out case studies to build up a strong case for culture in sustainability of cities was part of the Kanazawa Resolutions. The four case studies were carried out between 2000 and 2001. The studies, which covered four cities in the three major regions of Asia – South Asia, South-East Asia, and East Asia – were presented at the International Conference on Culture in Sustainability of Cities II: Creativity and Adaptation, held in Kanazawa in 2000. The four cities are Patan in Nepal, Penang (George Town) in Malaysia, Kanazawa in Japan, and Cheongju in Korea (henceforth referred to as PPKC). They make up the bulk of this part of the book.

The main focus of the studies is to examine how culture animates the cities mentioned above, and how it contributes to or what potential it possesses to contribute to sustainability. The four case studies thus offer a way to make sense of culture in an urban context and within the concern for sustainable urbanization. In doing this, four specific modes of engagement are examined. The concluding chapter in this section captures the different existing or potential pathways from culture to sustainable urbanization, and some of the common themes that have been addressed by the different authors.

5

Transforming cultural heritage into sustainable future: A case study of Patan, Nepal

Sudarshan Raj Tiwari

Introduction

The best way to see a city in totality is to get out of it and go far enough away to observe it as a whole unit. For mega-cities with a footprint global in dimension, this may be a difficult. However, for small towns, like those in Nepal, a walk of a few miles will demonstrate what is amiss within the city. About a century ago, when a similar situation prevailed in Britain, Ebenezer Howard may have taken a similar trip and thought of "quarantining the ugly technology and spice the city with nature and culture of the rural areas" in his "garden city".[1] Today we know that Howard's thoughts were quickly turned into wishful thinking. Yet "sustainability issues" are again making us revisit nature with a renewed wish to improve our urban systems.

We must remind ourselves that closed and self-perpetuating subcycles are unusual even in natural systems, making natural systems not "sustainable" in absolute terms of space and time. The concept must remain comparative and relate to the time horizon of human relevance. An action can be understood as being sustainable if the associated dynamic changes are not perceived to result in harmful fall-outs within a conceivable time-frame. However, because our knowledge and foresight are themselves limited, our understanding of urban sustainability will be *limited* since we are neither able to predict changes exactly nor assess the time-frame for these changes precisely.

Much like the dependency of man on Mother Earth, the root economy of urban areas is dependent on the rural hinterland. Whereas in early urbanization cities developed at the sites most advantageous for economic exploitation of this "rich and opportune" hinterland, with the successive growth of trading, industrial, commercial, communication, and information cities the hinterland has gone through a continuous process of expansion. It is now widespread, diffuse, and hazy. Yet the fact remains that cities, as economic entities, have their resource base outside their boundaries. Without this base there can be no city, and that a city cannot sustain itself by itself is an axiom.[2]

Exploitation of the hinterland beyond nature's capacity to sustain it and observation of imbalance in nature are behind the contemporary concept of sustainable development. The pattern of economic affairs of our age has sharply brought into focus two concerns, namely depletion of resources to a degree that would make future generations unable to exploit them to a similar scale, and difficulty in increasing exploitation commensurate to urban growth without causing ecological imbalance. Although urban activities are not the only causes, they certainly play a large part in these issues. Urban sustenance issues thus transcend the spatial boundaries of the city itself, and sustainability thoughts and actions need to play in an urban-rural continuum. We need to discard the concept of a bounded rural-urban divide as the first step towards urban sustainability. One of the objectives of this study is, therefore, to explore the extent to which the traditional culture of the city of Patan responded to the rural-urban continuum, and the extent to which current city actions or policies promote its continuation into the future.

Given that human-made urban systems have a short history when compared with natural ecosystems, it may be unreasonable even to expect the development of balance. In addition, the urban physical ecology exhibits characteristics so divorced from natural physical ecology, such as heat generation and retention, a dry subsurface, and concentration of supply and waste systems, to name just a few known examples,[3] that neither the principle of near balance nor how it is to be reached have yet been understood.

The city is a "concentrative system" (a system that concentrates resources and services within a defined space where the city is located) – it concentrates inputs from a wide hinterland, which is a function of technology, transport, and communication, and it concentrates outputs within the city itself. A portion of this output is waste, which creates, through its diffusion and disposal, problems in the physical environment. Thus, within a short time, in addition to the problems of resource sustainability modern cities have also brought to the fore problems of environmental imbalances. Like the resource base, environmental fall-outs, such as those related to air, water, and disposal of waste, also transcend the traditional boundaries of authority and responsibility of a city.[4] Thus from the perspective of city environment, sustainable management of cities demands an ability to reach outside of official administrative and political boundaries. The extent of this "outside area" varies between cities, but for each city the extent appears uniquely related to its cultural state.

One cannot but agree that a sustainable city has to move towards a lasting, sustained supply of the natural resources on which long-term development depends and defence from environmental problems that adversely affect development activities. Here, the word "lasting" should simply echo that it "meets the needs of the present without compromising the ability of future generations to meet their own needs", assured within the ambit of the knowledge of our time. It is important to note that the time-frame brought into focus by the word "lasting" transcends the present time and asks us to deal expressly with the "opportunities for the future". We could restate this by saying that the concept of sustainability in general transcends the present time, and solving current problems alone will be insufficient for attaining sustainability.

Thoughts about the time-frame for urban planning have only recently been extended from five years or so to perspectives or vision plans with time-frames of 20 years or so (i.e. one generation). Sustainability considerations would require it to be extended to span several generations. Empirical review also indicates that the objective period for sustainability is extended when economic progress objectives are coupled with social progress objectives. The objective of ecological progress will potentially extend it to much longer time-frames.

We must also add that "balance" between various groups in a society, particularly the rich and the poor, contributes to social sustainability. This balance is about equitable redistribution of wealth and equity. Among other things, this must be addressed through resource and environmental issues. In cities where heritage is important, as in Patan, it has been observed that the level of survival of traditional cultural practices in a section of the society is inversely proportional to the modern economic advantage that section has over another. It is also equally true that environmental imbalance in a city affects the poor adversely – the group where traditional culture survives to the highest order.

Overexploitation of resources or under-response to waste assimilation at any time, place, or location by any particular generation and/or by any particular social group or by a combination of these will lead to unsustainable development or decline. To arrest such a decline there needs to be "balance" between generations and between social groups through time and space.

Urban culture: Sustaining nature, economic pursuits, and social relationships

Culture has been aptly described as "a way of life and of living together in dialogical coexistence".[5] We should clarify the principles of this dialogue and the parties involved. Rural societies have been comparatively more sustainable than urban societies. While not denying the power and class dynamics of a stratified society, the rural way of life in contrast to urban life binds together a "more or less homogeneous" social group in a "more or less classless" society, which uses indigenous technology just capable of achieving subsistence-level economic self-sufficiency. Dialogical coexistence is sought between "nature and its provisions", "subsistence economy and its tools of indigenous technology", and "the homogeneous society of human beings". Both the subsistence economy and nature are homogenizing agents giving all three components similar dialogical strengths.

We may, thus, consider rural culture as a homogenizing guiding principle. Rural culture may be likened to an equilateral triangle within a larger equilateral triangle[6] whose vertices are nature, society, and economy. In contrast, modern urban life binds together a highly heterogeneous society, divided into many classes that use select technologies to affect economic growth through maximizing surplus. The equation of dialogical strength of the three basic players, nature, society, and economy, is dominated by economic action. Nature is not only distanced physically but also psychologically as economic actions get divorced from primary activities and focused on value addition and the creation of surplus wealth. In addition, the heterogeneity of society significantly reduces interpersonal relationships and replaces them with institutional relationships. The consequence of this is a general weakening of the dialogical strength of the society. If we represent this by a triangle, it would be a scalene triangle with surplus economy as the most influential vertex, and Morley's triangle[7] for urban culture gets closer to the dominant vertex (Figure 5.1), greatly reducing the dialogical strength of the other components. It would seem that traditional urban societies attempted to moderate the dominant status of economic pursuits and increase the social ties between the many specialized social groups through conscious cultural practices. Culture in traditional urban societies is, therefore, a summary applied knowledge that reflects its composite response to nature, economy, and social relationships. Recent urban societies, with overconcentration on economic pursuits, have reduced the positive nurturing of nature and social relationships, bringing sustainability issues into focus. Traditional urban societies show that culture-reforming activities were deliberate, and directed to reversing the negative results of reduced care for nature and social relationships.

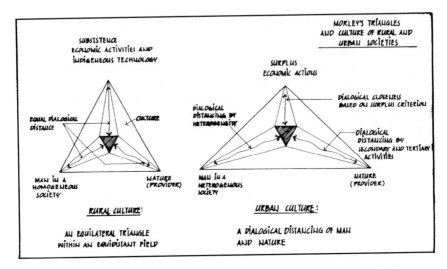

Figure 5.1 Morley's triangles and culture of rural and urban societies

The way cultural processes achieve sustainability is thus through striking a balanced dialogical existence between nature (resources and waste assimilation), economic pursuits (resource capitalization and waste generation), and social relationships (essential ordering of competition for resources and waste disassociation, i.e. separation of waste into its "components"). While we can see that balanced cultural processes were designed, developed, and practised in the past to support sustainability, a culture able to put the three elements together in the present-day context is only now being sought through international ethical norms and standards. City managers aim to provide for the "human needs" of city dwellers, generally defined through social, economic, and environmental objectives. Of these, the environmental objective is usually limited to the quality of physical elements such as air, water, land, and noise. While providing for a good physical environment is important, it should be equally, if not more, meaningful to provide for a good emotional environment for city dwellers. Likewise, while issues of neighbourhood and peace are addressed in the literature pertaining to sustainable cities, these have not been able to incorporate sufficiently issues relating to the culture of the people. Culture forms an important constituent of the emotional environment of a city, and demands activities that go beyond the concept of neighbourhoods. This is particularly important in the case of cities of long urban standing and strong urban culture, like the Kathmandu Valley towns. Devising ways of managing to sustain the cultural environment properly assumes a twofold significance: it can be a tool in sustainable development and can also provide an emotionally satisfactory environment.

In recent years, with the growth of tourism as the single largest global industry and its growing subsector of cultural tourism, the potential of culture in providing economic sustenance to cities with unique cultural heritage has significantly increased. With the promotion of "cultural industries", diverse means of economically exploiting cultural heritage have been proposed, tried, and developed. Yet one cannot but underscore that the business of cultural tourism needs to be approached with caution, as it is a two-edged sword that can hurt the culture itself. It has been severally observed that insensitive commodification[8] of culture can be a disaster to the recipient society, particularly if it is a living culture. As a theoretical issue, one needs to see culture as a continuum from the past to the present, and its transformation into some new form in the future is to be taken as a natural process. In that sense, all cultures may be said to be living cultures. Traditional culture includes past knowledge that is in present use. The larger objective of this research is to find ways of cultural transformation that would purposefully aim at urban sustainability.

Why Patan?

Exploitation limited only by the technology and culture of the times, depletion of natural resources, erasure of the economic base of urban settlements, precipitation of environmental problems, and squalor within cities are not issues specific to our generation. A cursory examination of historical urbanization will show that such imbalances existed even in ancient times. Societies tried to evolve ways of dealing with such problems. Preliminary research has shown that the Newar society, which led to urban development in the Kathmandu Valley and sustained itself over a period lasting for more than a millennium, did face "small-scale" urban problems but developed successful approaches to deal with them.[9] It would seem that the major reason for its sustained urbanism was development, as well as socio-cultural practices based on awareness of a delicate continuum between nature and town that needed to be continuously nurtured across time for the common good.

With a history as old as that of the history of settlement in the Kathmandu Valley itself, Patan[10] has been, and continues to be to this day, an important and vibrant part of Nepal's capital region. Throughout its long period of existence the city of Patan has played a paramount role in the political, cultural, and economic affairs of the valley and the country. Today, as the second largest of the five municipal cities in the Kathmandu Valley[11] and located besides its larger neighbour, Kathmandu metropolis, Patan physically and spatially forms a part of the larger Kathmandu-Patan megapolis. The banks and farmlands of the River Bagmati, which in earlier days divided and formed a fringe to both Kathmandu and Patan, are today more or less built up. Therefore, even as we look at Patan as a separate administrative entity today, it faces a rapid frenzy of development that will, at least in the spatial sense, turn it into part and parcel of the capital of Nepal. The city managers of Patan have seen this coming for some time, and have been seriously considering policy options available to them to ensure the retention of an individual city identity in the face of the inevitable physical homogenization. The prospect of "lasting and indelible identity" is offered by its cultural and historical background, and the mayor and his team are rallying around the slogan "Patan – The City of Fine Arts".[12] In this study, with its central objective of investigating options in creating possibilities of cultures for sustainability, the slogan is of immediate significance.

Kathmandu urban culture: Lessons in ecology and social agreements

Written evidence of urban settlements in the valley are found in inscriptions that start appearing in abundance from the middle of the fifth century AD, about 400 years after the institution of the Lichchhavi ruling house. The inscriptions refer to several settlements of long standing supported by many secondary and tertiary activities such as trading, mining, and manufacturing. Their well-developed urban services (water supply, street lighting, entertainment, hospital services, etc.) and supporting taxation leave little doubt that fair-sized, dispersed urban centres existed from several centuries previously.

The Kirata towns

Permanent constructions, necessary prerequisites to sustained settlement conglomerations and dating from as early as the second century BC, belonging to what is popularly referred to as the Kirata period, have been observed in archeological digs. The Kirata settlements, called *pringgas*,[13] were located on fallow high ground or hillocks. Many such settlements formed the nuclei of the present-day towns of the valley. Although they have been built over during the past 1,500 years and have been physically overwhelmed, their character remains to the present time. The Kirata religious faith included worship of the family of Siva, *yakshyas*,[14] mother goddesses, and ancestor worship, and their places of worship show significant reflection on the nature of settlement and the valley ecosystem.

It is important, from the perspective of general sustainability of agro-based urban centres, to note that the Kirata concept of siting *pringgas* on fallow and less-irrigated higher lands, called *tar*, was apparently to maximize the use of land suited for agricultural purposes. This very conscious ecology-sensitive tradition emphasized the preservation and use of *dole*, irrigable slopes, and *tala*, the fertile plain lands along the river banks, for agricultural purposes.

Towns in the Lichchhavi period

Palaces and temples were built in the towns of the Lichchhavis, and Buddhist *viharas* were generally located outside in natural settings. The Lichchhavi towns were apparently developed with either a palace or a temple as a central element and a strategically located tax collectorate in the immediate vicinity, around which the city conglomeration was planned. The townships of the Lichchhavis saw the development of ponds, fed by deep wells and canals brought over long distances, or naturally available water veins as reservoirs and depressed pit conduits for water supply. This major urban service element, "the stone water conduit", was also built at major road crossings.

As rulers at that time practised Vaisnavite Hinduism and the state was run on the basis of Vedic ritual doctrine, new Lichchhavi towns were laid out on the regulatory planning principles of Vedic prescriptions. Excavated and other remains show that the Lichchhavi capital city used grid-iron layouts of the *prastara* pattern as prescribed in traditional texts.[15]

With the Lichchhavi development, settlements started growing and *pringgas* may have expanded out to the farms – a problem that had to wait several centuries for a solution. Another problem they faced was that the simple spring sources, ponds, and the like, protected as *pith* outside the settlements, were not able to meet the water supply needs of expanding towns. Water was brought through canals that stretched from the foothills of the valley to towns to feed ponds, which in turn recharged supply to recessed pit conduits, a technology that is working to this day in Kathmandu. The town had entered the phase when its sphere of activities extended beyond the local micro-ecology to reach spots that were of macro-ecological significance to the valley and other settlements. Festivals[16] and rituals were framed to guide public behaviour for protection of far-away water sources and watersheds from the first days of the area's written history. These were in addition to legal strictures,[17] a management tool upon which we tend solely to rely these days. To ensure eco-logically sensitive behaviour, instead of legal mediation relying on the power of the state, managers in ancient times seem to used ritual media-tion, which was framed on prevailing religious faiths supported by ethics, individual faithfulness, and emotionally guided inner discipline.

Malla towns: Larger in size and wider ritual mediation

The basic structure of a *pringga* and the associated ecological behav-ioural pattern of rituals and festivals were inherited by the Mallas. How-ever, increasing population densities and large conglomerates demanded new ways of retaining social relationships and feelings of community. Larger water supply and irrigation systems were put in place that relied on more than one source, and these had to be shared with other settle-ments. At the same time, natural subsurface water systems around towns were affected. Clearly, the micro-ecology-based system of the Kiratas would not handle the new urban complexity.

The outwards expansion of towns damaged immediate economic and ecological resources and had to be decidedly curbed. This was tackled through a revised and reinforced version of the old Kirata system. Town boundaries were ritually defined through the use of perimeter goddesses – a creative use of culture to fulfil "town planning" objectives. The need to create a "micro-heat and waste substructure" appropriate to dense ur-ban areas seems to have been apparent to the Kathmandu Valley plan-ners and dwellers. More systems to collect, age, and distribute night-soil from the city to surrounding farms as manure were developed.[18] Interior courtyards formed by groups of houses were used as *sagahs* – a compost-ing place for vegetable waste matter. Periodic cleaning of *sagahs* and other city areas that tended to become polluted were given religious im-agery[19] that demanded unfailing cleaning cycles. By locating festivities in agriculturally lean seasons, the society mobilized and capitalized volun-tary labour in the guise of performing rituals for better life in the next birth (probably an allusion to future generations). Sensible design and lo-cal material usage, ensured through infusion of religious and physical "threats" incorporated in the working documents of design and construc-tion professionals, tried to take advantage of the warmer microclimate.

The location of dense towns on fallow ridges reduced the town to a no-greenery-inside situation. Apparently this was not acceptable once the town grew in size. Later towns consciously provided for lung space through several *khyo*, large chunks of open green space on the perimeter of the town. Town-level festivities were designed to congregate in such spaces in annual cycles, which helped ensure that town expansion in fu-ture did not wipe these out.

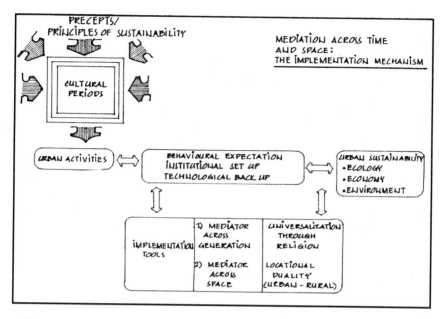

Figure 5.2 Mediation across time and space: The implementation mechanism

All this goes to show that socio-cultural codes and ethics of behaviour favourable to the health of the urban community and the ecological character of its supporting hinterland were *consciously charted and scrupulously followed*. The medium of implementation was through socio-cultural practices able to bring the town and its sectors to act together ethically (Figure 5.2). Often one wrongly believes that traditional societies were guided by universally agreed and unwritten moral codes – these cases certainly do not suggest so. The knowledge and codes were quite consciously built into cultural practices, which did not develop naturally over a long period of experimentation but were developed, timed, and implemented by those who were responsible for properly directing development. Such cultural practices, ensconced in the indigenous knowledge-transmission mode, were able to forestall negative individual action likely to damage community life, the city, or its ecological dependencies. In large part, it is these practices that led to sustainable cities in the micro-ecological setting of the Kathmandu Valley.

The Kirata and Lichchhavi concepts, rituals, and strictures were elaborated and extended by the Malla society, leading to the medieval town core structure that survives to this day in the Kathmandu Valley, of which Patan is an excellent example. What we see in Kathmandu today, the marvellous temples, *chaityas*, palace squares, monasteries, and the towns they perfected into art forms for living, are mostly handed down from the Malla period, which came to an end by the mid-eighteenth century.

The cultural degeneration process, which started around the mid-nineteenth century, has gained such speed in the last 50 years that the above cultural institutions/traditions have become museumized, i.e. showcased for the consumption of tourists – local, regional, and global. They have in effect introduced a distinction between what is termed "cultural heritage" and what is termed a "living culture". Although some aspects of the tradition survive as living culture, most of the eco-sensitive and complex nature-urban interface aspects have fossilized. Thus, today, festivals and rituals are seen as some archaic socio-religious drama of feasting and entertainment. Neither professionals nor urban managers have given thought to their larger ecological objective, which is conditioning appropriate social behaviour across time and space.

Patan town and its growth over history

The legendary founding of Patan

Like the other towns and villages of the Kathmandu Valley, the origin of the town of Patan is shrouded in legends and tales. Buddhist legends relate that the town was initially given a formal plan based on Dharma-Chakra, the Buddhist "wheel of righteousness", by the Mauryan Emperor Ashoka.[20] The four *thurs* or mounds located on the perimeter of Patan are ascribed to him through their popular name of Ashoka Stupas, and are venerated by Buddhists to this day. The *stupas* do seem to define the traditional sector of the town, and their general shape is also very close to the architectural typology of Ashokan *stupas*. The main arterial streets of Patan link the two pairs of *stupas* (east-west and north-south) and intersect at the Durbar Square, the city core of Patan, echoing the Dharma-Chakra layout. Despite these physical indicators, neither the visit of Emperor Ashoka to the Kathmandu Valley nor the presence of Buddhist monasteries[21] in Patan in the Lichchhavi period is historically substantiated. With the Buddhist population congregation starting around the ninth century, Patan did not become a predominantly Buddhist settlement until the mid-Malla period.[22]

The antiquity of the *thurs* is, however, not in doubt. Their role as Kirata funerary mounds has been suggested,[23] and the presence of many numinous stone shrines[24] thereabouts corroborates that the sites were a peripheral funeral space of Kirata settlements. A further affirmation comes from the Gaijatra festival of Patan, when the local *jyapus* visit the four *stupas* in memory of their dead in the early morning darkness.

The Kirata Patan

The Patan area almost certainly was settled in the Kirata period, and several imprints – such as Kirata places of worship,[25] several numinous shrines used by Newars for their ancestor worship rituals, and the *thurs* themselves – are still extant to prove the point. The existence of Kirata settlements in Patan is confirmed in Lichchhavi inscriptions, which name Kadapringga near the Pulchowk mound,[26] Gangula near the north *stupa*, Thambu near the Patuko mound, and Tegvala near Tyagal.[27] Popular folk memory in Patan is that the Kiratas and the Lichchhavis had their final war at Chyasal. The *jaat* groups inhabiting the area and some of their cultural practices do indicate Kirata precedence.

Patan in the Lichchhavi period

The Lichchhavi development around Patan was mediated by two main highways, one linking Lubhu in the south-east of the valley with the north-west (Konko-Vilva Marga) and the other linking Lele in the south to Deupatan in the north. The roads intersected about Swotha, defined by the Swotha-Narayana temple. Whereas the Asinko (current Khapinche and Guita) and Mulabatika (current Su-bahal and Mangal Bazar) settlements occupied the north-east quadrant, the south-west quadrant was occupied by Yupagrama (areas south-west of Mangal Bazar and Taha-bahal). Patan's location at the crossroads emphasizes its trading role, which grew steadily over history.

With the introduction of urban water supply in the form of depressed pit conduits[28] and irrigation canal systems[29] for intensive agriculture in the immediate hinterland of Patan, the resource linkage of Patan was extended to reach further out to the foothills in the south. Later, in 724 AD, the Mulabatika canal waters were further distributed among several villages to the east and south of these areas, reaching as far as Tyagal. The intake was apparently from a spring source[30] in the Bungamati area.

The heightened commercial activity in Yupagrama was supported, in part, by improved agricultural practices. Extensive irrigation led to Yupagrama's rapid growth, such that it amalgamated the settlements around to become a semi-autonomous urban area with the status of a *drangga* by 643 AD.

The Lichchhavi period saw a slow entry of both Vaisnavite Hinduism and Buddhism into the Patan area, but no major Hindu temple was built in the early Lichchhavi period. The annexation of Kirata sites around the north and south of Yupagrama seems to have begun with Buddhist settlements around the Yampi-bahal and Batuka-Bhairab areas, particularly during and after the rule of King Narendradeva (643–679 AD). A part of the Kirata population seem to have stayed with their tradition of mother goddesses and proto-Saivism, whereas others changed over to Buddhism or Hinduism.

Narendradeva further expanded the water system of Patan, and newer intakes were developed. Narendradeva also started the large festival of Rato Matsyendranath in Patan to commemorate these great waterworks. The route of the Rato Matsyendranath festival clearly demarcates the non-Kirata domain of Patan of that time and scrupulously excludes the Kadapringga, Thambu, Gangula, Tegvala, and Batuka Vairaba areas. The festival was apparently designed for the benefit of residents of Yupa-grama and Mulabatika, both Lichchhavis settlements, and the Buddhist population of the north-eastern sector, with whom Narendradeva had a special affiliation.[31]

Early medieval Patan

In the early medieval period, as the capital city of Nepal vacillated be-tween Hadigaon and Kathmandu, Patan remained a part of the state. The development of Buddhism and monasteries was apparently picking up fast in the north-eastern and central sectors of Patan, and monasteries undertook learned activities like producing religious handwritten books. The development of Buddhist settlement in Patan continued to concen-trate in the north-eastern and eastern sectors. The current central Palace Square area was popularly referred to as the Yankuli[32] sector or north-west corner, even as late as the sixteenth century. Similarly, the current Mahabaudda area was the Wonkuli sector or south-east corner. Seven major monasteries and their associated *sanghas* developed in the Yupa-grama and Mulabatika sectors of Lichchhavi creation. Containing only two of the seven monasteries, the development of Yupagrama was slow and it seems to have stagnated into Yupatole.[33] The power and importance of the seven monasteries led to the setting up of a semi-autonomous federal rule of the seven *sanghas*, or *sapta-kutumbajas*, in Patan which often defied Malla authority.

During this period, within Buddhism itself two kinds of changes seem to have started. Unlike the Lichchhavi period when Buddhist monas-teries were apparently located outside the cities, the transitional period saw the monasteries moving into cities. At the same time, celibate monks and nuns (*bhiksu* and *bhiksuni*) were converting to married status. It was these new developments that ultimately made Patan the most Buddhist of the three cities of the valley during the Malla period, even though the Malla rulers and also some of the Sapta-kutumbajas later took to Hindu-ism. The Tyagal area (Ganchanani), the eastern Kirata funerary site of Patan, apparently continued to be used as a site for setting up funerary memorials.[34] Tegvala and Kadapringga retained their Kirata population with minimum religious conversion.

The Malla Patan

Patan seems to have frequently asserted independence following the breakdown of the Lichchhavi ruling house. The rule of local governors, the *mahapatras*, provided the setting for sustained development in Patan. It would appear that the direct Tibetan trade and control of the stone quarries of Kotkhu led to a crafts specialization in Patan centred around bronze and brassworks, stone-carving, and, to a lesser extent, gold and silver crafts. Due to the concentration of the early population in the north-eastern sector of Patan, these specializations are located in the same areas to this day. With direct trade with Tibet and control of most of the areas south of the Hanumante, Bagmati, and Balkhu Rivers, Patan's economic strength grew remarkably compared to that of Kathmandu or Bhadgaon.

In 1349 AD, along with other towns of the Kathmandu Valley, Patan faced a wave of destruction at the hands of Muslim rulers from Bengal. They destroyed the Siva temple of Kumveswora and the Buddhist *stupa* of Pimbahal. Patan seems to have built a defence wall around the town immediately following this. The extent of the town wall shows that all the settlements were now united as one town (see Figure 5.3). The marriage of the visiting Prince Sthiti to the eight-year-old Rajjalladevi, the lone heir to the throne, and the strong rule that followed took Patan firmly under Malla rule by 1370 AD. The mark of this submission to Bhadgaon was the attendance of Jayasthiti Malla in the festival of Rato Matsyendranath of that year. Later again, the power of the Saptakutumbaja *mahapatras* increased and they virtually ruled Patan independently – Purander Singh being the last of the powerful *mahapatras*.

Major restructuring of Patan seems to have happened as the Mallas re-exerted their power when Siddhinarasimha Malla became king of Patan. This restructuring shifted the focus of the town from the north crossroads around Manihiti to the south. Patan had also very swiftly changed from being a predominantly Buddhist town to showing a marked Hindu character. The Mangal Bazar/Pulchowk section of street was made significant and its commercial function expanded greatly. Patan expanded to the north-west and west of Mangal Bazar. As the Hindu Gai Jatra was re-organized, so was the Mataya Baha Jatra, both of which tried to bring unity among their respective followings. The main streets of Patan were redefined and a common route for all city-level festivals influenced integration of the new and old sections of Patan.

With the increasing popularity of the Shakticult, the *piths* of the earlier

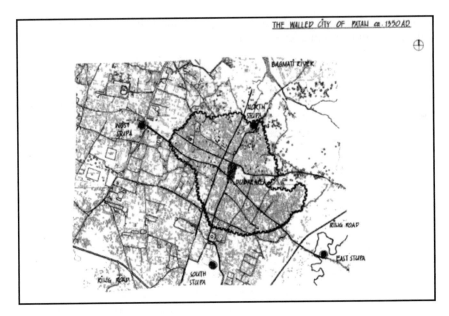

Figure 5.3 The walled city of Patan c. 1350 AD

period became more important, and more were added to create the
boundary set of the *astamatrikas*, the eight mother goddesses. At this
time the town seems to have been resectored to correspond with the
nine-square potent diagram of the *mandala*, the central square being occupied by the palace. Accordingly, Chysal was named so after its location
in the eighth square and Gustala became Guita to express closely its location in the ninth square. In a sense, a superimposition of a ritual cosmic
pattern over five or more small individual settlements was made to turn
them into a "complete" large town. The *jaat* sectorization of the town –
the spatial arrangement of "city professions" or social zoning – was crys-
tallized to bring finality to the town form. The professions more important to the palace were located to the west of the palace at Mangal Bazar.

The late Malla period also saw heightened cultural activity. Along with
expansion and resurgence of older festivities, many new festivities were
designed and popularized, giving the city varied religio-cultural entertainment. Apparently many of these festivities also incorporated good
city concepts such as public cleanliness, protection of water supply
sources and distribution systems, upkeep of wells and water conduits,
protection of trees and clumps of trees, etc. The earlier traditions were
evidently revised to take care of the growing town and its changing environmental demands.

Transformation of cultural accretions in the past

Many of the precepts and principles of urban living applied and developed in Patan over its long history might have been lost as the precepts and associated cultural actions themselves lost relevance to their practitioners. It is particularly of interest to note that, despite the changing religious faiths of the people, the town's history was characterized by continuous assimilation and adaptation of earlier practices. Even the two great religions, Hinduism and Buddhism, the latter being of more importance to the people of Patan, did not totally reject the faiths of the aboriginal Jyapu community. Their harmonious adaptation with each other can be seen most vividly still today in the Su-bahal area of Patan. Current cultural practices in Patan, like in other historic towns of Kathmandu, still carry quite a few traditions from different periods of its development. Although there is no doubt that the practices have been subjected to adaptation over time, their existence to the present day points to their continued relevance to living. Their long sustenance itself may be the reason behind the long-sustaining urban culture of Patan.

One can analyse some of these cultural traditions here to identify elements that have helped ensure sustainability in the town of Patan over its long history.

First cultural period

Dyochhen and pith: Recognizing urban-rural continuum and ecology

The Kirata settlement, the *pringga*, was built around a built-space-protector god, a temple or religious building which later came to be known as a *dyochhen*. The *dyochhen*, literally the house of god, had a counterpart natural spot outside the town called the *pith*, the natural abode of the godly spirit. The out-of-town symbol was of a nature protector. The *pith* was always located in an ecologically important site, such as a clump of trees, a spring source of water, a hillock, or the like, located in the agricultural hinterland of individual settlements. The in-town deity usually occupied the vantage central space of the settlement and the *pith* occupied an ecologically sensitive spot in the farms – the mainstay of their economy. The governing principle of sustenance and survival of the town was expressed tacitly in the requirement that every settlement must have a set of *dyochhen* and *pith*. A closer examination of the rituals and imagery shows that both spots are occupied by two aspects of the same tutelary protector, and the continuance of either of them depended on the well-being of the other. The linkage of the resource base, the surrounding agricultural land,[35] to the settlement was thus stated explicitly in the design of the settlement and the location of the twin-faceted deity in the town and in the farms at a spot of sensitive ecological significance. Indeed, the Kirata town makes it clear that without the ecology of the *pith* the farmland will not yield sufficient produce for the residents of the town, and the town itself will ultimately not be sustainable. Conceptually, therefore, the Kirata town clearly recognizes its dependency on resources outside the boundary of the settlement. The importance of the *pith* to the survival of the town led it to be ensconced in the faith.

Through religious faith, the Kiratas sought constantly and continuously to remind city dwellers that the sustainability and prosperity of the town was dependent on the protection of nature and its place-specific micro-ecology. A dispersal of a group of similarly conceived settlements, each aimed at sustaining local micro-ecology, ensured that urban expansion did not tamper with nature.

It has already been pointed out that at least four Kirata *pringgas* were located in the Patan area, namely Kadapringga, Thambu, Gangula, and Tegvala. Two more, which may have gone by the names of Yugvala and Jajje, were also nearby. The long intervening time has obliterated some of the elements forming the *dyochhen* and *pith* of these settlements, and their association to particular settlements is difficult to establish firmly now. However, based on the location and religious ritual affinity traces in the farming communities of Jyapus, such as the Maharjan, Prajapati/ Awa and Dongol, and the Nau, all thought to be descendents of the Kiratas, various *dyochhen* and *pith* sets seem to have belonged to certain settlements.

Even today, the ecological significance of most of the *piths* for the continued health of the agricultural economy is evident. The importance of these places to the farming communities of the Jyapus is recognized to this day in festivities popular with them. It may be shown that later waterworks linked these very places and further augmented the irrigation provision for the farmlands associated with various settlements.

The festivals: Ensuring follow-up across generations

One of the most ancient groups of festivities in Patan relates to worship at *pigan* sites. Literally, *pi* means located outside the town and *gan* stands for numinous stones. The *pigan* is the *pith* of the Kirata town. These folk festivals, mostly celebrated in the Chaitra Dasain period (March–April) and mainly by the Jyapus, are location-specific and must start from the spot of the in-town tutelary protector and process to the *pigan* or *pith*, associated images and stones along the way getting their share of worship. It is obvious that through these rituals and location-specific festivals the ecological significance of these sites and the importance of maintaining them for posterity were driven home to the farmers. The annual ritual prevented the sites being forgotten as a mundane matter.

Thus we see that the ecological relations of the farm with water and the farm with the town, established in the system of twin tutelary protectors, were constantly restated, and their sustenance as the key to the continued survival of the settlement was itself reiterated and perpetuated through cultural behavioural patterns in exacting rituals and festivals. The latter, as a set of social agreements or rules of behaviour, ensured the regulatory controls would be administered through several generations into the future.[36]

The following three festivals, belonging to Thambu, Yugvala, and Tegvala of Kirata days, have survived fairly intact in the spirit of the Kirata days and the Jyapu communities, even as the site of Balkumari shows overlap with later religious developments:

- the Pigam-Puja of Varahi
- the Jatra of Mahalaxmi[37]
- the Jatra of Balkumari.[38]

These festivals have been able to sustain the understanding and appropriate social-cultural behaviour commensurate with the concept of ecological dependence of urban areas on natural agricultural hinterland across generations. This is simply because they were built into religious practices, which people usually do not discard unless great external threats or economic débâcles come into play. The other sites and their festivities have not survived due to the displacement of the Jyapus or their annexation into the folds of Buddhism (e.g. Pulchowk Stupa, Racheswori, North Stupa, and Naudon) or Hinduism (e.g. Purnachandi, Vaisnavi, Chinnamasta, and Sikubahi).

Second cultural period

The guthi: Assuring institutional and financial sustainability

The institutionalization of management, operation, and maintenance of religious, social, and cultural artefacts and activities in the urban area seems already well developed, as Lichchhavi inscriptions appear on the scene in Patan and other places in the valley. This was done by the system of *gosthi* or *gosthika*, which was a corporate body "financed to perpetuity" through land grants or other "fixed deposits". Such bodies were created by both the government and private citizens to ensure that the operation and maintenance of the artefacts and activities set up as a community service by them did not suffer in the future either for lack of funds or after their death. The institutions of the *gosthi* built financial and institutional sustainability of such surety that they have survived to this day as the *guthi*.

It was usual for anyone setting up a temple or a religious activity to allocate a piece of agricultural land, cultivate it under tillage, and require the tiller of the land to provide a fixed portion of its agricultural output, variously referred to as *ma, pima, pindaka, pindakama*, etc., annually to the operators of the temple to cover costs of daily worship (*karana-puja*), maintenance (*khanda-futta-pratisamskara*), and its ritual and festive activities (*yatra*). The right of the tiller was recognized as permanent and could only be transferred to legal heirs and not sold, as the ownership of the land was kept with the temple and its activities. This concept of institutional ownership, possibly arising out of the republican nature of the Lichchhavi rulers, although commonplace today, was remarkable for that time. Often the management of the annual funds was assigned to a committee constituted particularly for the purpose. Such trusts were either composed of relatives (*svajana-gosthika*) of the person setting up the grant, or a known private citizen and his appointees, or the *sangha* in the case of Buddhist institutions. Even government funds were allocated to private trusts for similar purposes. Some of the trust funds, which were based on encashed agricultural products, also followed the recurrent deposit system (*Dhana-briddhi*), suggesting possibilities of corporate investments. This system not only assured a perpetual flow of resources (*aksyaya*)[39] for the continuance of cultural practices and a lasting institutional set-up for its management, but also brought in community participation in the upkeep of culture. Through the *guthi* system, citizen participation in keeping the city clean was also developing as a cultural practice. There is a dated record of 1172 AD of a private person setting up a land trust, *guthi*, for street cleaning in Patan city. The *guthi* system was further widened during the Malla period to cover city services, clan activities, and social functions. Indeed, it would appear that by the end of the Malla period the role of the state in maintaining the city, its temples and festivals, its social functions, and even activities on a national scale was reduced to a minimum and the continuity of cultural accretions was managed and adapted by the community for whom they had come into being in the first place.

The cultural tradition of the *guthi* has been crucial in developing, operating, and sustaining the town's religious, social, and physical infrastructure over the last 1,500 years. More than the religious faiths, it was the *guthi* and its structuring that led to the overall sustenance of community services buildings, water supply, cleanliness, and drainage. The *guthi* effectively channelled "individual wealth" into public endowments managed by committees recognized as permanent entities. It is important to note that the rights of the donor ceased with the formation of the committee, and it was the rights of the latter that continued into perpetuity. It is also apparent that the extended family system of social organization prevalent in the traditional society led to a continuous expansion of the *guthi* members, ultimately making it look like a wide community organization. The latter resulted in fuller clan participation in maintenance and operation of local services. Although capital investments, in principle, were not sought from the committee and it was only expected to utilize, operate, and maintain the facilities created, the trust resources were also voluntarily enlarged by the community as its size increased with natural growth.

The farsightedness and tenacity of the system is more than attested by the fact such institutions have survived intact almost to this day. It is also to be noted that many of the *guthi* associated with Buddhist institutions of Patan suffered under the political changes following 1768, when their *guthi* lands were apparently granted to others.

The Rato Matsyendranath festival: Recognizing water as an urban resource

Large waterworks, for both irrigation and drinking water, were installed at various times in the middle Lichchhavi period. This system, with its earliest intake located at Bungamati, about four kilometres from Patan, was later expanded with additional tapping of water from as far away as Nala. It survived well up until recent times, and has gone into disuse and destruction today only around the town of Patan. The overflow runoff of these great waterworks was apparently canalled across the town and into the Bagmati River.

According to legends, an extensive festival of Sri Bungma Lokeswora, now known as Rato Matsyendranath, was initiated and popularized in the Lichchhavi period by King Narendradeva and his priest following a monsoon failure that had caused a long dry spell and famine.[40] The faithful were told that the cause of the dry spell was Guru Gorakhnath, who had imprisoned the *nagas*, the agents of rain. As a ritual solution, Sri Lokeswora was to be brought to the valley. They were guided in this quest by the serpent king Karkotaka. As Sri Lokeswora arrived at Bungamati, Guru Gorakhnath got up to pay his respects to the new arrival and released the *nagas*, who instantly made it rain and saved the valley. We can interpret that an extreme drought had adversely affected agricultural output[41] and state intervention was called for. The festival timing (April–June) indicates that the shortage of water was during the seeding and planting of rice and the intervention had brought water for the planting season. Although the legend is about divine intervention, in reality it seems to have been concerned with the extension and reconstruction of a large irrigation canal system for Patan. Inscriptions provide evidence that the waterworks were extended between the rules of Jisnugupta and Jayadeva, when Narendradeva was also in power. The legend appears woven around the act of expanding the waterworks system and bringing an increased supply of water for irrigation to the town of Patan and its immediate hinterland, assuring the well-being of its agricultural economy and people.

There is little doubt that this festival is a socio-religious version of an annual visit undertaken for necessary repairs to the intake, stone aqueduct,[42] canal, city reservoir pond, and distribution system. Indeed, for the proper conduct of the festival water must be available at Lagankhel and Pulchowk ponds and the stone water conduit of Sundhara must be running well. Even the reservoir overflow canal had to be flowing. In other words, prior to the festival the system must be maintained and made operational.

The festival of Rato Matsyendranath, a cultural activity, is therefore not just an archaic religious festival, but incorporates essential mundane activities required for the maintenance of waterworks. It was developed to serve a utilitarian function, and if the waterworks had survived the practical gains for the city could have been as vivid as the festival's ritual enactments. This is an example of a creative use of culture *par excellence* aimed at sustainability in historical times.

Third cultural period

The astamatrikas *and* dasa-mahavidhyas: *Bounding urban growth*

Several simple mono-cellular Kirata towns and small Lichchhavi settlements amalgamated into the town of Patan. The combination of the individual *dyochhen* and *pith* structures was conveniently adapted into the cult of *astamatrikas* as the latter gained in popularity. Consequently the earlier *piths* of the Kirata townlets were adapted into Vaisnavi, Mahalaxmi, Balkumari (Saraswoti), Chamunda, and Varahi, and three new sites were added on the banks of the Bagmati River for Indrayani, Rudrayani, and Brahmayani to complete the perimeter set of eight *astamatrikas*, the mother goddesses. The corresponding *dyochhens* now occupied spaces in between the town centre and the boundary. The *piths* defined the outer boundary of the town itself.[43] Religious rituals and festivals were charted and popularized to ensure that the town did not extend beyond the *piths*. More sites of micro-ecological importance were identified and given religious association. Festivities and annual socio-cultural events were put in the calendar to link these spatially and emotionally to the town and its specific zones.

However, Patan being predominantly Buddhist, the imposition of the perimeter did not work as well as it did in the case of Bhaktapur, and only the older sites commanded an active ritual status. The concept of bounded urban growth, it seems, did not work for Patan, primarily because the *piths* were located very far apart and the concept itself had no linkage with Buddhism. The *piths* remained as agriculture/nature-protector sites. Additionally, an inner set of delimiting images, the *dasa-mahavidhyas*, were imposed as an urban boundary for the new areas to the west of the palace, where in the Malla period the Hindu development was concentrated, with Chinnamasta in Mangal Bazar[44] providing the eastern limit. It is within this area bounded by the 10 goddesses that concentrated town development occurred in the late Malla period.

As the town of Patan expanded and threatened to cross the religious limits, the town of Kirtipur was expanded and reorganized in a pattern similar to that of Patan and several families from specific *toles* were moved and resettled in Kirtipur. Patan thus provides the first example in Malla history of creating a satellite town to overcome the problems of urban growth. With this move the town effectively avoided heavy densification. To this day, the core density of the three towns of the Kathmandu Valley remind one of this wise move in history.

The Ganesha and town sectorization by jaat: *Homogeneous neighbourhoods in heterogeneous towns*

With the coming of the larger towns the heterogeneity of the town increased, threatening to break down social interaction and harmony. The town professions expanded greatly, possibly bringing about wide economic disparity between professions, and their interdependency on each other tended to be forgotten. The fast-developing secondary and tertiary activities in the town tended to lessen the public perception of the importance of agriculture. The 18 crafts of the Kirata period[45] were socially regrouped into 64 or more divisions.[46] This major social reclassification of population on the basis of professions, called *jaat*, and the rezoning of the city by *jaat* created pockets of harmony linked to family/clan and profession at the same time. At the same time, the location of similar trades in the same areas brought in greater efficiency.

The term *jaat*, often mistakenly associated with "touchability/untouchability" or "purity/impurity" conceptions in the Hindu caste system, simply means "born to a hereditary trade or profession". Within the same *jaat*, religious affiliation of particular families was a matter of personal choice. *Jaat* division primarily created a horizontal social structure with little "high or low" status significance in the beginning. It acquired vertical stratification traits only for a small section of the population at the top and bottom, and only towards the end of the Malla period.[47] As the palace and royal tutelary protector were located in the central area of the town, families subscribing to the professions of worship and rituals, administration, and politics were located around the palace. The other professions occupied separate *toles* around the core, equidistant from the centre – in a way physically translating the horizontal relation between the professions. The dispersal of *jaats* in the town was directly based on "proximity priority", related to frequency of consultation by the palace or the state. While not denying the role of power relations in this context, the resulting pockets of social neighbourhoods seem to have helped retain a sense of social agreement and understanding.

Patan was divided into 23 *toles* and a royal/administrative quarter, corresponding to the 24 broad trade groups. Each of the *toles* centred around a tutelary image of Ganesha, equally revered in both Hinduism and Bajrayana Buddhism, the two major religions of Patan.[48] In the areas where the farming community was strong, such as Su-bahal and Dupat, their tutelary image, the *nasahdyo*, shared the same public space. Location specificity of these gods added to the strengthening of community behaviour that was crucial in bringing about social sustainability of the town. At the same time, through the location of god images the city also achieved the side benefit of conservation of open space, as no one dared to infringe upon the spaces of the gods.

The Sithi: Keeping the city's public facilities in good repair

The festival of Sithi, celebrated in the month of May (Jestha Sukla Sasthi), is popular with the Newars, and in particular with the Jyapus, the farming community. In Patan, like elsewhere in the valley, this festival marks the end of about a month-long celebration. Primarily a festival honouring ancestors (*digu puja* or *Dewali*), Sithi is also the socially agreed period for construction of new buildings and public facilities and repair of deteriorated ones. Thus, along with general feasting, the festive activities include a mundane component – cleaning of wells, waterholes (*kuwa*), ponds, and drainage ditches.

Although the tradition of worshiping Kumar is very ancient, the Sithi festival seems to have been celebrated from the late Malla period, the earliest reference to *Sithinakhata* occurring in a *thysafu*[49] record of the year 1664. The "traditional period" of annual repair of old buildings and cleaning of water sources and bodies extends from Baisakh Sukla Tritiya to Jestha Sukla Sasthi. We find Jayasthiti Malla undertaking the largest waterworks repair known in Malla history on Baisakh Sukla Tritiya (*Akshya-tritiya*) of the year 1381 AD.[50] Several Malla-period inscriptions related to repairs and construction were issued on this date. The Rato Matsyendranath festival, also related to repairs of waterworks, starts a day after this date and is generally completed within the same period. The timing in the driest period of the year clearly relates to the repair of buildings. The incorporation of the cleaning of wells, ponds, and drainage ditches must also relate to the period when, along with the stone water conduits, wells became an important part of the urban water supply system. Although wells had been used in the valley since before the Malla period, they seem to have become numerous enough to demand an urban cultural practice of annual maintenance as the town size increased. Also, with the specialized trade zoning and homogeneous neighbourhoods, the stagnant water of wells must have become acceptable even in the religious context of "purity" usually associated only with flowing water.

The growing city demand for maintenance of these public water supply systems was seemingly addressed through full public participation and coupled with repair of old buildings. The urban utility of water and its maintenance was given the same status as repair of temples, *patis*, and other religious-cultural edifices in the town. At the same time, it seems, the responsibility of extant *guthis* was extended to cover those parts of the water supply system that did not have such a provision.[51]

The festival of Sithi and the extension of its utilitarian component are thus a crafty incorporation of an urban activity into extant cultural practice and show a management sense geared towards overall sustainability of the urban system. The importance and timing of the rituals are doubled up by linking cleaning the wells to agricultural water demand. This must have been done to ensure appropriate urban behaviour from a primarily agriculture-based population. It must be for such reasons that the cleaning of wells is tied up with an additional belief that the act is an honour to the goddess of agriculture, Basundhara. The large-scale cleaning of all urban water utilities must also have resulted in the irrigation of agricultural land for the immediate sowing season. It is this crafty cyclic linkage that has led to the tradition being sustained for centuries.

Ponds have dried up due to unprecedented urban expansion and wells no longer constitute a major source of water. Many wells are not cleaned these days in Sithi, and building repairs are also common throughout the year. Yet the utilitarian component of the festival of Sithi had remained. Even today, in sectors of towns with a majority farming community, cleaning of wells is joyfully undertaken on the day of Sithi.

The tradition of Luku-Mahadeo, Pasachahre: Removing garbage from the dump sites of the sagahs

Pasachahre[52] is a dry-season festival celebrated for three days in Chaitra Krishna Chaturdasi (April). This ancient festival of Ajima[53] seems have undergone several ritual additions over history. Our interest is on the starting rituals of the festival, when a god called Luku-Mahadeo commands the first offer of worship. Luku-Mahadeo, a form of Siva worshipped by both Hindus and Buddhists among Newars, concerns a *puranic* incident in which Lord Siva had to go into hiding. Early in the morning on the first festival day the faithful go to their hiding place, dig the garbage around to expose Siva-*linga*, and offer worship to it.

It is interesting to note that this Siva is sited in courtyards and open spaces used for dumping garbage in the city, and the festival serves the practical function of annual garbage removal from these pits. As the traditional garbage was mostly organic, the courtyards and dumps served as composting places and the festival also made manure available to the farms as a by-product. It seems that the festival of Pasachahre was adjusted in medieval times with the inclusion of this new ritual as the garbage problem in the town must have acquired not only a visible dimension but may also have caused disastrous health problems. As agriculture-based towns, many garbage-dumping courtyards, called *sagahs*, had developed inside the towns, and the higher ambient urban temperature quickened the process of composting garbage for manure: such composting would not have been possible in the open farms in the cold winters of the valley. However, its timely removal was important to avoid health hazards, and seemingly the tradition of Luku-Mahadeo was invented and popularized as a folk festival to avert such a situation.

In recent times, when the worship of this god was reduced to a purely functionary ritual and with the erosion of the agricultural base of the town, the *sagahs* of Patan and other towns of the valley have become such a problem of city sanitation that hundreds of trips by solid-waste-removal trucks have to be organized to clean them. In the not so distant past, however, such a situation did not occur in Patan or other towns of the valley simply because the festival of Pasachahre made regular garbage recycling a part of community behaviour, strongly enforced by the mediation of Luku-Mahadeo, the hidden Siva.

Lessons from Patan's past in the creative use of culture in urban sustainability

This chapter has identified above eight cultural activities that have survived into modern times and have been crucial in creating the sustained urbanism of Patan. These cultural practices conditioned appropriate social behavioural patterns through several generations and through changing cultural periods. In several instances, the developments of later cultural periods can be seen as restatements of earlier practices to maintain a co-relation with newer economic activities, changed ecological conditions, and growing urban waste and heat problems. One can observe that they also conditioned appropriate social regroupings so that individual and specialized group behaviour patterns suited the increasing urban population and the town's complexity. The practices incorporated elements that sought to mediate behaviour through time and space.

From the earliest cultural period there are surviving landmarks of the *dyochhen* and *pith* and the associated *pigan-puja* festival. As the resource base expanded in the following Lichchhavi period, the institution of the *guthi* was developed to ensure institutional and financial sustainability for activities of a community scale. For Patan, the importance of Bungamati as its source for water for agriculture as well as urban uses was driven home to the citizens through the institution and popularization of the Rato Matsyendranath festival. As urban growth continued in the Malla period, several new urban cultural elements were set up. They tried to ameliorate problems that were only natural in urban areas which were increasing in size and heterogeneity in socio-economic standing and limited in waste absorptivity. These problems were successfully moderated through the incorporation of the *astamatrikas* and *dasa-mahavidhyas* to delimit and bound urban growth; of the Ganesh and zoning by *jaat* principle to create homogeneous neighbourhoods in an otherwise heterogeneous town; of Sithi to keep the city public facilities in good repair; and of Luku-Mahadeo to clear garbage from the *sagah* dump sites.

The end result has been *sustainable development* of the city over centuries. Not only do the practices show ecological, economic, and environmental sense, but also each activity included components applicable to each of these areas. These have been critical in ensuring economic, social, and environmental sustainability in the town function.

By wrapping the cultural practices around religious beliefs and faiths, an assurance of general acceptance of the activities was built in. Legends and folk stories were apparently thought out to strike a religious chord, although all of them seem to have had fairly mundane end-result objectives. For a population steeped in various religious faiths, this seems like a crafty manipulation of cultural practices to attain harmonious acceptance and gain general popularity. God images such as Ganesh,[54] Basundhara,[55] and Luku-Mahadeo[56] were sought out or even improvised for the purpose. Clearly, the municipal managers were using the "religious faith" of the people as a vehicle for implementing their plans and programmes. It is precisely because of the use of rituals as an implementation tool that the festivities continued to yield expected behaviour and results over a long period of time spanning several generations. Couched in religion, the activities sustained as long as the god images themselves continued to rule the hearts and minds of the people.

In conclusion, one can say that cultural practices tied to the concepts dearest to society at any moment, and adapted as emerging realities unfold, sustain best. They contribute to the sustainability of a town if linked to actions designed to resolve urban problems of resources and waste. The past of Patan shows that this was done through the Lichchhavi and Malla periods but failed to be adapted afterwards, leading in modern times to not only loss of culture *per se* but also to unsustainable towns.

For now, our cultural practices need to be adapted to arrest unsustainable trends like a dwindling resource base, growing waste accumulation, and social discord. However, culture can be adapted only if everyone uses it creatively and positively.

Present moves towards transforming and creatively using cultural heritage

The cultural practices which had previously successfully maintained urban life in Patan are now languishing. Such a situation appears to have been caused mainly by gradual erosion of active religious beliefs and their conversion into mere rituals; the growth of other sectors of economy, the reduced importance of agriculture, and consequent change of profession in the farming group; and the dwindling of traditional crafts with a fall in internal demand for these products. These factors may be seen as two faces of the same coin: the changing economy. With the Shah unification of Nepal, Patan's wide agricultural base and commercial activities reduced and the town was left with its limited domestic craft industries. Unfortunately its cultural practices had not consciously nurtured this aspect of the economy. Consequently, Patan started to decline and urban degeneration set in.

Creative use of culture to bring about community participation in managing the environmental and waste problems of the present, and in circumventing the problems themselves, has been relatively limited in Patan in modern times. The cultural practices of the past have only recently been revisited for possible adaptations and adjustments.

In the last 10 years or so creative transformation of the cultural heritage of Patan to affect overall sustainability is gaining strength in three particular areas: cultural tourism and resurgence of the domestic craft industry; heritage conservation as part of the city development strategy; and community participation in conservation and in operation of local community heritage, facilities, and services. While cultural tourism has been used as a tool of economic development and a source of municipal revenue, it has also contributed significantly towards the generation of employment and the augmentation of personal income of city residents. What is more important for Patan is that cultural tourism has generated employment in the traditional skill sector along with the modern sectors. The surviving family trades, particularly metal crafts and painting, have got a new lease of life due to tourism and souvenir sales. Policies and actions appear guided to create a distinct cultural identity of Patan as a city of monasteries[57] and metal crafts. For about a decade now, Patan, with international assistance, has embarked on a programme of development and conservation. The mode of implementation of this programme is largely community-based. This approach has incorporated measures to transform the earlier form of cultural participation into a modern mould of community participation in creating ownership of cultural heritage as well as development inputs.

In effect, they show constructive creativity in the use of "cultural heritage" for the purposes of economic development (income, employment, revenue, etc.), social development (cultural revival, cultural identity formation, etc.), and political development (local governance, decentralization, etc.).

Cultural heritage tourism

Nepal's marvellous natural attractions, such as the highest mountain in the world, Mount Everest, and pristine highlands and tropical lush forests in the plains within its small territory, are matched by an equally marvellous asset of cultural heritage. Ever since 1951 international visitor interest in Nepal has been growing unabated, and in recent years it has attained such proportions that tourism earnings are a significant portion of the total national earnings of foreign exchange. Cultural heritage tourism (CHT), or "travel concerned with experiencing the visual and performing arts, heritage buildings, areas and landscapes, and special lifestyles, values, traditions and events",[58] has come to be a major industry in Nepal today. With the recognition of this heritage as "unparalleled in the world" by UNESCO through the listing of seven monument zones, including Patan's Durbar Square, as the Kathmandu Valley World Heritage Site in 1978, Patan's CHT has received an added impetus.

At least one-quarter of total tourist arrivals in the country visit Patan every year. Visitors to Patan in 2000 totalled about 100,000. Since the beginning of 2001 a tourist entry charge[59] has been levied on visitors to Patan, and the money is deposited in a Heritage Conservation and Tourism Development Fund. Apart from conservation of monuments and spaces, some of these earnings will also be allocated for conservation of intangible heritage. Other than the city entrance fee charged by the municipality, the Golden Temple (Hiranya Varna Mahabihara) has also been charging a small entrance fee of Rs 25 to tourists since 15 December 1998. This fund is managed by a monastery committee.

Economically, tourism seems to be fourth in importance, after commerce, agriculture, and industry. This conclusion is drawn from the results of a small research survey[60] conducted in major tourist-frequented streets in Patan to assess businesses associated with tourism, numbers of citizens directly employed by the industry, and their approximate earnings. The survey was generally contained within the traditional sector of the town: the areas between Kumbheswor in the north, Mahaboudha in the east, and Pulchowk in the west. It is estimated that the surveyed businesses cover about 85 per cent of the total.

Individual capitalization of cultural resources

Apart from tourist visa fees and entrance fees, tourism as a consumer of cultural heritage, artefacts, and skills also contributes indirectly by providing employment and business to the private sector and the community at large, and has become a new means of economically sustaining the city.

Hotels, restaurants, and travel agencies

The first-ever hotel in Patan, Hotel Narayani, was established in the late 1970s. At present a total of nine hotels and guest-houses provide a total of 690 beds to different classes of tourists. Hotels Himalaya, Summit, and Narayani provide facilities of higher international tourist standards, while the Mahaboudda Guest House and Third World Guest House provide accommodation amid the heritage setting itself. The latter type of accommodation has been growing in popularity with the saturation of Kathmandu's medium-class tourist places. However, as the peak tourist season is limited to about six months – three months each in spring and autumn – the occupancy rate in the hotels year-round is not more than 40 per cent. This underscores the need not only to promote tourism in lean periods but also to make extra effort to bring tourists to stay overnight in Patan. The hotels now provide employment for about 750 persons. Although this is not a significant number, it is observed that the smaller hotels in the city core of Patan employ more local people as a percentage of the total.

Patan Café, started some 15 years ago, was the first restaurant to be explicitly targeted at tourists. As the number of tourist arrivals in Patan increased, several more restaurants were established. Today seven of them provide a variety of food, from continental to Nepali. Some of them also serve typical Newari food like *bara, chhoyela* etc. These restaurants have been able to generate employment for about 90 people, of whom 21 are local to Patan. The restaurants are not utilized to capacity. The situation underscores the need to extend tourist attractions within Patan.

Only five travel agencies operate out of Patan, handling a small number of tourists, as many travel agencies and tour operators are concentrated in nearby Kathmandu. Substantially high rents and shortage of rental space in Kathmandu are the key reasons behind travel agencies being located in Patan.

Workshops

With the fame and skill of Patan, making it synonymous with the "City of Fine Arts" and the "House of Artisans", the quality of handicrafts produced in Patan is rated highly by tourists. The ancient method of metal casting, the "lost wax process", is still used in making metal statues in Patan. Along with bronze and copper statues and statuettes, hand-carved wood and stone items are popular as souvenirs with tourists.

As most of the handicraft works are made through skills inherited from ancestors, workshops are located in specific areas (*toles*) and almost all are family managed. Metal-casting and carving works are done in the Mahaboudha area; stone-carving is done in Chapat and Bhinchhebahal. Apart from the products, the workshops and work processes have also acquired a heritage dimension as attractions to tourists used to mechanized production. Other skills like woollen carpet-weaving, *thanka* painting, and *aquaral* painting workshops are scattered across the town.

Handicraft stores

Apart from the workshop sales outlets, several handicraft stores dot Patan's tourist-frequented areas and are an ever-growing phenomenon. Along with metal statues (bronze, copper, brass, and silver) and wood carvings, new items such as woollen carpets, dresses, paintings (watercolour and traditional *paubha*), pashmina shawls, handmade paper products, paper masks, postcards, and stone carvings have been added to suit tourists' tastes and budgets. Most handicraft shops are concentrated in the Durbar Square area, where almost 90 per cent of all commercial space has already been converted into handicraft shops.

Like the workshops, most shops are small enough to be family managed and provide additional income to the traditional residents. Silver handicrafts, watercolour and *thanka* paintings, and wood carvings seem to be the best-selling items. The monthly sales turnover in these shops varies, the highest turnover reaching as much as Rs 450,000 in some cases.

Raw material supplies to these shops come mostly from within the valley and provide additional employment. Almost all the metalcraft items sold in Patan or other places in Kathmandu are supplied by workshops in Patan itself, while about 80 per cent of wood carvings come from Patan and the remainder from other parts of the valley.

Tourist peddlers (hawkers)

Alongside the regular handicraft shops there are quite a number of hawkers seen in the main tourist spots such as the Durbar Square, the

Golden Temple, and around the bus stops at Pulchowk and Patan Dhoka. They sell wooden or bone-made ornaments, passport bags, flutes etc. The hawkers, mostly women or children, are estimated to number around 100. Although they provide a service for tourists, it is felt that they should be allowed to sell their things only within a specific area so they do not become a harassment.

Creative use of skills and culture: Product adaptation

The practice of arts and crafts was at its peak during the late Malla period. It was competition among the kings of Kathmandu, Bhadgaon, and Patan that resulted in a profuse addition of beautiful temples, community buildings, shrines, and monasteries and heavy demand for crafts products. Recruitment of craftsmen from Patan to other parts of the country by these rulers sustained craftsmanship within Patan. After a gap of three centuries, growing tourism and the appreciation of traditional skills by tourists are playing the same role. Craft has once again become a source of inspiration and income. Thus in the area of traditional crafts and arts, the capitalization of cultural heritage has added advantage to a traditional economic sector. Through creative innovations in their cultural products and adaptations, the traditional craftsmen and artists are further capitalizing on cultural tourism. Traditional painting has found a new expression, and several shops located in the Patan Durbar area frequented by tourists display collections of new watercolour paintings depicting scenes of local life. Souvenir and craft shops in the tourist-frequented sections of the town as well as traditional workshops of metalworkers and woodworkers in town and in Patan's industrial district provide a significant array of new products directed towards the tourist market and exports. To a minor extent, these innovations have also created a domestic consumer market.

The key crafts and skills that have been creatively experimented upon by the traditional skills sector are bronze, brass, and copper working, paintings, *thankas* and *paubhas*, wood-carving, ricepaper crafts, and gold and silver jewellery. Products ranging from watercolour paintings, chessboards and pieces, and notebooks to lampshades, miniature carved windows, and temple lions, etc. show a wide and varied innovative adaptation.

A very large Tibetan refugee camp that was established in the 1960s in the south-western outskirts of the old core of Patan has now become an important site for craft products. Carpets produced in this area have a significant market in European countries and provide a vibrant economic base for Patan.

Cultural identity formation

With wide competition between Bhadgaon, Patan, and Kathmandu for CHT and the growing popularity of Bhadgaon as a cultural city, Patan is making conscious efforts to form its own distinct identity as a town of Buddhist monasteries. Patan can rightfully make this claim, with as many as 166 monastic establishments or their shrine remains and the largest and most active monasteries of the valley located in the city.

In physical terms, quite a few monasteries have turned into residences and workshops of the family of the last *thapaju*, leaving only the main shrine, some religious objects in the courtyard, and occasional rituals to remind one of the Buddhist monastery. Despite the generally degenerate status of the traditional *guthi* as well as the *sangha* of many monasteries, the Buddhists of Patan are still a better-organized group than those of other towns in the valley. A revivalist trend in religion is evidenced by the strong and colourful participation in several festivals, such as *yala-pancha-daan*, *mataya*, and *baha-puja*. The growing participation in *baha-puja*, visits to the monasteries to worship, is particularly notable. Although they appear ritualistic, and are sometimes also feared as having a fundamentalist tendency, these festivals are cultural expressions that help strengthen the identity of Patan. One of the first monasteries to have been "reconstructed with modern grandeur and functionalism", the Yakhse-wor Mahavihar, is a matter of pride for Patan. The reconstruction of I-baha-bahi monastery with Japanese assistance is a notable conservation work in Patan.

Like the newly conserved monastery of I-baha-bahi, some other monasteries with reduced religious activities have also been adapted as schools for local children, leaving the shrine and the *agam* room for religious usage as occasionally needed. This adaptive use as schools should be seen as a creative manipulation of the traditional role of Buddhist learning. Architecturally, the form and design of the monasteries suit this new function quite effectively.

Moderating heterogeneity

Like the Buddhist festivals, several other festivities have also gained wider resurgence. The festival of Bhimsen is celebrated with a gaiety and participation unseen in recent times. Interviewees among general residents along the festive route expressed the feeling that the festivals and their revival have improved the quality of life in Patan. Similarly, cultural programmes with a mix of traditional musical and dance presentations and modern interpretations, particularly in the Durbar Square area, have increased in frequency. Residents have donated generously to offset the cost of such festivals. Along with the traditional *guthi*, positive growth of participation of secular community clubs in the management of religious events has been observed in the past few years. This has helped in removing the "fundamentalist" tendency. At the same time, such revival of celebrations with the participation of new groups has contributed to developing a heightened level of feelings of togetherness.

Regular municipal allocations are made to top up *guthi* resources for organizing cultural festivals. Some endowment funds for festivals with small resources have been established. For example, in 2000 about US$6,000 for the Mataya festival, US$2,000 for the Astamatrika festival, US$1,500 for the Kartik Nach dance festival, and US$500 for Buddha Jayanti celebrations were provided.

Unlike in the area of crafts, secular performing arts have not been ably made into a tool for economic upliftment of the people. Attempts at inducing contemporaneity in dance and music forms are just beginning to take place in some of the performing arts presentations.[61] A few recently formed cultural groups have taken initiatives to present traditional and folk dance shows. There is an attempt to revitalize unused monasteries and residential courtyards for music and dance performances as a new product in tourism.

Recreating community participation

The land-based *guthi* system got a severe set-back when the generalist Land Reform Act 1961 was enforced in Nepal. Although the primary intent of the Act was to recognize the tillers' rights to land, it also nullified and eroded the resource base of the *guthi* system. The problems precipitated by the Land Reform Act were supposed to be resolved through the setting up of the Guthi Corporation in 1964. However, in the preceding century only the land property of the major Hindu religious institutions and the associated *guthi* had been preserved through royal interventions,[62] and the Guthi Corporation was detailed to manage only these trusts. Problems within the Act and inefficient management of the corporation contributed to the disappearance of community-led operations and conservation traditions. Heritage and associated socio-religious functions started to face bad days, as the Act had brought close to 85 per cent of the total heritage of the nation under the corporation. Poor management by the corporation turned participation into a mere ritual affair.

It is quite obvious, given the large volume of heritage extant in Patan, that new efforts to bring about community participation in the management and operation of heritage are called for. The Patan Conservation and Development Program (PCDP) has been designed and implemented to create a real opportunity to bring community participation into cultural heritage conservation.

Patan Conservation and Development Program

This action programme,[63] financed under assistance from the Federal Republic of Germany and implemented in Patan between January 1992 and June 1998, primarily sought to integrate the conservation actions and needs of the heritage of Patan with its developmental needs. This integrated approach was an expansion of experiences gained during a 15-year programme of conservation and development implemented in Bhadgaon. The programme used innovative approaches to conservation and development works to evolve and use participatory processes. This mode of operation is very much like a "light reinterpretation" of the traditional community participatory management of urban elements, spaces, and activities ensconced in the *guthi* practice.

Working within a city-scale programme framework that included documentation of heritage, area preparation, and problem-specific action plans incorporating development needs, institution-building, capacity-strengthening, and awareness-generation activities, its every activity became a forum for the participation of public and private sectors in conservation and development. To facilitate the involvement and development of the capacity of municipal and neighbourhood-level institutions, the donor agency took a back seat.

By integrating conservation of built-heritage elements and spaces with development works and expanding them further to embrace other aspects of urban management, the PCDP infused the relevance of living into conservation action. The usual conservation of monuments alone had led the community to think that conservation was for CHT or the benefit of travellers from distant lands. But the PCDP approach showed that the benefits of conservation could also accrue to the people.

Patan Sub-Metropolitan City Office led the group of participating organizations, which included the Department of Archaeology, the Department of Urban Development and Building, the Ministry of Local Development, the local community, and several NGOs, both international and local.

The identification of activities and details, their timetable, and the implementation mechanism were left to the participating institutions and beneficiary groups. Participatory processes, development, and follow-up of improved working styles to reach commonly accepted objectives rather than outputs were used as success indicators. To ensure that actions sustained after the "project" officially ended, the programme was embedded in related existing institutions and sought to add to built-in sustainability. A mandatory community contribution towards the cost of the activity was required to ensure sincerity of participation and seriousness of purpose in the activity itself. Thus both the process of identification of appropriate activities and beneficiary groups and demanding a contribution as a mandatory requirement gave the programme a unique feature and contributed to its institutionalization and governance.

Components of the Patan programme

The initial focus of the programme was on documentation and inventory of cultural heritage – primarily the components of built environment – as this was seen as a prerequisite to safeguard the heritage of Patan endangered by the process of new physical development. Documentation was done of Buddhist and Hindu monuments such as the *bahas*, *bahis*, *chaityas*, and temples, and other secular monuments including *hitis* (public water-spouts), *dabulis* (platforms), *inars* (dug wells), *jharus* (water tanks), *patis* and *sattals* (pavilions and rest-houses), etc. A guidance/ strategy plan incorporating key environmental, development, and investment concerns was prepared to provide an overall planning framework. The documentation was used as an official inventory, a "community listing of property", which provided a basis for preparing local area conservation and development plans. Several detailed action plans ranging from traffic reorganization in the city core area to conservation, development, and management of sites of historical and architectural importance were then prepared. In order to safeguard the cultural environment, including streets and street embellishments, a "building control component" prepared appropriate by-laws, building designs, building permit mechanisms, construction supervision, etc. for wider application by town planners and managers. The projects included restoration of monuments and rehabilitation of important public places, *hitis*, and ponds among other things.

   Pilot projects were designed with two components, a turnkey component and a replication component to be undertaken by existing institutions. The turnkey component was designed specifically to generate awareness of conservation among the people, to demonstrate the desirable quality of work and approaches necessary for conservation and development, and to train the craftsmen and technicians accordingly. Pilot projects included both conservation and development-related projects. Several small works needing emergency interventions were designed as a separate component called "emergency repair of monuments". Like the pilot projects, the emergency repair programme was also designed with a turnkey element and replication action. Under this programme more than 60 major and minor repairs were carried out. Traditional *hitis* (public water-spouts) and ponds, some as much as 400 years old, have been rehabilitated and are now used to supplement the water supply system of Patan. Due to the overwhelming participation from the community, this type of support has been continued into the follow-up phase.

The "integrated neighbourhood improvement programme" component sought to mobilize locally available resources to plan and carry out basic improvement initiatives as the first step towards increasing community awareness and encouraging participation in development. Pilot actions were designed and implemented to provide a model for entire neighbourhoods (*toles*) in Patan. The activities explicitly included development components such as installation of private toilets, solid-waste collection and disposal, street cleaning, sanitation and health education campaigns, small-scale repairs, eye-care camps, informal education programmes, and skills development and training. The integrated *toles* improvement programme (ITIP) was introduced in 1992 at Subahal in Ward No. 8, and ITIPs are now being implemented in 32 *toles*. Within the framework of this programme, 485 individual toilets have been constructed and 359 *sagahs* (semi-private waste-dumping yards) have been rehabilitated.

What is sustaining after the project?

Since 1993, through the PCDP, more than US$1 million has been spent in a variety of conservation and development works in Patan. The various institutions set up or activated are now operating as regular outfits, with finances from the government, municipality, and/or community. The PCDP Steering Committee is functioning without any external support and continues to provide an environment for coordinating activities, especially those related to the conservation of monuments and sites. The Community Development Section of Patan Sub-Metropolitan City Office is operating well, regularly organizing coordination meetings with donors and NGOs involved in the development of Patan. The Patan Durbar Maintenance and Supervision Office, a branch of the Department of Archeology and Patan Sub-Metropolitan City Office, is engaged in meaningful sharing of responsibilities in Patan. At the community level, 32 groups have been formed and are working with the municipality together to manage conservation, development, and social service programmes with little or no external support.

The project has also significantly raised local professional capacity for developing conservation and development action plans. The quality of works produced has been comparable. A special study on Chyasa and a feasibility study of traditional water supply systems have been of remarkable quality.

At the initial stage of the programme it is interesting to note that the local people of Patan and even the municipal administration gave a very low priority to conservation action, and little or no participation was forthcoming. The pilot activities were crucial in creating public appreciation for conservation as a tool for neighbourhood improvement. Public participation grew steadily and so impressively that, in the closing year of the programme, local and municipal contribution exceeded GTZ[64] direct inputs to component activities. Public contributions in small emergency repair activities were even higher, sometimes reaching as much as 70 per cent of costs.

Creating pride in the past through adaptive reuse

The changing economy and perceptions led many traditional houses to be replaced. They were rebuilt using new design and construction materials and methods, much to the detriment of the built cultural environment of the town. The general attitude towards the form and architecture of the traditional house has not been one of pride. Concrete structures that largely fail to empathize with the past are becoming commonplace. Changes are often also associated with the inability of the traditional form to cater to the needs for and of commercial space. It has been felt that one of the ways to demonstrate the usefulness and commercial viability of traditional houses is to commodify the material design and form and market it. With this in mind and with the support of UNESCO, the PTDO, and local entrepreneurs, three large traditional houses are to offer bed-and-breakfast facilities for tourists.

Such activities and facilities enable tourists to observe and live in a style similar to local people. This enhances a feeling of international brotherhood and at the same time is expected to inculcate pride in local people's perception of their lifestyle and a better understanding of themselves.

With the above and other cultural conservation activities in Patan, popular participation in conservation of culture has grown remarkably. Partly due to the higher rentals traditional houses command and partly due to growing pride towards culture, many buildings in tourist-frequented areas are in the process of getting a new veil of a traditional façade.

Adaptation of pati, sattal, *and* chapa

Pati, the community rest place, *sattal*, the community rest-house, and *chapa*, the community centre, are like built ornaments of the physical environment of historical Patan. There are many of them still around. *Patis* are normally used for *bajans* (prayers) when located near a temple and this function is slowly coming back, providing a lively evening environment in the town. Today, following the PCDP, most of these buildings are used and maintained by the community. Some, like Lampati Sattal in the southern part of the Durbar Square, Jhatapol Pati, Lalitapur Sattal at Jhatapole, and a *pati* in Pulchowk, have been recently restored. Adaptations of similar traditional community buildings for modern purposes such as libraries, youth clubs, or even bus stops have been observed elsewhere.

Display of historical and cultural artefacts in a royal setting

It was mentioned above that some of the Buddhist monasteries have been put to use as schools for children. However, the most important traditional building to undergo adaptive reuse is the third court of the Patan palace itself. Called the Manikeshava-Narayan Chowk, this royal residence has been "conserved" and "reconstructed" to house a cultural museum of historical artefacts. Severely criticized by conservationists as flaunting international charters of conservation, but widely acclaimed by the general public as a meaningful and impressive adaptation, the Patan Museum has quickly become a priority spot for tourists and also an attraction of value to local visitors. The resources accruing out of entrance proceeds go to the government of Nepal and are budgeted back to the museum.[65]

NGOs and CBOs in conservation: Patan Gate Visual Improvement

The importance of culture and cultural heritage and their conservation in the sustenance of Patan have been recognized and seriously taken up by several NGOs and citizen body organizations (CBOs), such as the Lalitpur Heritage Society, the Lions Club, the Rotary Club, etc. Several stone water conduits, temples, and other community buildings have been conserved through their support and coordination. The Lalitpur Heritage Society raised more than sufficient public donations to clean, repair, and seal the joints of the landmark temple of Krishna Mandir in the Patan Palace Square.

One case of joint community and institution action of interest is the Patan Gate Visual Improvement programme. Started as a simple class project for the students of architecture at the Institute of Engineering, it has developed into a demonstration project being implemented by a community group, the Patan Gate Committee, assisted by another NGO, the Patan Tourism Development Organization (PTDO). The primer funding for the project, US$9,000, was contributed by UNESCO, and it is expected that the municipality, the community, and other development agencies will add to the funds to complete the improvement works and bring back the visual environmental ambience of the ancient gateway to Patan. Apart from leading to improved living for local people, it is expected that Patan Gate will be a key entry point for tourists.

Patan Tourism Development Organization: An NGO with a mission

The PTDO, established in 1995 as a NGO, is dedicated to tourism promotion in "a healthy manner without disturbing the original cultural and architectural fabric of the city". It has since been involved in a variety of activities such as publishing guidebooks, promoting alternative heritage tours across Patan, organizing special music and dance programmes, exploring new tourism products, converting traditional Newar houses into quality tourism accommodation as pilot projects, etc.

The adaptation of traditional Newar houses into quality tourist accommodation has been taken as a project and is a major endeavour of the PTDO. Gravely concerned about traditional houses losing their full appreciation by the community and quickly taking note of the fever of "cement concrete construction", the PTDO has identified a few excellent old houses and embarked on a programme of supporting the owners of such houses in restoration and development. Such houses will be adapted to suit the requirements of tourists.

The PTDO has so far identified three architecturally and historically important houses and its tireless efforts in seeking funds for support finally attracted the attention of UNESCO (after five years). Through UNESCO, the National Federation of UNESCO Association in Japan (NFUAJ) has now provided US$30,000 for Shrestha House, one of the three proposed houses. Restoration of Shrestha House at Kulimha is in progress. Likewise, the NFUAJ has also already approved the same amount of money for Rajbhandari House, situated near Hiranya Varna Mahabihara at Kwalakhu.

It is hoped that with their commercial success, private citizens will be inspired, will acquire a positive attitude towards their historical heritage, and will be forthcoming to restore, maintain, and/or adapt their traditional houses.

Conclusion

This discussion of the past and present ways of using culture for the sustainability of a city captures a number of differences. Whereas in the past culture and cultural practices seemed to have been used to cause appropriate community behaviour towards sustaining ecology, environment, and social relationships over longer periods of time, current practices relate to creative exploitation of cultural practices as resources by themselves and aim at immediate economic gains at the individual, community, and institutional levels. While the latter approach has potential for sustaining the cultural environment and its conservation, providing necessary resources for its maintenance and other development works, its help towards environmental sustainability and waste absorption is limited. The reinstitution of the participatory process, albeit in a different garb as compared to the *guthi* system, may provide limited sustainability across time to the next generation. As a commodity for tourism the new approaches seem to have worked well. However, apart from the economic capitalization, community participation, and the reestablishing of past traditions in the area of environment and ecology, the gains are limited or non-existent. What seems warranted most is reforming cultural practices and establishing new transformed ones that follow the approach seen in the examples of the past. The sustainability of Patan would gain greatly if culture could be used as a way of life, fully interlinking economy, ecology, and social structure in a composite system.

Perceptions of historic environment as a simple legacy/heritage of the past are based on the presumption that there is a break between the past and the present. Its relevance to present times is then given the status of the proverbial "grandfather clock" and tangible elements become historical monuments to be conserved for memory and tourism, the latter giving it an economic resource role. The presumed break in "continuity of time" presupposes spatial, psychological, and cultural distance of present citizens from those of the past. This presumption would hardly be true about living cultures such as those of Patan and other Kathmandu Valley towns. Ideas and works of conservation of historic monuments or zones or even cities are guided by this concept of a break, and do not see historic environments as important constituents of the present life of a town and its inhabitants. As a consequence, the "software" of culture, the intangibles like rituals, festivals, and social relationships which link people to the artefacts, is left to languish. Indirectly, the current mode of historic environment management has encouraged adverse community and individual behaviour towards the ecological environment. Conservation as practised today neither mitigates cultural degeneration nor helps develop cultural processes. Providing for the needs of the citizen in town may be a matter of economic investment, but its sustenance needs to be approached through culture-building processes and should maintain continuity with past cultural mechanisms. Internally guided regeneration and not externally supported revival should be the basis for creative use and management of historic environments.

Culture-forming activities with the objectives of social, resource, and environmental sustainability should be implemented through media that are agreeable to the majority, or all, of the society to ensure success. Such media must be able to cut across sectors and direct individual actions in desired directions. Legal mechanisms used these days rather universally were developed in Western society with little cultural bearing for Eastern societies. In countries where a law-abiding culture is not yet strong, actions mediated through legal arrangements alone have tended to fail. In historic Patan, ritual mediation was practised and was not transgressed by the citizens, as religion pervaded society. Precisely for that reason, the practices sustained for generations. For Patan, where traditional culture still persists and is being systematically revived, there is a higher propensity towards voluntary conformity than in the case of modern legal provisions.

One may add that creative redefinition and development of historic culture and cultural practices could be used as media for managing changes more successfully than through mere legal provisions. For such reasons, over the past few years the Department of Architecture Institute of Engineering (Tribhuvan University) has been exploring ways of urban regeneration through the medium of cultural processes such as festivals or other surviving indigenous knowledge systems (such as related to water supply systems, local domestic industries, drainage and irrigation, etc.) of potential relevance to physical planning. Guided by analysis of cultural practices and their visible strong respect for and ties with the valley ecology, these conscious efforts at taking such cultural practices further will also help in restoring a sustainable interactive relationship between the people, their town, and their environment. Starting with one or more of such processes and their spatial linkages as points of departure, efforts are being made in these regeneration exercises to incorporate modern-day needs and positive social practices (e.g. festival routes and their activation, school and children's play parades, open spaces, modern community sports and entertainment, etc.). The community response to these planning exercises has been very encouraging.

The argument is more and more convincing that for towns and cities with a dominant "historic environment", cultural practices and processes can be used as a powerful tool to overcome effectively not only the current social disintegration but also the resource and environmental problems.

Notes

1. Howard, Ebenezer. 1898. *To-morrow: A Peaceful Path to Real Reform*. London: Swan Sonnenschein,
2. See also Kano, Katsuhiko. 2000. "Observations", in *Report of the International Conference on Culture in Sustainability of Cities*. Kanazawa: IICRC, pp. 38–40.
3. Fitch, James Marston. 1990. *Historic Preservation, Curatorial Management of the Built World*. Charlottesville: University Press of Virginia.
4. For these reasons, city systems must either incorporate exclusion of waste or invent a subsystem for its conversion into a resource. Although both approaches were in use in ancient cultures (such as that of Patan), they are in infancy or at the experimental stage in modern society.
5. IICRC. 1999. "Main research project proposal". Kanazawa: IICRC.
6. If each of the angles of the triangle is trisected, each dividing ray representing the equally important stance of each vertex in relation to the others, the intersections will result in an equilateral triangle in the centre, which we may liken to "culture". (Morley's theorem states that if angles of a triangle are trisected, the intersection of the trisection lines forms an equilateral triangle.)
7. Weisstein, Eric W. 2005. "Morley's theorem", in *MathWorld – A Wolfram Web Resource*, available at http://mathworld.wolfram.com/MorleysTheorem.html.
8. Commodification of culture is not possible within the culture itself as it is not internally consumable and only assists in consumption of other commodities. However, particular cultures may be commoditized for people belonging to a different culture (tourists) from outside.
9. Tiwari, S. R. 1999. "Kathmandu Valley urban capital region and historical urbanism – Historical environment management: Lessons from history", paper presented to Thirteenth Biennial Conference of the Association of Development Research and Training Institutes of Asia and the Pacific (ADIPA), Managing Asia-Pacific Mega-Cities: Policies to Promote Sustainable Urban Development in the Twenty-first Century, Bangkok.
10. The city of Patan also goes by the name of Lalitpur. The indigenous people of the valley, the Newars, call it Yala.
11. The national urban classification system makes Patan a submetropolis. Kathmandu, which is much larger in both income and population, is a metropolis. The other three, Bhadgaon, Madhyapur, and Kirtipur, are municipalities.
12. Conversations with the mayor and his team; also official brochures and profiles on Patan.
13. Slusser, Mary. 1998. *Nepal Mandala*, reprint. Kathmandu: Mandala Book Point, pp. 84–85. According to her, *pringga* is a terminology synonymous with permanent settlement.
14. Although only a few *yakshya* images have been found, they are still significantly remem-

bered in the socio-religious practice of "Chhwasa" worship in Newar traditions. Apparently, *yakshyas* were site-specific deities.

15. Tiwari, S. R. 2001. *The Brick and the Bull*. Kathmandu: Himal.
16. The festival of Satyanarayana of Hadigaon, coming down from Lichchhavi times, is one such ritual/festival that links the town to spaces in the valley important for the supply of water, and ensures through participatory strictures proper social behaviour to protect and keep clean the water sources, reservoirs, and recharging ponds.
17. Royal orders restricting felling and burning of trees, carrying charcoal, and cutting of branches for animal fodder in watershed areas are seen in inscriptions from seventh-century Kathmandu.
18. A similar practice is still successfully followed in Milwaukee. In 1991 Shanghai's Bureau of Environmental Sanitation collected as much as 90 per cent of human waste and converted it to manure. For further current relevance see Smit, J. 1996. *Urban Agriculture: Food, Jobs and Sustainable Cities*. New York: UNDP.
19. The religo-cultural imagery of Luku-Mahadeo can be taken as a neat example, as this form of Siva was comfortable under garbage but required light, air, and sun on ritual occasions.
20. Wright, Daniel. 1966. *History of Nepal*, reprint. Calcutta: Ranjan Gupta.
21. An undated inscription in Lichchhavi script located in the Chapat area of eastern Patan suggests that a Mahayana Buddhist nunnery existed thereabouts. This appears as an exception, and could be reflecting a relocation act of the transitional period or later. A minor monastery was located around current Yampibahi near the northern *stupa* of Patan.
22. Tiwari, S. R. 2001. *The Ancient Settlements of the Kathmandu Valley*. Kathmandu: CNAS.
23. Slusser, note 13 above, p. 96.
24. These are popularly referred as *digu-dyos*, and are associated with ancestor worship rituals of the Newars.
25. Mahalaxmi of Tyagal, Uma-Maheswora of Tikhel, etc.
26. The current reflection may be seen in the name Ku-pon-dole (Kadapringga-dula).
27. Slusser, note 13 above, p. 97, wrongly also places Gullatangagrama in north-eastern Patan, quoting Dhanabajra Bajracharya's *Lichchhavikalka Avilekh*. Careful analysis of the inscriptions will show that Gullatangagrama was located in the Deupatan area.
28. The earlier water supply system was apparently based on use of shallow wells and ponds. The two systems are still in use to date.
29. The Lichchhavis used a non-Sanskrit term, *tilamaka*, for its irrigation canals. This is apparently a Kirata term. Given that the Newari term for depressed water conduits is *hi-ti* (*hi* standing for moving and *ti* a degeneration of *tila* or conduit), even though there is no physical evidence available to prove it, the knowledge of depressed pit conduits as well as irrigation may be said to have existed in Kirata days.
30. This is inferred from recurrent references to the place as a waterhole and the nature of the site itself.
31. Their importance is still enacted in the festivities of Degu Jatra at Sundhara as part of the Rato Matsyendranath festival.
32. The word is also used to indicate "headman" in historical documents. This usage is possibly related to the *si-kayegu* festival.
33. This reference occurs in a manuscript dated 1150 AD.
34. A memorial image of Uma-maheswora was set up here in 1012 AD. See Regmi, Dilli R. 1965. *Medieval Nepal*. Calcutta: Firma K. L. Mukhopadhyay, Part III, p. 3, Ins. IV.
35. This is a case of the use of "mediators through space". Since the resource base of urban centres has always been, and remains so to this date, outside of the urban area or in the

rural hinterland, for any sustainability to be achieved in a real sense the rules of survival need to be applied outside the urban boundaries. The Kirata town recognized this resource linkage with its economic base, the agricultural fields, and thus some of their cultural practices that mediated across the boundaries led to ecological sustenance of the urban area.

36. Here festivals and rituals appear to have been used as "mediators across generations" or rules that will continue to be implemented through several generations in future, an important reason for the town's sustainability.

37. Possibly because of the near-total obliteration of Naudon, the festival of Mahalaxmi starts from the *pith* and, after going round the south-east section of town, including worship at the Naudon area, returns to the starting point of the *pith* itself.

38. The festival of Balkumari has also been extended to the palace area following the annexation of Balkumari as a Saraswoti site in the Malla period.

39. This word used in the inscriptions is best translated as "that would last for ever" and worked as an endowment.

40. Locke, J. 1975. *Rato Matsyendranath of Patan and Bungamati.* Kathmandu: CNAS, p. 46, also Chapter 3.

41. A side-plot in the story talks about how the paddy crop had yielded only rice husk, and how with the grace of the "god" it had subsequently been possible to grow full-grained paddy.

42. Legends refer to the stone aqueduct as Sailanadi, the canal as Karkotaka Naga, etc.

43. The first capital of the Mallas, Bhadgaon, combined three *pringgas* into one city and expanded its ritual structure by using the *dyochhens* and *piths* for eight mother goddesses. Here *piths* were used for perimeter definition. In the case of Patan, however, the *piths* were used more as nature protectors and remained out in the fields.

44. In some accounts, Balkumari of Tyagal is also taken as Sodasi.

45. Cf. *Asta-dasa-prakritin* of Basantadeva's inscription at Thankot.

46. Different records give different figures. See Regmi, note 34 above, p. 641.

47. For Patan, "untouchability regulations" were enforced only after the reign of Siddhinarasimha Malla.

48. The discussion on Bajrayana Buddhism needs to be specified, in that this form of Buddhism was the earliest form of the Vajrayana branch of Buddhism as witnessed in Ladakh, Jammu and Kashmir, and Nepal. The form and content of esoteric and tantric rituals and practices changed. Buddhism moved to China, Central Asia, Korea, and Japan. The influence of Ganesha was a remnant from early forms of Mahayana Buddhism.

49. Regmi, note 34 above, Part III, "Thyasapu G", p. 120. Slusser (note 13 above, p. 121) makes a belaboured case to suggest that the tradition may have been there since the Lichchhavi period. But the fact remains that the inscription to which she refers makes no mention of any repairs at all. A little later, an edict of Srinivasa Malla of Patan located at the temple of Rato Matsyendranath in Tamgah, dated 1673, mentions Sithi.

50. Malla, Kamal P. (ed.). 1985. *The Gopalarajavamsavali.* Wiesbaden: Nepal Research Centre Publications, folio 58.

51. It is more than likely that wells started as a private facility and as the city grew the utility took a public garb and wells also became a public facility. This is a likely scenario for the fact that *guthis* were not organized for the maintenance of wells in the first place.

52. The first direct reference to the Pasachahre festival is made in the royal edict of King Jitamitra Malla, who ruled Bhadgaon between 1672 and 1696. See Maskey, Soni. 2042 BS (1985–1986). "Kathmandu Upathyakaka Newar Samudayale Manaune Chadparva", *Nepali Samskriti*, Vol. I, No. 3.

53. The faith of Ajima belongs to the first cultural period.

54. Ganesh seems to have gained stature as a major deity of the townspeople around the twelfth to thirteenth centuries at the beginning of the Malla period, although worship of Ganesh as a minor deity in Hinduism is a much older practice.
55. Bajrayana Buddhism incorporated Basundhara as a Laxmi/Sri-Laxmi equivalent. The concept was similar to the still older symbol of the Earth Mother.
56. Luku-Mahadeo, the hiding Mahadeva, is mentioned in the *Purana*. The *puranic* period in the Kathmandu Valley must be seen as post-Lichchhavi or even early Malla, as we start finding written documents called *puranas*. The Mahadeva hiding under the garbage is, however, a local innovation and must belong to the late Malla period, when garbage in towns would have assumed unhealthy proportions.
57. The contribution of the present mayor, Buddhiraj Bajracharya, should be recognized specifically for this identity development.
58. Jamieson, Walter. 2000. "The promotion of culture and history in the APEC region", paper presented at APEC seminar, Manila, June, unpublished.
59. The charge is about 35 cents for visitors from SAARC countries; other visitors pay about US$3.
60. This supporting research for the current study was made by Dilendra Raj Shrestha, president of the Patan Tourism Development Organization, a Patan NGO. His contribution is gratefully acknowledged.
61. One of the latest to be put on as a public performance in Patan Durbar Square was "Kumari ballet and Svarsudha music" during the 2000 festival season. It attracted both Nepalese and foreign audiences.
62. Called Raj Guthi, these trusts were primarily set up by the ruling class in earlier historical periods. They were redesignated with certain additions and deletions during the early Shah period.
63. The programme ended in June 2001.
64. Deutsche Gesellschaft für Technische Zusammenarbeit GmbH (GTZ) is an international organization involved in sustainable development.
65. The entrance fee charged with effect from 28 October 1997 is Rs 120 for tourists other than SAARC nationals, Rs 30 to SAARC nationals, and Rs 10 to Nepalese citizens.

6

Culture of sustainability: Multicultural reality and sustainable localism – A case study of Penang (George Town), Malaysia

M. Nadarajah

Introduction

The discussion on sustainability appears within certain "social sites" consisting of ways of thinking, social practice, and institutions. This study of Penang identifies five such social sites – governance, market, conservation, human rights, and culturalist – and shows that the development of a cultural practice for urban sustainability in Penang is just beginning to take shape. Furthermore, the study articulates eight principles for creating a culture of sustainability.

Introduction to Penang

Locally referred to as Pulau Pinang, Penang is a state in the north of peninsular Malaysia (see Figure 6.1) and consists of an island and a strip of land on the mainland, each governed by separate local municipalities. The Penang state government is now situated on the island, though there is an effort to locate it on the mainland. Both a ferry system and a modern bridge join the island to the mainland; although there is a great deal of resistance against it, a third link is being considered.

For over two centuries Penang attracted settlers from the Indonesian archipelago, India/South Asia, and China, emerging from the nineteenth century as a city with one of the most culturally diverse communities. Poised at the gateway to the Straits of Malacca, Penang served as the first

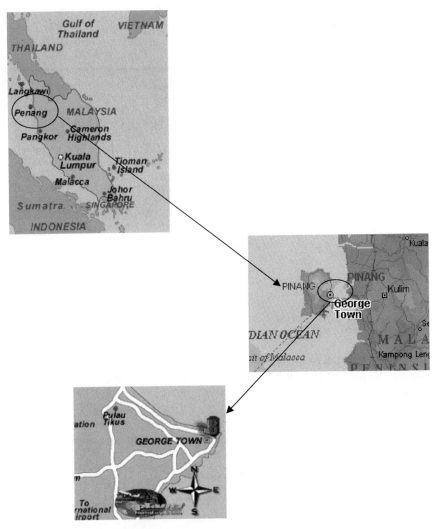

Figure 6.1 Map showing Penang and George Town on the island of Penang

port of call, east of India, for transoceanic ships. For the populations of Acheh, north Sumatra, and south Thailand, it was an entrepôt of tin, rubber, and tropical produce and a gateway to the West. Penang also evolved into an important investment centre for the Nanyang Chinese.

Penang has sought to become an industrial hub in the north. With the development of a free-trade zone in the 1970s, the state was a site of investment and industrial development monopolized by the electronics industry. This has led to it being identified as Malaysia's "silicon valley". It is also one of the most promising and economically dynamic areas within the Indonesia-Malaysia-Thailand Growth Triangle (IMT-GT),[1] a trade promotion initiative in the region.

Politically, Gerakan,[2] a multi-ethnic party with predominant representation of the Chinese community, manages the government with the political support of the Barisan Nasional (National Front). The Barisan Nasional is seen as a coalition party made up of communal parties. Being close to the Barisan Nasional, Gerakan has to work with the United Malay National Organization (UMNO) in addition to the Malaysian Chinese Association (MCA) and the Malaysian Indian Congress (MIC). The MCA sees Gerakan as a serious contender for Chinese votes, which has caused a bit of a friction between Gerakan and the MCA. Another political issue is that there are areas in which the state is subordinate to the central government's interest. These dynamics have implications when considering sustainability issues.

Sustainable Penang Initiative

Penang is of particular interest to understanding of the role of culture in sustainability of cities because of its experience with a project called the Sustainable Penang Initiative (SPI). Officially launched between November 1997 and December 1999, the SPI was a long-term project conducted by the Socio-economic and Environmental Research Institute (SERI) with support from the UNDP-TUGI programme (UNDP's Urban Governance Initiative), the UN Economic and Social Commission for Asia and the Pacific (UNESCAP), and the Canadian International Development Agency (CIDA). The SPI objectives were to establish a broad set of sustainable development indicators to monitor development in Penang, incorporate these indicators into integrated and holistic development planning, and educate the public about sustainable development. In contrast to city-based programmes like Sustainable Seattle, the SPI had a *state-wide* focus. In a sense, this case study is an "evaluation" of the project in relation to culture in sustainability of cities.

Examining the "discourses of sustainability" in Penang

In examining the role of culture in the sustainability of Penang, this study identifies various discourses within which the issue of sustainability figures. Here discourse is understood as "constitutive – as contributing to the production, transformation, and reproduction of the objects . . . of social life. This entails that discourse is in an active relation to reality, that language signifies reality in the sense of constructing meaning for it, rather than that discourse is in a passive relation to reality, with language merely referring to objects which are taken to be given in reality."[3]

This approach was selected because at the time of this study discussions on sustainability were ongoing and parallel. There was no single voice or institution that was engaged in a coherent articulation on sustainability, but rather many voices and institutional media through which the idea was expressed. In addition, the cultural angle to the sustainability of Penang is only an emergent discourse. Thus the exploration of the various discourses of sustainability offers us a view into the various agencies involved in its articulation. It not only reveals the contestation over the notion and its practice, but also the near absence of a culturalist discourse on the sustainability of Penang.

The governance discourse

The Sustainable Penang Initiative: Local and global context

The Sustainable Penang Initiative developed within a specific global and local context: Agenda 21/Local Agenda 21; Sustainable Seattle; growing urbanization; and a willing state government. A consideration of these factors demonstrates the importance of *governance* in the SPI.

Agenda 21 was the output of the UN Conference on Environment and Development, and was adopted by 178 governments in June 1992 at Rio de Janeiro, Brazil. Termed the Earth Summit, the conference's primary focus was on the need to arrest environmental degradation and develop a shared commitment to strategies for preserving and enhancing the environment well into the twenty-first century.

Among its 40 chapters are many that are particularly pertinent to sustainable cities, including those combating poverty (chapter 3), changing consumption patterns (chapter 4), protecting and promoting human health (chapter 6), promoting sustainable human settlements development (chapter 7), and environmentally sound management of toxic chemicals, hazardous wastes, and solid wastes and sewage-related issues (chapters 19, 20 and 21).[4]

Chapter 28 of Agenda 21, entitled "Local Authorities' Initiatives in Support of Agenda 21", has given rise to what has come to be called "Local Agenda 21". In the extract from the chapter below, why "local" in "Local Agenda 21" will become clear.

Because so many of the problems and solutions being addressed by Agenda 21 have their roots in local activities, the participation and cooperation of local authorities will be a determining factor in fulfilling its objectives. Local authorities construct, operate and maintain economic, social and environmental infrastructure, oversee planning processes, establish local environmental policies and regulations and assist in implementing national and sub-national environmental policies. As the *level of governance* closest to the people, they play a vital role in educating, mobilising and responding to the public to promote sustainable development.[5] (Emphasis added.)

While Agenda 21 set the framework for focus on governance issues, it was the successful Sustainable Seattle project that linked governance concerns to their measurability. Founded in 1991, Sustainable Seattle's mission is to protect and improve the long-term health and vitality of Seattle, thus critically linking economic prosperity, environmental vitality, and social equity through the concept of sustainable development. Sustainable Seattle developed the "report card" system, which uses indicators to measure sustainability in order to make sense of long-term trends in the region. This system was created through the efforts of hundreds of volunteers from the Seattle area, who invested time running into thousands of hours for design and research. After Agenda 21 brought attention to the importance of local governance, this "citizens' report card" soon became an important way to measure government performance and has become a popular tool the world over.

The Report Card as a tool for measuring public agency performance, getting user feedback and initiating reform has been employed in a number of cities across the developed as well as developing world ... Used to evaluate local governments' performance as seen by citizens, it is being acknowledged by governments as an important aid in obtaining public feedback on efficiency and efficacy of service delivery mechanisms and in making substantive systemic improvements.[6]

The report card technique was central to the Sustainable Penang Initiative.

The rate and implications of urbanization in Asia were another important factor behind the SPI. TUGI states that 4.2 billion of the world's 7 billion population in the year 2010 are projected to reside in the Asian and Pacific region; about half (45 per cent) of all global GDP growth will take place in Asia; and 43 per cent of the Asian population will live in cities.[7]

The Penang state government, under the leadership of the Gerakan party, proposed five strategic thrusts "to meet the various new challenges to achieve the mission of making Penang an advanced and modern city" for a period covering 10 years, 1992–2002.[8] Among the five strategic thrusts, the second and third are of particular importance to understanding sustainability in Penang.

The Second Strategic Thrust therefore places emphasis on environmental conservation and the provision of facilities for waste management and treatment as well as proper land use and land development ... [The] Third Strategic Thrust aims to promote an even more equitable, integrated and caring society in Penang.[9]

This official position of the state government was certainly helpful to the sustainable development agenda, and to activists in particular.

The process of developing indicators for a sustainable Penang

From late 1997 to early 1999 the SPI organized a series of popular roundtables on sustainable development issues. The roundtables brought people together to identify issues of sustainable development related to five themes that have relevance for "good" governance: ecological sustainability; social justice; economic productivity; cultural vibrancy; and popular participation.[10] These roundtables were organized specifically to develop indicators to "measure" these areas. Altogether about 500 concerned persons – mostly Penangites – from diverse backgrounds spent over 4,000 people-hours at the roundtables, follow-up meetings, and workshops. They identified the first set of issues and indicators of sustainable development that can be used to promote sustainable governance to realize a sustainable Penang.

Launched in June 1999, the Penang People's Forum was the culmination of the series of SPI roundtables. It set out to engage people from all walks of life, as well as the press and the government, to ensure that the results of the SPI process were communicated to a wider audience. The forum consisted of a large, one-day popular exhibition, along with workshops and presentations of the results of the visioning and indicator project. These sessions contributed to the development and use of "report cards" to assess the governance of Penang in relation to sustainable development/urbanization.

The impact of the Sustainable Penang Initiative

The most significant impact of the SPI was to spark the creation of a number of new networks that contribute to the governance and sustainability of Penang. Growing out of the SPI, these entities have taken on their own identities and manage their own activities.[11] Three of the groups are detailed below.

SILA (Sustainable Independent Living and Access)

SILA (Sustainable Independent Living and Access) is a network of organizations for people with disabilities, and is committed to promoting an environment that is friendly to the disabled and physically challenged. The group was formed in February 1998 as a result of the SPI roundtable on social justice (14 February 1998). In the Malay language, *sila* means "please" and denotes access, as in "please come in". With access, people with disabilities can have better prospects of living and independence and so be able to sustain themselves physically, mentally, and spiritually, contributing towards social sustainability. SILA is significantly multi-ethnic, multilingual, and multi-religious, representing the main cultural groups in Malaysia.

STEP (Sustainable Transport Environment Penang)

As is the case in most cities in Asia, the traffic and transport situation in Penang is getting worse. A product of the SPI, STEP (Sustainable Transport Environment Penang) was formed in response to this situation, and has promoted a variety of activities and projects. The Ideal Bus-Stop Project involves conceptual design for an ideal bus stop for Penang, and has been undertaken with a group of student volunteers from Australia and the Penang Heritage Trust. A proposed cycling action plan for George Town and Bayan Baru has been submitted to the Majlis Perbandaran Pulau Pinang (Penang Municipal Council); if approved, the study would be a joint project of SERI/STEP/Interface for Cycling Expertise (Netherlands) with partial funding by the Royal Dutch Embassy in Kuala Lumpur. A "cycling day" was organized in the Pulau Tikus neighbourhood in association with schools, shopping complexes, and residents' associations. A photo survey of the KOMTAR bus station was exhibited at the Penang People's Forum and SPI day, and also became the basis for a memorandum to the Penang state government.

WaterWatch Penang

Water supply is a growing problem in Malaysia, with most cities facing the danger of water shortage. WaterWatch Penang (WWP) is attempting to address this critical problem in an effort to contribute to the sustainability of Penang. WWP is a voluntary citizens' organization set up to promote the awareness and practice of water monitoring, conservation, and protection of water resources. The ultimate goal of the initiative was the creation of Penang as a water-saving society. Activities include publications; promoting public awareness by organizing field trips, educational camps, seminars, forums, conferences, lectures, and talks; providing a link between government, water companies, NGOs, and the public; conducting research; and liaising with other societies dedicated to similar aims and objectives.

To conclude, the discussion on the governance discourse highlights the importance of "good" governance and the need for people's participation. Thus for a city to be sustainable, it needs to put into practice good governance principles and engage citizens in the process.

Conservation discourse

Repeal of the Rent Control Act

George Town, the capital of Penang Island, is everything a thriving city should be: a historic environment of residences, shops, religious buildings, and civic spaces; varied ethnic groups occupying distinctive neighbourhoods; and overlapping streetscapes with vibrant street life. George Town has an urban history dating back to 1786 when a British trading post was established on Penang Island. It has maintained its original town plan and some first-generation brick buildings in the oldest historic core (1790s–1830s) and inner city (1840s–1870s), as well as most of its second-generation buildings (1880s–1930s). In addition to vernacular shophouses, townhouses, and handsome public buildings, there are over 100 temples, shrines, and mosques built by different migrant groups. The George Town Historic Enclave is a heritage area consisting of almost 5,000 pre-Second World War buildings – some of the 8,259 pre-war houses located in George Town. It is a living heritage city with one of the largest surviving ensembles of pre-war buildings in South-East Asia. But like most historic urban centres, George Town faces severe development pressures – new, unsympathetic intrusions, conversion of residences into offices, overwhelming traffic, and developers eager to demolish "vernacular treasures".

George Town's built heritage faces man-made threats: a speculative property market; a high redevelopment plot ratio resulting in pressures for high-rise redevelopment; negative environmental impacts of new developments (piling, flooding, etc.); blanket commercial zoning resulting in decreased residential use; increased traffic and air pollution; increasing illegal use of properties for warehouses; and inadequate maintenance and general urban decay.

The vernacular buildings were protected by the Rent Control Act of 1966, which made removal of tenants difficult. The 1994 Census showed that Penang had 12,453 rent control premises, with 8,259 located in the heart of George Town, 2,395 located outside George Town, and the rest in Seberang Perai (a strip of the state of Penang on the mainland). This Act was repealed with effect from 1 January 2000, and this has the potential of destroying the heritage of the George Town area. It places the agenda of conservation right in the middle of a possible tragedy involving the heritage – material and communal – of Penang.

The repeal of rent control has been estimated to affect 10,000 families. It is a complex issue with a number of serious consequences. It is a social housing issue. The rent control tenants had been paying rents below market levels, and had benefited from social housing in the inner city for the last 50 years. The problem is that this "social housing" was not provided by the government but by unwilling private property owners. And with the repeal of the RCA, only the market will determine rents. It is also an urban renewal issue. The rent control and below-market prices had led to owners neglecting their properties in the George Town area. Many of the premises are in need of repair and renewal. Tenants, of course, will not invest heavily in improving their tenements unless they have a long lease on the place. Landlords, on the other hand, relieved to get their properties back after 50 years, may not be willing to grant long leases or to reinvest in their properties to make up for 50 years of catch-up maintenance.

The only alternative offered to rent control tenants facing displacement is the possibility of purchasing low-cost flats outside George Town. This opportunity, however, can only be taken advantage of by people of low-to-medium income, not by those in severe poverty. Even for those who can afford low-cost housing there is a waiting list of up to 20 years, since low-cost housing is not a priority for most house developers. In such a context, the city of Penang is certain to see the formation of squatter settlements inhabited by former rent control tenants who have nowhere to go. The problem also unfolds as a planning issue. If all the tenants move out of the inner city, the area would be dead at night. There would no longer be any local residents to support or operate the many small businesses. With George Town being zoned as commercial, landlords expecting commercial rents would rather leave their properties empty than rent them out to residents. This will certainly depopulate the inner city, destroying material and non-material heritage. Many shophouses would be converted into warehouses, which are fire hazards. Lastly, the repeal of the RCA presents a transport problem, since residents who moved out of George Town have to commute to work in the town.

Penang Heritage Trust

The Penang Heritage Trust (PHT), formed in 1987, is an organization that has done much to focus world attention on George Town. The Trust, unlike the institutions that managed the Sustainable Penang Initiative, is not the site of governance discourse but rather conservation discourse. Conservation relates to preserving and making wise use of what is here and now, so that we do not waste or pollute or exhaust the availability of resources. This implies that we also conserve what comes to us from the past so that this heritage may be handed on to future generations. The conservation focus essentially has a "local" flavour.

The PHT has made efforts to include George Town on the UNESCO list of World Heritage Sites. In addition, the Trust has contributed to discussions on the Penang Heritage Guidelines under the auspices of the Penang state government, voicing the opinions of civil society regarding the heritage of the George Town area. The guidelines aim to regulate the development of the George Town area so that there is some protection of heritage and careful development of the area. There has been some success in this effort and it has resulted in colour zoning the area, indicating which areas have to be preserved and which areas can be developed and how this can be done.

Through its participation in the UNESCO Local Effort and Preservation (LEAP) programme, the PHT has been active in mobilizing support for the conservation of *waqf* buildings and a Muslim lifestyle in the inner city of George Town.[12] *Waqf* refers to "charitable endowment", in which a person dedicates his/her property to Allah for all time to be used for a beneficial purpose specified by the donor. The charitable gift becomes public property that cannot be given away, sold, mortgaged, inherited, or otherwise disposed of. When all other purposes fail, poverty relief is the ultimate purpose of every *waqf*.[13] According to Abdul-Razzaq Lubis, *waqf* is an Islamic approach to sustainability.[14] The PHT effort has included a workshop on "Memories – Lifestyles and the Women in George Town" and student field and research projects.

The market discourse

The market discourse on sustainability has the power effectively to silence other discourses in the name of economic growth and general well-being. While the genesis of the modern market discourse takes us to Europe, colonialism, and industrial revolution, the discussion here will be limited to the context of Penang. In the Penang state government's strategic plan for 1992–2002, one can delineate the articulation of a market discourse of sustainability.

The policy statement focuses on material growth. In this context, aspects relevant to sustainability are articulated from the point of view of "sustainable growth". The institutional locations of this market-driven discourse on sustainability are the state government, businesses, and business associations such as those representing the interests of property developers. Even groups such as the association of architects eventually fall into this discourse, even though there are conservation-sensitive architects who are doing a great deal to conserve, recycle, and reuse pre-war buildings and spaces in Penang. Even as the market discourse has adopted concerns for sustainable development/urbanization, the consequences of this discourse have materialized in the threat it poses to many important heritage sites, buildings, and communities in the George Town area.[15] An added complexity to this discourse is the reality of globalization. Penang's aspiration to be a global city and to benefit from globalization pushes it further down the road of the growth strategy. While one cannot deny the benefits of globalization, the dangers to local culture are also evident.

The human rights discourse

Save Our Selves (SOS) is a coordination centre for residents who have been affected by the repeal of the Rent Control Act of 1966. It has been in the forefront of defending poor tenants who are faced with the reality of eviction, something neither SERI nor the PHT is seriously addressing. The effort is led by Ong Boon Keong, popularly called "Organic Ong", who had previously spearheaded the organic farming movement in Penang. SOS and Ong are of the opinion that heritage is not just about buildings, but rather must be about people in relation to buildings, living areas, and neighbourhoods. SOS and Ong are critical of both the state government and the PHT for lacking sincerity about sustainable development and heritage. They invariably side with the developers and put poor tenants, now residents of George Town, at risk of losing their homes and being forced to live far from their workplaces.

The discourse which animates Ong and SOS comes from concern for human rights, and articulates a position located in the development of the modern state and linked to the global movement for human rights in general and the right to shelter/housing in particular. It is not that SERI and the PHT are unconcerned about human rights, but they are not addressed on the ground as a serious political issue governing the problem of shelter for the poor community in George Town. The discussion on protecting individual and collective rights, particularly the right to shelter, affirms the agenda of sustainable urbanization as a critical component in the discourse of human rights.

The (emergent) culturalist discourse

The culturalist discourse emerging in Penang builds on the concern for sustainable urbanization. For now this discourse is being shaped within the institutional environment of the PHT, some of whose activities go be-

Table 6.1 Events and status of culture in Penang

Year/stage	1994	1997	2001/2002
Event	Twenty-fifth anniversary of Penang Development Corporation	Sustainable Penang Initiative (SPI)	The Penang Story
Status of culture	Culture articulated as part of economic growth	Culture articulated as part of sustainable governance	Culture articulated as part of cultural diversity/ multiculturalism

yond the concerns of the conservationist discourse. This emergent cultural discourse in Penang witnessed a high point in early 2002 with an international conference called "The Penang Story" organized by the PHT and *The Star*, a national English daily in Malaysia. The conference was a cultural excavation exercise *par excellence*, stating that "embracing the stories of local communities, the 'Penang Story' is a celebration of Penang's historical diversity". Table 6.1 shows critical events in Penang and the articulation of culture[16] shaping a culturalist discourse.

The Penang Story offers genuine potential for cultural diversity, including unique cultural hybrids, to take root. This development offers opportunities for the recovery and reconstitution of ethno-cultural institutions and the (indigenous) knowledge systems surrounding them. For instance, it can allow the development of *kongsi*[17] or *waqf*, which are ethno-cultural and religious institutions respectively that support cultural diversity and sustainability.

The concern for ethno-cultural diversity also allows for the development of the "road of harmony" and other local models for multicultural and religious negotiation and coexistence, a model that is still to be understood historically and/or semiotically. The symbolic "road of harmony", which was originally called Pitts Street and is now called Kapitan Kling Road, accommodates, within walking distance, a Protestant church, the Goddess of Mercy Chinese temple, the Mariamman Hindu temple, and the Kapitan Kling mosque, in addition to two other places of worship. The accommodation seems to suggest multi-religious coexistence, a culturally sustainable scenario. There are other such experiences available. The Dato'Kong is a shrine found in a number of places in the George Town area on the roadside, usually under a tree, where Chinese and Islamic religious symbols coexist. Yet another model is Bangsawan, a dance form which accommodates themes from different ethnic groups. These models present different approaches to complex and productive cultural transactions and hybridization. The examination of all these institutions offers a pathway for redefining multicultural diversity in the making of a sustainable urban society.

Culture of sustainability

In order to understand the contribution of a culturalist discourse to sustainability efforts in Penang, an attempt is made here to pursue a framework for a culture *of* sustainability in contrast to a culture *for* sustainability. The culture *of* sustainability has two components.

- Local cultural practices, knowledge, and institutions that influence a people's everyday life, in particular their interaction among themselves, with other groups, and with nature.
- A set of principles that provide a "guide" to determine whether these practices, knowledge, and institutions are sustainable or not.

The culture *for* sustainability is seen as part of a global sustainable agenda which articulates at a local level. What is promoted as sustainable is part of a global culture – practices, knowledge, and institutions – for sustainable development. In this approach there is no concerted effort at recovery of local cultural institutions. With this brief distinction, let us examine eight principles.

Eight principles for a culture of sustainability

The principle of the "symbolic universe"

As human beings, we live within a symbolic universe.[18] We make sense of ourselves, other people, and the "physical" world through "meaning complexes", which are the stuff of the symbolic universe. The principle recognizes that we live within a symbolic universe and respond to the world that appears to us as a "meaning-scape". Whether there is a physical, objective world "out there" is dependent on what we make of it.

Furthermore, the principle recognizes that we are physically located, and are inevitably embedded in a distinct ecological context. This comes to be wrapped with meanings, a development that transforms three-dimensional physical space into a place. Being in a specific location, responding to the specific ecological context, we all develop distinctive response patterns, produce distinctive meaning complexes, and consequently evolve different highly complex "ethnic cultures".[19] These kinds of development are also closely associated with individual and communal needs for identity. A city therefore can be understood as a complex symbolic order, a distinctive "meanings complex" having a character of its own. And it offers, and will need to continue to offer, increasing numbers of people a sense of themselves, their communities, and their living-working place.[20]

The principle of wholeness

This principle captures the connections across both space and time among the components that make up nature and society. The first aspect of this concept is interconnectedness within the spatial-temporal context. Thus a group acting on a decision they have made in rural England can affect people in rural India,[21] and what we did yesterday has an impact on us today and may impact negatively on future generations. The second aspect is related to how we imagine our relationship with nature, which can be seen in terms of *immediacy*,[22] *duality*,[23] and *mediation*. The idea of wholeness relates to mediation: a "mediated relationship is to be contrasted with both immediacy and duality. Mediation is an 'interceding' between adversaries, with a strong sense of reconciling them. This reconciliation is not a 'neutral' process of the interaction of separate forms, but an active process in which the form of the mediation alters the things mediated ..."[24] The important issue is how this mediation is achieved. It is the author's contention that traditional cultures, largely guided by non-materialist value systems, are usually sustained by a notion of the sacred or a clear idea of deep interconnection or wholeness. Thus consumption is not seen as just an isolated act but one contextualized in a complex network of acts involving the past, present, and future against the circularity of time. Such acts of consumption are more sustainable than those which drive modern industrial society: the materialist ethics of profit-making and of possession and having in the context of linear time.

The principle of development

Development has been very often confused or conflated with *growth*, to the extent that they have become synonymous. But are they? Growth deals with the material expansion of human life and is supposedly aimed at the satisfaction of (primary) human needs. The health of an economy has been and still is to a large extent measured by growth, using the quantitative measure of GNP. This has been critically addressed and is now increasingly seen as relating to "inauthentic development". Authentic development, on the other hand, is seen as a composite of both *material* and *ethical* progress.[25] Communal and individual well-being cannot be defined or located purely in "the material" and need to be relocated in another field, "the non-material". In most cultures, this means recovery of a strong tradition. In simple terms, my happiness defined by possession will confront the inevitable, the finitude of the material. This comes along with all its consequences. My happiness defined by the non-material is a state of being without the limiting horizon of crass possessiveness.

To take another step forward, authentic sustainable development must be separated from a growth-based discourse. Authentic sustainable development is a moral project[26] to create an intentional social world guided by a "dematerialized value system" and practices and a "decommoditized economy".[27] This effort requires a rude rupture of the temporal sequencing of progress by careful recovery of forgotten, marginalized, and neglected traditions that constitute critical resources and pathways to a sustainable future. It is looking back to move ahead.

The principle of democracy

Institutional power needs eventually to be located within communities and exercised through direct communal involvement, decision-making, and participation. Democracy should be an "environment" that allows people the right *and* the ability to interpret events, behaviours, and texts to create alternative political narratives. For such a possibility to be realized, the units involved in direct democratic activities need to be small – not large, bureaucratized social entities.[28] There is certainly a need to rethink organizational forms and promote those which are democratic and sustainable.

There is also the need for a strong media to encourage a participatory, self-conscious democracy built on the principle of social criticism and societal self-learning.[29] This is critical for sustaining sustainable development. All these processes contribute to the achievement of equity and democratic governance.

An interesting discussion on social learning has been put forward by Anil Agarwal.[30] Consider Figure 6.2[31] and the discussion provided by Agarwal:

The x-axis represents time and the y-axis productivity. At any point in time, we want to use natural resources at least at its level of natural productivity. Now let us assume that there are four societies: A, B, C and D. Society A uses its natural resources base and starts degrading it at a particular point in time because of a combination of circumstances, but then it reaches a certain point when it *realises* it is making a mistake. It then starts self-correcting and goes back to the natural level of productivity. The other curves show that society B takes a longer time to the stage, society C even longer, and society D does not learn at all, which means that the resource base is irreversibly degraded.[32]

In the discussions on democracy there has also been a trend of arguments, particularly by authoritarian political leaders in Asia, that Asian notions of democracy and human rights are different from the Western

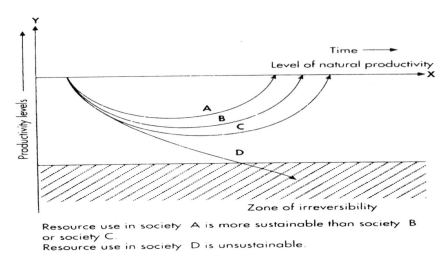

Figure 6.2 Social learning loops and sustainable development (*Source:* Agarwal, 1997)

model, creating in the process the cultural roots and rationale for authoritarianism. However, Amartya Sen,[33] for instance, has challenged this by offering us an alternative reading of Asian culture and cultural roots of participatory democracy. Such notions are not the monopoly of the West, as they are made out to be.

The principle of circularity

In a discussion on metabolism, Herbert Girardet observed that the "metabolism of most cities is essentially linear, with resources flowing through the urban system without much concern about their origin and about the destination of wastes; inputs and outputs are considered as largely unrelated".[34] To continue along this line of thinking, it is instructive to look at models of sustainable consumption found in various cultures.

Industrial capitalist society has made consumption an end in itself, in a sense to keep the economy dynamic. In many societies, traditional models of consumption were different. To understand this it would be useful to look at consumption as an event consisting of a pre-consumption stage and a post-consumption stage. This can be represented as shown in Figure 6.3.[35]

Within traditional consumption models the three stages appear in a "circular" form, as shown in Figure 6.4.

Consumption takes place within a symbolic universe. There is also a model the author has summed up as "consumption as the transubstantia-

| Pre-consumption stage | Consumption stage | Post-consumption stage |

Figure 6.3 Three stages of a consumption event

SYMBOLIC UNIVERSE

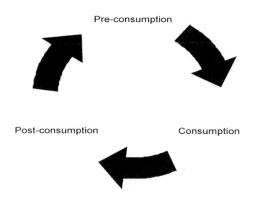

Pre-consumption

Post-consumption   Consumption

Figure 6.4 Traditional model of consumption

tion of the sacred".[36] This model, obtained by a close examination of sacred groves, offers an idea of the circularity principle that treats consumption as a link between two other stages. Consider the following example from Himachal Pradesh in the north of India:

Protection from earthquake and abnormally high and low precipitation/temperature are the major concerns fostering protection of sacred sites. People believe protection from catastrophic events is provided by the supernatural powers residing in the sacred sites ... Apart from spatial connotation of sacredness, people consider many species sacred. Seven species are used as incense on various religious-cultural functions, six species are valued for offering their flowers to the deity and 12 species are believed to be preferred by the deity all across the landscape ... religious and cultural importance of these species is a factor promoting their sustainable utilisation as well as conservation. Management activities critical to the survival of the people such as sowing, harvesting, migration to alpine meadows for grazing and medicinal plant collection are undertaken following religious functions in and around sacred sites.[37]

The pre-consumption and post-consumption stages influence the consumption stage. The notion of the sacred guides production, distribution, and consumption, and in the end conserves nature. Thus the metabolism in a city needs to be shifted from one marked by unilinearity to one informed by circularity. At one level, by doing this we influence consumption by sensitizing ourselves to the consequences of pre- and post- stages of consumption. We also, at another level, encourage societies to move through recycling and reuse to zero-waste situations.

The principle of diversity

The negative underside of globalization is homogenization/standardization: the tendency to create regimes based on homogenization/uniformity. This has taken place in both the biological and cultural spheres, forcing "monocultures" as a standard in place of diversity. A commodity-based, profit-oriented economy primarily drives such a tendency. Biotechnology and new communication technology destroy diversity, both biological and cultural.

This principle recognizes that cultural diversity and biodiversity are intrinsically a good thing.

Plants, animals, and even the invisible micro-organisms around us, sustain and recreate the quality of the water we drink, the air we breathe, and the soil on which we grow food. It is our forests, lakes, rivers, grasslands, coasts, seas, and agricultural lands that provide us with oxygen, water, and fertile soil, with food, medicine, clothing, housing, energy, and other materials needs. Most of the oxygen we breathe comes from marine algae, whose existence is dependent on a complex chain of diverse life forms and inanimate matter. Where would we be without all this? ... Agriculture, which provides 32 per cent of the gross domestic product in low-income countries, may have of late become technologically sophisticated, but it still depends on traditional crop varieties, and on wild plant relatives of crops. In the 1970s, a wild rice species found in India was found to be resistant to one of the most dangerous pests (a species of plant hopper); genes from this plant were used to save millions of hectares of cultivated rice in South and Southeast Asia from being destroyed by a major epidemic. Diversity within agricultural systems is also crucial to the stability of farmers.[38]

The diversity of "ecological contexts" has contributed to cultural diversity, producing a diversity of languages, dance forms, dressing styles, cuisine systems, kinship patterns, indigenous knowledge systems, etc. All these are at risk of destruction if the homogenizing tendency of globalization is not recognized and confronted. In fact, the present form of civil war within multi-ethnic and multi-religious nations seems to be a reaction to cultural homogenization by both the state and global forces. There is an increasing tendency for ethnic groups to assert their cultural identity. The principle of diversity mobilizes our intellectual and emotional energies for the protection of diversity, which supports the sustainability agenda.

The principle of localism

This principle recognizes that human life is embedded within distinct eco-logical contexts and is not free-floating. The importance of localism is highlighted in the concluding remarks of a report on a nine-country study of consumption patterns.

Development policies have encouraged a shift from agriculture to industry and services. It is against such a scenario that we made growing one's own food an in-dicator of sustainability. What is the role of growing one's own food, in terms of promoting a sustainable lifestyle? In growing one's own food, energy is saved in production and marketing. Food need not be transported over long distances. Garden plots are more labour intensive. It is also probably easier to avoid the use of chemical fertilisers and pesticides. Such a practice plants the value of local-ism. A revealing example will be useful here. After the collapse of the Soviet Union, Cuba was faced with a crisis. With no ability to continue the import of fer-tilisers and pesticides, Cuba transformed nearly all of its agriculture. To address the food situation in the cities, residents were encouraged to grow food on avail-able land. Incentives were given to encourage people to move to rural areas and work on farms. Cuba thus managed to avoid famine and at the same time make its agriculture more environmentally sustainable.[39]

Knowledge production is another example of localism, as it is pro-duced at all levels as people build patterned responses to their ecological contexts, i.e. the natural and social worlds. Knowledge indigenously pro-duced covers a wide area, and is produced in context-specific situations. Many of these systems of local knowledge feature sustainability not as a concept as we have these days but as a *lived* activity.[40]

Global processes can affect local developmental decisions and lead to the loss of localism. To what use a plot of land here will be put can be influenced by decisions elsewhere in the globe. The present international economic regimes can affect and weaken sovereignty with regards to sus-tainability, as the recent movements against the WTO meetings in vari-ous parts of the Western world showed.

Against such development, we need to consider "enlightened local-ism" as much as "enlightened globalism". An additional concern is rec-ognizing that in the design of complex systems, "globalization" always presents a danger of indiscriminate interconnectedness and interdepen-dence. There is thus a need to *modularize* as well. There is certainly an affinity between modularization and localism.

The principle of spatialization

Spatialization is the process whereby what we understand as physical, ob-jective, three-dimensional space becomes a place, endowed with mean-

ings. To understand this process, it is worth looking at the phenomeno-
logical notion called "place-ballet".

First, it joins people, times and space in an organic whole and portrays place as a
distinct and authentic entity in its own right. In the past, many approaches to the
person-environment relationship have been piece-meal and mechanistic: place is
only the sum of the behaviours of its individual human parts. In contrast, place-
ballet depicts a whole greater than its elements: place is a dynamic entity with
an identity as distinct as the individual people and environmental elements comprising that place. Place-ballet, in other words, is an environmental synergy in
which human and material parts unintentionally foster a larger whole with its
own special rhythm and character. An outdoor marketplace, for example, may
be grounded in economic transaction, but is considerably more than just those
transitions. The marketplace takes on an atmosphere of vitality, camaraderie,
and excitement – even gaiety.[41]

It is this level of practice "that materially grounds the experience of
'space' and transforms it into 'place' ... 'Place' is eventually transformed
into 'home', 'home' into 'homeland' ..."[42] The same process can be applied to what one makes out of a city, which is where more and more of
us are being born and begin our social life, and where our identities are
formed and stabilized.

Today, the socio-cultural process of spatialization takes place through
interest articulation of various subgroups inhabiting a city environment.
In an unequal society such a dynamic of interests leads to a hegemonic
process[43] resulting in the monopoly of spatialization by a dominant
group or clique of powerful people, so there is a need to democratize
the process of spatialization. The principle also draws attention to the
socio-cultural process of "democratic spatialization".

Problems of local governance

The effort of creating a sustainable Penang is greatly affected by local
political dynamics. While multiculturalism contributes to sustainability,
it can also create obstacles. As a multi-ethnic/multicultural society that
operates within multi-ethnic politics, local action and governance are
complex. This leads to a phenomenon of taking only those issues that
are not particularly controversial or something very generic, and cultural
and religious issues in particular tend to be ignored. Given the dynamics
of the local community in Penang, three pathways to approaching these
issues are electoral constituencies, traditional non-governmental constituencies, and issue-based constituencies.

Electoral constituencies come under particular political parties, which are greatly influenced by the ethnic diversity in Malaysia. Actions have to be carried out through the mediation of the dominant political party that is in charge of a constituency. The success of local action is determined by political dynamics, which are complicated by the role of ethnicity and religion.

Alternatively, the local community can be approached through the established networks of NGOs that have build up a tradition, like the Penang Heritage Trust. Penang has a reasonably well-developed network of NGOs, which have their own constituencies within civil society for implementing their projects. For instance, the PHT actively mediates in approaches to the local community in the inner-city area of George Town. Other NGOs have membership across local communities, and this allows for mobilization on a larger scale over critical social issues. Most of these NGOs are not organized along ethnic lines and invariably show a positive aspect of the rich possibilities of multiculturalism. Other groups that can be approached are the members of trade/business organizations and a number of cultural organizations.

Issue-based open constituencies are local community groups that have been established through active interaction with persons who are associated with a specific issue. An example of this is Save Our Selves, discussed earlier, which came into existence to address the repeal of the Rent Control Act and the problems faced by poor tenants in the inner city of George Town. These constituencies consist of members from a specific community or communities whose problems are being addressed.

Local action undertaken by the state government is complicated by the fact that the ruling state government is a political party whose continued political survival depends on a number of other ethnic-based political parties cooperating in a ruling coalition. This arrangement severely limits local action, and is a threat to local efforts for sustainability. In addition there is the problem of the centre-state relationship: the central government has the power to overrule action by the local state government, and such actions are easily influenced by business lobbies or political parties.

Conclusion: Heritage, culture, and sustainability

Heritage is highly contested in Penang. This has become even more the case since the repeal of the Rent Control Act, which puts many heritage sites in jeopardy. There is little consensus among the various interest groups, which each define heritage differently. Given the situation, two aspects are of particular importance.

Despite the ideology of "stakeholder discourse", there is serious conflict between the conservationists and cultural and sustainable development activists on one side and the agents of economic growth on the other, whether they act for business or state government interests. While the state government is sensitive to sustainability issues, its concrete actions seem to be shaped more by techno-economic growth solutions, guided by business interests, rather than conservationists or sustainable development interests. Many activists doubt the sincerity of the state government even as they engage with it.

The second aspect brings us to the concerns of the Kanazawa Initiative, namely "How do we make a case for culture's role in sustainability of cities?" In attempting to answer this question, there is a need to realize the implications of the debate and contestation over heritage defined by the activities that are going on in the George Town area in general and the inner city in particular. The George Town heritage issue offers evidence of the difficulty locally, nationally, or regionally of setting a cultural agenda for the sustainability of cities. While the Sustainable Penang Initiative does not offer a case for an active cultural localism for promoting the concerns of sustainable development, the George Town/Penang case is an opportunity to evaluate the theoretical and practical issues – including governance issues – surrounding such an effort.

The efforts to look at local cultural forms also mean that there is a great need to develop linkages between the global sustainable development discourse and the local cultural discourse on sustainability. This demands that the "culture *of* sustainability" of city activists must understand the very basis of the local cultural forms of life, their knowledge systems, their institutional life, and their developmental trajectory. There is a need to redefine, recover, or reinvent culture for the purpose of promoting local culture and the sustainability of cities. This also means that there must be a careful working out of the relationship between a culture *for* sustainability (global discourse) and a culture *of* sustainability (local discourse).

The Penang case study is useful to understand the difficulty of developing a radical local cultural approach (cultural localism) to sustainable urbanization through *active local municipality action*. While the city has certainly benefited from the Sustainable Penang Initiative, there is hardly anything in this effort in terms of concrete action to suggest that local cultural institutions have been or are being revived, recovered, redefined, or reinvented to be employed in the sustainable urbanization efforts.

A serious problem is that the use of sustainable governance principles in the effort to promote sustainable urbanization in Penang is not seen as coming from within local culture but rather as a set of principles that are "imported" from outside. While this in itself is not necessarily bad, the real danger is that instead of acculturation between the global and local sustainable development discourses and eventually institutional practices, it may lead to assimilation in which local cultural forms may be substituted by organizational innovations that promote sustainability based on a completely different ethos. This will certainly be sustainable urbanization indeed, but one without the cultural "soul" of a locality.

The Penang case study illustrates that the culturalist discourse is far from being the "dominant" discourse on urban sustainability. While the more established discourses – the market discourse, for instance – with their institutional support seem to direct present activities related to sustainability, there is a growing realization of the importance of institutionalizing the culturalist discourse. In Penang, quite ironically, the most serious obstacle to a culturalist discourse is the governance discourse of the Sustainable Penang Initiative. This focus on governance as an end in itself does not further the agenda of local culture or multiculturalism. It places local cultural knowledge, social practices, and institutions at risk of marginalization and eventual loss to the community. There is a need to tame the governance in Penang to serve the interest of local culture and multiculturalism through "sustainable enlightened localism". And through that achieve urban sustainability.

Acknowledgements

The author gratefully thanks the following for their help: Salma Khoo Nasution, Penang Heritage Trust, Penang; Chong Li Mei, Help College, Malaysia; Prafulla Pradhan, UNDP-TUGI, Kuala Lumpur; Abdul-Razzaq Lubis, UNESCO-LEAP, Penang; Anwar Fazal, UNDP-TUGI, Kuala Lumpur; Alagar Mathi, Ipoh, Malaysia; Professor S. Kusune, Kanazawa, Japan; Professor Ratna Rana, IICRC, Kanazawa, Japan.

Notes

1. The IMT-GT is an economic network of three regions in Indonesia (north Sumatra and Acheh), Malaysia (Kedah, Perlis, Penang, and Perak), and Thailand (Satun, Narathiwat, Yala, Songkla, and Pattani) which share many similarities in both social and economic perspectives.
2. "With its non-racial approach in serving multi-racial Malaysia, Gerakan has been an anomaly of sorts within Barisan Nasional, the ruling body politic comprising largely communal parties." See the Gerakan website at www.gerakan.org.my/mainindex.htm.
3. Fairclough, Norman. 1992. *Discourse and Social Change*. Cambridge: Polity Press, pp. 41–42.
4. Satterwaite, David. 1999. "The key issues and the works included", in David Satterwaite (ed.) *Sustainable Cities*. London: Earthscan Publications, p. 13.

5. *Ibid.*
6. UN TUGI. 2000. "Assessing urban governance: Citizens' report cards", *Urban Voices*, No. 29, April, p. 2.
7. See www.tugi.apdip.net/.
8. Koh, Tsu Koon. 1996. "The Penang Strategic Development Plan", in ASLI *Penang into the 21st Century*. Petaling Jaya: Pelanduk, p. 5. Koh Tsu Koon is the chief minister of Penang.
9. *Ibid.*, p. 6.
10. SERI. 1999. *The Sustainable Penang Initiative: Penang People's Report 1999*. Penang: SERI, p. 7.
11. Several factors contributed to the success of the SPI. The state of Penang (the island in particular) is a compact, relatively developed, and urbanized state with the human and infrastructural resources to sustain a broad-based citizens' initiative; in part because of that, the state of Penang has had a longstanding tradition of NGO activism. Indeed, Penang provides the home base and headquarters for a remarkable number of international and regional NGOs. Local voluntary organizations are similarly active, and the accumulated experience and networks between such organizations as well as individuals were crucial to the SPI's rapid launch. The SPI project employed highly competent and enthusiastic staff, and experienced and motivated supporting staff and volunteers. Finally, liberal, open-minded elements within the state government leadership were receptive to ideas of broader-based governance.
12. *PHT Newsletter*, No. 65, November 1999–January 2000.
13. Khoo, Salma Nasution. 2002. "Colonial intervention and transformation of Muslim *waqf* settlement in urban Penang: The role of the Endowment Board", *Journal of Muslim Minority Affairs*, Vol. 22, No. 2, p. 299.
14. In an interview in a documentary entitled "Sustainable Penang", produced by Cahayasuara, Kuala Lumpur, 2001. Lubis was also the manager of the UNESCO-LEAP programme on *waqf*.
15. See Nagata, Judith. 2001. "Heritage as a site of resistance: From architecture to political activism in urban Penang", in Maznah Mohamad and Wong Soak Koon (eds) *Risking Malaysia: Culture, Politics and Identity*. Bangi: Penerbit University Kebangsaan Malaysia, pp. 190–193.
16. Nadarajah, M. 2002. "Cultural diversity and sustainability: Preliminary notes toward a 'theory' of Penang", paper presented at International Conference on "The Penang Story", Penang, 18–21 April.
17. Wang, Tai Peng. 1994. *The Origins of Chinese Kongsi*. Petaling Jaya: Pelanduk Publications.
18. Inspired by Berger, Peter L. and Thomas Luckmann. 1967. *The Social Construction of Reality*. Harmondsworth: Penguin.
19. See for instance Tonnesson, Stein and Hans Antlov (eds). 1996. *Asian Forms of the Nation*. London: Curzon Press; Ramakrishnan, P. S., K. G. Saxena, and U. M. Chandrashekara (eds). 1998. *Conserving the Sacred For Biodiversity Management*. New Delhi: Oxford and IBH Publishing; Bruun, Ole and Arne Kalland (eds). 1995. *Asian Perceptions of Nature*. London: Curzon Press; Faure, Guy Olivier and Jeffrey Z. Rubin (eds). 1993. *Culture and Negotiation: The Resolution of Water Disputes*. New Delhi: Sage Publications; Vitebsky, Caroline and Piers Vitebsky. 1997. *Sacred Architecture: Models of the Cosmos, Symbolic Form and Ornament, Traditions of East and West*. London: Duncan Baird Publishers.
20. See for instance Oncu, Ayse and Petra Weyland (eds). 1997. *Space, Culture and Power: New Identities in Globalising Cities*. London: Zed Books.
21. Historically this kind of situation developed with the development of industrial capital-

ism and the growth of capitalist markets. Such a development linked the most remote village with metropolitan urban centres.

22. Part-whole relationship: "someone who argues that man is nothing but a part of nature, a natural being subject to natural laws, is taking the position that man is in immediate unity with nature". Arthur, C. J. 1986. *Dialectics of Labour: Marx and His Relations to Hegel.* Oxford: Basil Blackwell, p. 5.

23. External relationship: "someone who takes a dualistic position, representing man as separate from the natural realm, developing himself spiritually, and struggling against the power of nature latent in himself as well as the influence of external determination, is taking man to be immediately opposed to nature". *Ibid.*

24. See Williams, Raymond. 1988. *Keywords: A Vocabulary of Culture and Society.* London: Fontana, pp. 204–205; Meszaros, Istvan. 1975. *Marx's Theory of Alienation.* London: Merlin Press, p. 82.

25. See for instance Lutz, Mark. 1992. "A humanist approach to socio-economic development", in Paul Ekins and Manfred Max-Neef (eds) *Real-Life Economics: Understanding Wealth Creation.* London and New York: Routledge, p. 166.

26. For a related argument see Nadarajah, M. 1997. "Bringing in the value system", in *Consumers in the Global Age*, proceedings of the International Conference on Consumer Protection, 22–24 January, New Delhi. Penang: CI-ROAP.

27. A decommodified economy is not based on exchange values determined by demand and supply pressures of the market, but uses values determined by actual needs of the people, arrived at through a collective and democratic process. A decommodification process can involve for instance the shift from private to public transport, or the promotion of paperless offices. In these cases it is also a process of dematerialization.

28. See for instance the idea of "radical municipalism" put forward by Bookchin, Murray. 1992. *From Urbanisation to Cities: Towards a New Politics of Citizenship.* London: Cassell.

29. For this argument see Dreze, J. and Amartya Sen. 1989. *Hunger and Public Action.* Oxford: Clarendon Press; Sen, Amartya. 1987. *Food and Freedom.* Washington, DC: CGIAR. This discussion has been used effectively in trying to deal with serious collective or societal problems like hunger. For this see Banik, Dan. 1998. "India's freedom from famine: The case of Kalahandi", *Contemporary South Asia*, Vol. 7, No. 3, pp. 265–281.

30. Agarwal, Anil. 1997. "An environmentalist's perspective: Political dimension of sustainability", in Anil Agarwal (ed.) *The Challenge of Balance: Environmental Economics in India: Proceedings of a National Environment and Economics Meeting.* New Delhi: Centre for Science and Environment.

31. *Ibid.*, p. 13.

32. *Ibid.*, p. 12. Agarwal's discussion touches on sustainability "as a *relative* issue" when he compares the four societies. The purpose of the diagram is to consider the reality of social learning and the need for democracy to encourage it, an issue of which Agarwal is not unaware.

33. Sen, Amartya. 1997. "Human rights and Asian values: What Lee Kuan Yew and Li Peng don't understand about Asia", *The New Republic*, Vol. 217, Nos 2–3, 14 July.

34. Girardet, Herbert. 1999. "Sustainable cities: A contradiction in terms?", in David Satterthwaite (ed.) *Sustainable Cities.* London: Earthscan, p. 417.

35. Developed based on Aaker, David A. and George S. Day (eds). 1982. *Consumerism: Search for the Consumer Interest.* New York: Free Press.

36. In Christian understanding, transubstantiation relates to the transformation of bread and wine offered by the priest into the body and blood of Christ. However, the term has a larger application. By extension here, it simply means that which human beings

need is the transformation/transubstantiation of the sacred. See Nadarajah, M. 1999. "Two models of sustainable consumption", paper presented at the International Experts' Meeting on Sustainable Consumption Patterns: Trends and Traditions in East Asia, 27–29 January, Cheju Island, Korea.

37. Singh, G. S., K. S. Rao, and K. G. Saxena. 1998. "Eco-cultural analysis of sacred species and ecosystems in Chhakainal watershed, Himachal Pradesh", in P. S. Ramakrishnan, K. G. Saxena, and U. M. Chandrashekara (eds) *Conserving the Sacred For Biodiversity Management*. New Delhi: Oxford and IBH Publishing, pp. 307–308.

38. Kothari, Ashish. 1997. *Understanding Biodiversity: Life, Sustainability and Equity*. New Delhi: Orient Longman, pp. 3–4.

39. CI-ROAP. 1997. *A Discerning Middle Class: A Preliminary Enquiry of Sustainable Consumption Trends in Selected Countries in the Asia Pacific Region*. Penang: CI-ROAP, p. 74.

40. When human behaviour starts to conform to concerns of sustainability it goes through a conscious stage. Once behaviour conforms to sustainability it becomes a norm, and usually the conscious role is diminished. Normative behaviour is patterned and lived.

41. Seamon, David. 1980. "Body-subject, time-space routines and place-ballets", in Anne Buttimer and David Seamon (eds) *The Human Experience of Space and Time*. London: Croom Helm, p. 163.

42. Nadarajah, M. 1999. *Culture, Gender and Ecology: Beyond Workerism*. Jaipur and New Delhi: Rawat Publications, p. 199.

43. For an interesting discussion on this see Benko, Georges and Ulf Strohmayer (eds). 1997. *Space and Social Theory: Interpreting Modernity and Postmodernity*. Oxford: Basil Blackwell. Also see the work of the Marxist scholar Lefebvre: Lefebvre, Henri. 1991. *The Production of Space*. Oxford: Basil Blackwell.

7

Creating cultural identity for sustainability: A case study of Cheongju, Korea

Sang-Chuel Choe

Introduction

Cities, culture, and sustainability are the key notions that will influence the twenty-first century: culture will serve both as a barometer of the quality of life and livelihood and as an agent for sustaining the rapidly urbanizing world. However, the three notions are so broad and so closely related that a comparative study on culture in sustainability of cities needs some conceptual underpinnings. The three concepts have rarely been brought together into one agenda, although the combination of a pair has been one of the favourite agendas for international dialogue and academic discourse in recent times. The interplay of the three concepts is schematically represented in Figure 7.1.

The theme of cities and culture has long been a cherished research topic, whether it is the cultural economy of cities or the culture of cities. The former usually views culture as a means of urban development, while the latter is more or less focused on urban culture *per se*, including cultural identity, creativity, and excellence of culture of cities. Likewise, the interface between cities and sustainability has also been widely debated and suggested for the design of sustainable cities. The interpretation of culture and sustainability leads us to another dimension of the present enquiry into culture in sustainability of cities. It can be approached from two different perspectives: the sustainability of culture and the culture of sustainability. The elaborate construction of a general theory of the interaction of these three concepts goes beyond the scope of this study. Thus,

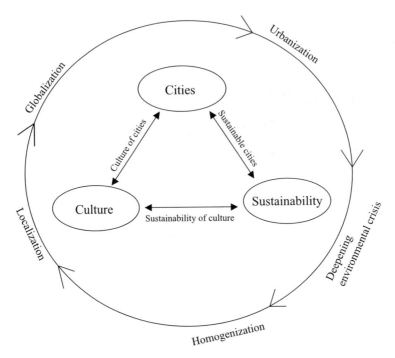

Figure 7.1 Cities, culture, and sustainability

this case study on Cheongju in pursuit of culture in sustainability of cities is organized into six parts.

The first part will begin with the conceptual context of the interplay of cities, culture, and sustainability. The second part is largely a profile of Cheongju city, in terms of both historical evolution and current issues. The third part covers the cultural system of Cheongju and its cultural sustainability. Part four focuses on the cultural implications of sustainable urban development, mainly from the perspective of culture as a way of life. The fifth part highlights the interface of global and local culture, which is becoming one of the most critical issues for cultural sustainability of cities. Finally, it is intended to investigate some comparative dimensions of the case study cities and identify certain differences in the pursuit of a culturally sustainable urban policy in Cheongju.

Cities and sustainability

Most of humanity will soon live in cities, and the trend of urbanization is irreversible. The urban population in 1990 amounted to 1.7 billion, or 38 per cent of the world total, but by the outset of the twenty-first century a half of the world's population lived in urban areas. Globally the urban population is currently increasing by about 65 million a year, which is roughly equivalent to adding an urban population larger than the population of France. Rapid urban transformation over the coming decades will be a grave challenge to the world. As urban conditions are difficult to control and predict, cities have the potential to become and/or already are a threat to the environmental, economic, and social stability of a nation and the world. The possibility of catastrophe cannot be excluded. The years between the 1992 UN Conference on Environment and Development in Rio de Janeiro and the 1996 UN Conference on Human Settlement (HABITAT) in Istanbul featured a unprecedented number of initiatives and scholarly works on the sustainability of cities. Going beyond conceptual discussions, many practical suggestions have been made for sustainable urban development.[1]

Multiple dimensions characterize the paradigm of sustainable development. Early theoretical frameworks concerning sustainable development focused on the integration of economic and environmental dimensions. More recently, sustainable development theorists have argued for the inclusion of other dimensions, particularly the cultural dimension. Recognizing that global environmental problems have local origins and impacts, cultural heterogeneity has attracted international attention. Global environmental debates now generally embrace the notion that traditional forms of knowledge and organization, or culture as a "cake of customs", will greatly facilitate attaining the sustainability of cities. Culture, playing an intervening role and forming a cross-sectional hinge in the interaction between cities and environment, can support the objectives of economic and environmental sustainability.

Culture and sustainable development

Within the conceptual framework aforementioned, culture in sustainability of cities can be interpreted as implying that people in a city have their own cultural sovereignty. Culturally sustainable development in an urban context implies urban development that is shaped by shared ideas, beliefs, and values as well as the intellectual, moral, and aesthetic standards of a city. The World Decade for Cultural Development, which was proclaimed by UNESCO in 1988 and continued until 1997, came up with four main objectives for culturally appropriate development: to assert the cultural dimension in development; to enhance cultural identities; to broaden participation in cultural life; and to promote international cultural cooperation.[2]

Elsewhere, Spaling and others have elaborated five principles for attaining cultural sustainability: diversity, change, holism, identity, and relativity.[3] To elaborate these principles, the rationale of cultural diversity is simply that human potential is too rich to be perceived with a single measuring rod. While biodiversity is one main focus for ecologists influenced by sustainable development, much less attention is paid to the maintenance or promotion of cultural diversity as a strategy for sustainable urban development.

Culture is never static, but is dynamic. Cultural change is certain and inevitable. The dynamic nature of culture is understood as creative adaptation evolving over time. Cultural sustainability of cities is therefore not achieved by building museums of the city, but by creating a system that promotes and perpetuates creative change through which people can determine the nature and means of cultural change.

The third principle of cultural sustainability is cultural holism. Critical to cultural sustainability is the notion that the various subsystems of urban culture have to be harmonious. Cultural lag between material and spiritual cultures and the superficiality of cultural assimilation is more than common, resulting in deviant and harmful patterns of urban culture. Cultural sovereignty (identity) is embodied by the right of self-determination of the people in a city to decide what represents a good life for them. No one should impose on them a culture that is alien, except through active dialogue. Groups and individuals should have the pride and responsibility to maintain their own culture and be engaged voluntarily to sustain their cultural heritage. And finally, cultural relativity is also one of the principles for cultural sustainability. The presence of cultural differences has often resulted in ethnocentrism, which leads people to make judgements according to their own cultural standards. Cultural relativism suggests that we have to understand, evaluate, and possibly appreciate the behaviour of others in the context of their own culture.

Cities and culture

According to UNESCO, culture is defined as the whole complex of distinctive spiritual, material, intellectual, and emotional features that characterize a society or social group. It includes not only the arts and letters but also modes of social life, value systems, traditions, and beliefs. It can be iterated into two dimensions in operational terms: culture as artistic expression, and culture as a way of life. Arts and letters can manifest its most uplifting and ennobling sense in artistic expression, nurtured and directed by art, whether painted, carved, sung, danced, or written. A way of life or mode of life is strongly embedded in the behavioural and value systems of a society and socially accepted norms or the "cake of customs".[4]

Although "culture as expressive arts" should not be underestimated in its relevance to the sustainability of cities, the present enquiry emphasizes "culture as a way of life". However, it is hardly possible to separate neatly the two conceptions of culture, because artistic expression is very much instrumental in the change and nourishment of modes of life, values, and behavioural patterns in cities. Culture when articulated as a mere abstract concept would not explain sustainable urban development. But it will have strong explanatory power when it is permeated into other sectoral and functional concepts like governance, economy, environment, spatio-physical structure, and societal systems. This is because all the functional sectors are also culture-bounded. Good urban governance is generally characterized by efficiency, effectiveness, fairness, transparency, and civic engagement and participation. For a sustainable city, economic growth, stability, full employment, and income generation of the city are more than necessary. Environmental sustainability is widely discussed and relatively well documented. Spatio-physical sustainability of urban structures is also greatly debated among urban and regional planners, with the aim of arriving at a desirable urban structure and development pattern in terms of density, land use, transportation, and urban community. As the city is one of the main human settlement systems, it should be equitable, secure, and inclusive to sustain itself from social disintegration. These norms are interdependent, mutually reinforcing, and culturally determined. Culture cannot stand alone, but is meaningfully substantiated by other sectoral areas of the urban system. A conceptual framework is schematically suggested in Figure 7.2.

Historical and cultural characteristics of Cheongju

The city of Cheongju is located 70 kilometres south-east of Seoul and is the capital of Chungcheongbuk-do province. It is one of the most rapidly growing cities in Korea: its population has almost quadrupled over the last three decades, from 147,000 in 1970 to 582,158 in 2000. The urban population of its commuter catchment area, including contiguous townships, amounts to 700,000. Cheongju is also a historical city dating back to the sixth century. As the Cheongju region was bordered by three kingdoms during the Three Kingdoms period in Korea's history (from the first century AD to 676 AD), it created some unique cultural characteristics of its own in a blending of the three kingdoms (Silla, Paekjae, and Kokuryo). After the unification of the three kingdoms by Silla in 676, the region centred at Cheongju was dominantly influenced by the Silla culture, which was basically patterned from the eastward dissemination of Buddhist culture from Nepal via northern China to the Korean peninsula

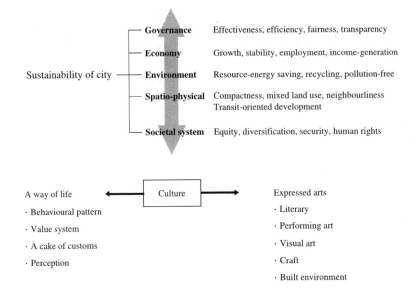

Governance — Effectiveness, efficiency, fairness, transparency

Economy — Growth, stability, employment, income-generation

Sustainability of city — Environment — Resource-energy saving, recycling, pollution-free

Spatio-physical — Compactness, mixed land use, neighbourliness
Transit-oriented development

Societal system — Equity, diversification, security, human rights

A way of life ← Culture → Expressed arts
· Behavioural pattern — · Literary
· Value system — · Performing art
· A cake of customs — · Visual art
· Perception — · Craft
— · Built environment

Figure 7.2 Conceptual framework for cities, culture, and sustainability

and Japanese archipelago along the Silk Road. In this regard, three of the case study cities covered in this volume, Patan in Nepal, Cheongju in Korea, and Kanazawa in Japan, share some cultural legacies and common cultural denominators.

Since Buddhism was almost a state religion throughout the Three Kingdoms period and the Unified Silla kingdom (676–918), the printing of the *sutras* (Buddhist scriptures) was a matter of utmost importance for teaching and dissemination of Buddhism. And the cultural legacy of Cheongju would not be complete without mentioning the development of movable metal-type printing technology in 1240, 200 years *before* Gutenberg's Bible. *The Selected Teachings of Buddhist Sages and Zen Masters* (Pulcho Chikchi Simche Yojol) was printed and published in Cheongju with this movable metal-type printing technology. Metalcraft flourished with the introduction of Buddhism to Korea in 372 AD, as ritual instruments such as temple bells, gongs, incense burners, water cisterns, *sarira* cases, and the like were in great demand. Before movable metal-type printing was invented, wood-block print, which was not durable, had been used. The Unified Silla kingdom was succeeded by the Koryo kingdom in 918, which patronized Buddhism, the state religion. During the Koryo period (918–1392) many temples were constructed and complete sets of Buddhist scriptures were carved on wood blocks for printing. Cultural remnants found in Cheongju today, including two temples and movable metal-type printing, were largely built and created during the Koryo period.

The subsequent demise of the Koryo kingdom witnessed the decline of Buddhism. The Choson kingdom (1392–1905) introduced Confucianism as the state religion, although private devotion to Buddhism persisted passively. As Cheongju and its region were a stronghold of Confucianism during the Choson kingdom, Buddhist temples and legacies were destroyed or neglected. Lack of maintenance and renovation ruined them. The old part of the built-up area of Cheongju's central business district today was originally temple sites. Only stone walls, foundation stones, and a iron flagpole remain.

One of the first attempts at restoration involved the iron flagpole at Yongdu-sa Temple. Urban renewal around the iron flagpole was carried out by a group of citizens led by Professor Hyo-Sung Choi of Cheongju University in the late 1980s. The iron flagpole was erected in 962 during the Koryo kingdom: the date of construction was inscribed in the third cylinder of the flagpole, which was originally composed of 30 cylinders. A campaign by a small group of citizens led to the municipal authority of Cheongju purchasing land around the pole and clearing some obstructive buildings. This led to the creation of the Chuldanggan Plaza (Iron Flagpole Plaza) in the very centre of downtown Cheongju. It is a success story of how a historical heritage can be saved, renovated, restored, and eventually preserved by citizens' initiative. Another example was the restoration of the Heungdeok-sa Temple site where the oldest movable metal-type printing was made – and despite the fact that the original buildings had been torn down and the printed *sutra* removed to the Louvre Museum in France, with only parts of the original displayed in Cheongju.

More than 65 per cent of Cheongju citizens (see Table 7.1) are very proud of the fact that Cheongju was the first city to print with movable metal type, and much earlier than Gutenberg's innovation which contributed to great advances in Western civilization. With this rich heritage the city of Cheongju, aspiring to be reborn as a city of printing and publication, hosted the International Printing and Publishing Expo 2000 from 22 September to 22 October 2000 and has also built the Cheongju Early Printing Museum. Through the expo the city attempted to uphold its urban identity as a cultural city and create a sense of belonging for its uprooted citizens. It has done this with the slogan "From *Jikji* To Digital", designed to create the image of a high-tech city as well. There are very few places in the world today that can be satisfactorily understood or explained in isolation from the national and global contexts in which they are located. The historical incidence of movable metal-type printing technology in *Jikji* finds material continuity in the modern and global digital world in the economic revitalization of Cheongju through high-tech industries.

Cheongju, as a seat of the prefectural governor seconded from central government throughout the Choson kingdom, became the provincial capital of Chungcheongbuk-do in the late nineteenth century. It was already an educational city with many universities and famous high schools, including Chungbuk National University. Government functions and educational institutions were a backbone of the urban economy in terms of employment and income generation until the late 1970s. By taking advantage of spill-over resulting from the government's punitive industrial relocation policies designed to disperse industries from the Seoul metropolitan region (SMR) – where about 50 per cent of industrial establishments and more than 45 per cent of the nation's population are concentrated – Cheongju has undergone transformation from a sleepy administrative and educational city to a vibrant and multifunctional city. Since the early 1970s the government has introduced a variety of measures to control the influx of industries and population into the SMR. The government delineated the boundary of the SMR's restrictive controls, like tax penalties and an outright prohibition of development permits; falling outside this boundary, Cheongju gained a relative locational advantage and has eventually become a haven for new and relocated industries because they can still enjoy the agglomeration economies offered by the SMR. Since then, Cheongju has benefited from rapid growth. Many universities and higher-education institutions have been relocated or built a second campus there. A quiet administrative and educational city has suddenly become a boom town with good access to newly built express highways.

With such a development, immigrants now outnumber the natives. The population of Cheongju has quadrupled since 1970. The culture of a city cannot be built in a day: despite the resiliency of the indigenous people, the rapid urban growth overwhelmed existing cultural assets and has resulted in the loss of cultural identity. People are culture-bearing beings, but where people are anonymous and transient and thrown together in a mass, culture based on traditions is difficult to build or sustain. Cultural identity could disappear because it has been swallowed by "mass culture". The majority of citizens think that cultural consciousness is relatively low (see Table 7.1), and respondents who have lived more than 40 years in Cheongju are greatly concerned about the cultural uprootedness of the new immigrants and their lack of "my-home-town" spirit. The natives want to keep Cheongju's image as a "cultural-educational city", while the majority of citizens, especially the young and middle-aged newcomers, want Cheongju to be a city with diversified functions.

Survey on the cultural perceptions of Cheongju citizens

To discover the views of Cheongju citizens on the current status of culture in their city, a questionnaire survey on their cultural perceptions was conducted from 28 September to 2 October 2000 with the help of Professor Hee-Yeon Hwang and students of Chungbuk National University. A stratified sampling of 315 was made by age, sex, occupation, and period of living in Cheongju. Table 7.1 shows a simple enumeration of the questionnaire survey, but cross-tabulation and analysis are not complete.

Cultural system and cultural sustainability

Even without referring to Gravier's famous eulogy of *Paris and the French Desert*[5] – which means that Paris is culturally so dominating that the rest of France is almost a "cultural desert" – it can be seen that Korea is not greatly different from France. Seoul has always dominated the local cities. More than 50 per cent of cultural events and artists are concentrated in Seoul, where patronage of cultural activities and a market for cultural products are readily available, as shown in Table 7.2. Cultural workers ranging from scholars to traditional artists serve as catalysts for comprehending and addressing the needs and aspirations of individuals and communities. Their roles are essential in preserving traditions and collective memories. Cultural workers and artists are vital to community resiliency. They help people withstand and respond to the stresses of migration and cultural adaptation in a rapidly growing city like Cheongju – which has a very meagre share of the nation's total cultural activities and artists.

In addition to cultural centralization, Cheongju is located just within the cultural watershed of the powerful SMR and finds it hard to maintain its own cultural identity and market. Historically, Korea has been characterized as being a highly centralized country in terms of political and administrative systems. Top-down command and bottom-up obedience have been the rule in every sphere, including cultural affairs. This is somewhat different from Japan, where the feudal system during the Edo period allowed a certain degree of local autonomy in the economy and culture, which directly encouraged local or regional culture with some distinct local characteristics. The historical legacy of centralization dies hard in Korea, and thus regional cultural identity has been weak from the outset of modernization and this persists to the present day.

Consequently, there is an absence of local cultural diversity – a situation that can easily be subjected to uniformity. The identity of "place" or "locality" is formed largely by the history of relations with other

Table 7.1 Cultural perceptions of Cheongju citizens

Q1 What do you consider to be the level of cultural-mindedness of Cheongju citizens in general?

	No.	%
Very high	10	3.1
High	116	37.4
Low	180	57.9
Very low	8	1.6
Total	315	100.0

Q2 Cheongju is famed as a cultural-educational city in Korea. What makes it so famous?

	No.	%
High level of cultural consciousness	24	7.6
Many cultural assets and remains	51	16.2
Numerous schools and students	203	64.5
Many cultural events and festivities	14	4.4
Excellent cultural infrastructure	6	1.9
Others	12	3.8
No answer	5	1.6
Total	315	100.0

Q3 The city government has staged many cultural events like expositions, performances, and exhibitions. What is your evaluation of these?

	No.	%
Too many and too often	31	9.8
Government-led and lacking citizen participation	155	49.2
Not greatly contributing to urban economy	79	25.1
Low level of citizens' cultural-mindedness	37	11.7
Others	5	1.6
No answer	8	2.5
Total	315	100.0

Q4 What is the most critical problem for Cheongju in aiming to be a cultural city?

	No.	%
Lack of cultural infrastructure	73	23.2
Inactive artists and performers	36	11.4
Lack of financial support and investment	111	35.2
Lack of citizens' cultural education	60	19.0
Lack of care for historical cultural assets	25	7.9
Poor accessibility to cultural facilities	3	1.0
Others	7	2.2
Total	315	100.0

Table 7.1 (cont.)

Q5 What is the most desirable policy option for the development of Cheongju in preparing for the twenty-first century?

	No.	%
Strengthen economic base by high-tech industries	85	27.0
Expansion and improvement of urban infrastructure	95	30.2
Creation of urban identity by cultural development	126	40.0
Other	9	2.8
Total	315	100.0

Q6 By what means do you find out about cultural events and cultural activities in the city?

	No.	%
Television and radio	147	46.7
Placards, posters, and handouts	149	47.3
Personal contact	14	4.4
Other	5	1.6
Total	315	100.0

Q7 What is the most urgent action to be taken for the cultural development of Cheongju?

	No.	%
Expansion of cultural facilities and spaces	69	21.9
More support for cultural institution and artists	27	8.6
Urban economic development by cultural products	176	55.9
Strengthening of citizens' cultural education	43	13.6
Total	315	100.0

Q8 What is an alternative for the cultural development of Cheongju?

	No.	%
Decentralization of Seoul-oriented cultural activities	51	16.2
Creating cultural identity of the city	127	40.3
Internationalization of local culture	65	20.6
Recovery of Cheongju's role as a regional cultural centre	62	19.7
Rebirth as a historical city	5	1.6
Others	5	1.6
Total	315	100.0

places and localities. Diversity and uniformity can be understood as two sides of the same coin, in which two centrifugal and centripetal forces can be held in tension with each other.[6] A pattern of extreme centripetal political dynamics, resembling a vortex, swept all active elements of the society upwards towards central power and culture in Korea until the early

Table 7.1 (cont.)

Q9 What is the proudest cultural asset in Cheongju?

	No.	%
Iron flagpole of Yongdu-sa Temple	37	11.7
Sangdang Mountain Wall	61	19.4
Movable metal-type printing	206	65.4
Prefectural governor's house	2	0.6
Namseok stone bridge	3	1.0
Others	6	1.9
Total	315	100.0

Q10 Which is the most impressive cultural event undertaken recently?

	No.	%
Cheongju Aviation Expo	30	9.5
International Craft Biennale	80	26.3
Cheongju Printing and Publishing Expo	121	38.4
Citizens' Day Festival	15	4.8
Restoration of the iron flagpole at Yongdu-sa Temple	23	7.3
Performance of the opera "Chikchi"	22	7.0
Others	10	3.2
No answer	11	3.5
Total	315	100.0

Q11 What do you consider to be a desirable future image for Cheongju?

	No.	%
Cultural-educational city	160	50.8
Diversified regional city	112	35.6
Industrial city	14	4.4
Tourism city	19	6.0
Administrative city	10	3.2
Total	315	100.0

1990s. However, Korea has now restored a local autonomous government system and has been in the process of decentralization. Since then, almost all localities and cities have attempted to create their own cultural identity and market their areas for economic development. In this general process, Cheongju is no exception.

In an important sense, culture is a state of mind of the people who are the consumers and final beneficiaries of cultural products. To conceptualize this relationship, the cultural system in a city can be thought of as composed of four components: producer, consumer, mediator, and infrastructural facilitator. Expressive artists are the main producers of urban culture and the general public are the consumers. Cultural mediators are

Table 7.2 Number of cultural producers and artists

	Literary events	Music performance	Drama/ballet performance	Fine art exhibition	Literary writers	Musicians	Fine artists
Nation	196 (100.0)	795 (100.0)	596 (100.0)	1,872 (100.0)	2,684 (100.0)	3,940 (100.0)	857 (100.0)
Seoul	73 (37.2)	373 (96.9)	349 (58.6)	967 (51.7)	1,468 (54.7)	2,521 (63.5)	635 (74.1)
Cheongju	– (00.0)	10 (1.3)	7 (1.2)	2.5 (1.3)	36 (1.3)	15 (0.4)	5 (0.6)

Source: The Yearbook of Culture and Art, 1996

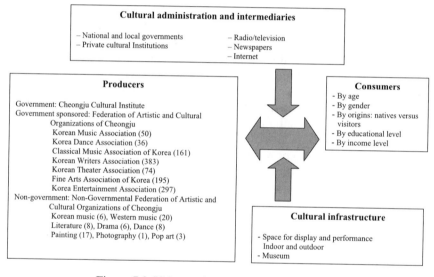

Figure 7.3 Urban cultural system of Cheongju

an intermediary linking cultural producers and consumers. They can be mass-media professionals or journalists or other citizens' groups. Cultural infrastructure includes facilities and spaces for cultural performances, displays, and dissemination. Cultural administrators can be public or private institutions which promote and manage cultural activities. The cultural system in a narrowly defined sense is the interplay of four major components, as shown in Figure 7.3. Its governance depends greatly on how the various actors work out their relationship in a city.

In Cheongju there are a good numbers of cultural producers: governmental and non-governmental, and also government-sponsored or subsidized cultural institutions. The most important players are the Cheongju Cultural Institute, which is under the municipal government of Cheongju, and the Federation of Artistic and Cultural Organizations, the Cheongju branch of a nationwide organization, which is heavily dependent on subsidies from national and local governments. The federation has eight subcommittees and the total membership is 1,470, by no measure small. However, its activities are quite nominal and the annual budget is less than $100,000, which is barely enough to cover the operation of the office and secretarial services. As by their nature artists and cultural organizations want to be free from any governmental interference, there is another Federation of Artists and Cultural Organizations that is non-governmental, although it is not always anti-governmental.

Throughout the 1990s Cheongju's cultural infrastructure, which includes museums and indoor and outdoor facilities for display and performance, has been overly expanded and built to contribute to an image of a cultural city. Most facilities have been underutilized because of a lack of cultural activities. They also suffer from budgetary deficits, even for day-to-day operation. As the cultural survey shows (see Table 7.1), only a small number of citizens complained of a lack of cultural facilities; more were concerned about the productions to be performed and displayed in those facilities. Mass media plays a very important role in disseminating information on cultural activities taking place in the city. Increasingly, citizens have come to know about cultural events, exhibitions, and performances by means of mass media like television and radio. Placards, wall bulletins, and leaflets are also very effective means to bring citizens to the venues of cultural activities. Websites and the internet are becoming popular among youngsters in the city as a way to get information about cultural events. Customers of cultural products are also becoming diversified by age, sex, income, and education. Locals and visitors tend to have different perspectives on what the city offers by way of cultural activities.

A generative system of culture seems highly dependent on how the four subsystems (see Figure 7.3) work in a city. The aim of governance of the cultural system is to bring the four actors together into a long-term synergy in order that it may lead to cultural development of cities. Learning from the experience of Cheongju, the urban cultural system does not work as it should. The expertise of cultural administrators has to be strengthened. Cultural media, including local television and newspapers, have to give more time and space to local cultural affairs. Cultural producers in Cheongju have to overcome their inferiority complex, which is the result of the powerful centralized cultural system dominated by Seoul. They have to find a niche for local cultural identity, preparing for the era of localization and devolution. This is beginning to happen. Against this background, economic consequences of local cultural development have to be given fair consideration. Mundane local economic development, including place marketing, commodification of local culture, and creation of urban artefacts, needs attention.

Culture of sustainable urban development

Korea has gone through drastic changes during the past half-century. The population has almost doubled. Per capita annual income has increased about 100 times from $100 in 1960 to $10,000 in 1998. Automobile numbers have increased from 15,000 to 11 million during the same period. Average life expectancy has increased from 50 to 74: Korea is becoming one of the ageing societies where the age cohort over 65 is expected to exceed 15 per cent of the total population within the next decade or so. Consumption patterns of energy, electricity, and water have become quite alarming, accelerating the depletion of available resources and forcing dependence on imported materials and foodstuffs. Environmental degradation is all-pervasive, leaving irreversible scars on land, inland water bodies, and coastal areas, and threatening the very sustainability of the Korean people.

Sustainability is originally an ecological concept. It applies to a situation where the death rate is equal to the birth rate and where resources for achieving a good livelihood are not exhausted. As a global agenda, the concern for environmental sustainability first appeared at the UN Conference on Human Environment in Stockholm in 1972. Subsequently, the UN Environment Programme, based in Nairobi, established the World Commission on Environment and Development which was headed by Gro Brundtland, the former prime minister of Norway. The report of the Commission, entitled *Our Common Future*, was released in 1987.[7] In this report, sustainable development was defined as development that meets the needs of the present without compromising the ability of future generations to meet their own needs. Since then, the term "sustainable development" has emerged as a key concept and has been discussed and debated extensively in academic circles and international organizations.[8]

The notion of sustainable development is, however, not always clear and/or uncontested. It has become a multidimensional concept covering the environmental, the socio-economic, and the cultural. Its meaning and interpretation seem to vary according to the perspective or discipline from which one is looking. However, the meeting point in the debate has been to suggest that society cannot take out more resources than are put in over time. The sustainability of human settlements in general and cities in particular was brought on to the international stage at the UN Conference on Human Settlements in Istanbul in 1996. It confirmed that sustainable urban development will be the most pressing challenge facing humanity in the twenty-first century, and that cities will occupy the centre stage in the environmental drama. The World Assembly of Cities and Local Authorities was created to coordinate and implement UN policies and programmes for sustainable urban development. Many national governments have established a national commission for sustainable development, with cities and local authorities preparing their own action programmes. Korean cities are actively contributing to these ends.

Korean cities and citizens were alerted to the situation by the IMF bailout from the foreign debt crisis in 1997, and more recently by soaring oil prices. In the process of overall restructuring of the national economy, many firms have closed. The urban economy is on the verge of total collapse. Until recently few people were seriously concerned about the implications of habitual and unsustainable patterns of consumption. The patterns of consumption that were being embraced, as a consequence of economic affluence, were largely those that Americans followed – an influence of the images of American consumption as sold over the Korean mass media. Korean urbanites have, however, been slowly awakening to the fact that they may not be able to sustain the present unsustainable pattern of living (Figure 7.4).

Korean cities' consumption patterns in the domestic sector have followed – and in fact exceeded – those of the USA and Japan. Household electricity consumption per capita is already above that of any advanced country. It has become obvious that Korean cities, including Cheongju, are no longer frugal societies. Household appliances such as refrigerators, air conditioners, washer-driers, microwave ovens, rice cookers, and colour televisions are becoming necessities in everyday life. Korea does not produce a single drop of oil and is entirely dependent on imported fuel. It spends one-third of its hard-won foreign currency reserve to meet its needs for electricity for household appliances and petrol for automobiles. A drastic turnabout in people's consumption behaviour is needed to sustain urban Korea, and maintaining a comfortable and convenient urban habitat will only come with the development of an alternative way of life.

Per capita water consumption in Korean cities is the highest in the world. Bathing and kitchen facilities are patterned on American standards and are usually installed even in low-income housing units. A well-to-do house has more bathtubs and flush toilets than the number of family members. This must be seen in the context of a grave water situa-

QUALITY OF LIFE

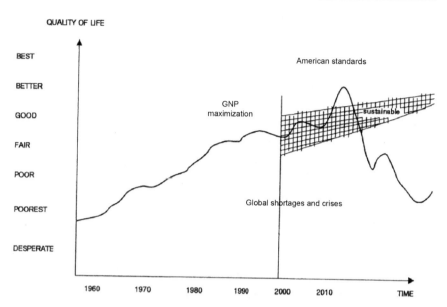

Figure 7.4 Alternative futures for urban Korea

tion. The monsoon may fail in many cities in the years to come, and there will be a shortage of water. A more reliable supply of municipal water can only be obtained by building and expanding reservoirs and upstream dams. That means flooding some of the best agricultural land to meet water consumption needs. In Chungcheongbuk-do province, productive land covering four counties had to be flooded to meet the urban water requirements of downstream cities. Thus, in addition to water-saving measures, including the recycling of water for intensive commercial farming in urban fringes and fish-ponds, Korean cities have to introduce drastic changes in the pattern of water consumption.

Many Koreans are, for instance, quite amazed by the smaller size of Japanese bathtubs and washers, which use only half the water consumed in a Korea bathroom. Korean urbanites have to learn from Japan how to live in a city where land and water are the most precious and expensive resources. The culture of consumption produced by Western civilization is clearly as devastating for underdeveloped countries which import this vision of life as for the developed societies which originated it.[9]

The automobile population in and around Korean cities has exploded from 61,000 in 1970 to 12 million in 2000. Each vehicle requires 20–25 square metres of parking space near home and roughly an equal amount that it shares at work and other destinations. Therefore, each new automobile in Korean cities demands about 50–60 square metres of space in order for it to function. Some 5 million units of housing have been built to accommodate new migrants into cities, encroaching on and using fertile agricultural land for residential purposes. A total of 22,099 square kilometres of agricultural land has been converted to urban uses. Unplanned urban development is taking place in and around Cheongju. If this trend continues in every city, Korea as a nation cannot be sustainable in terms of food production, environmental quality, and resource availability.

As the Korean economic miracle was fading away and the economic crisis came close to a financial moratorium in 1997, austerity measures became a part of daily life for Korean urban dwellers. Everybody is realizing that they cannot afford the urban life they enjoyed during the heydays of economic prosperity. They are trying to find an alternative way of life, naturally retreating to the humble and frugal life which Buddhist and Confucian thinkers have long cherished. Many may give up their private cars. Others may take serious steps to reduce resource consumption by adopting more traditional consumption patterns. Yet others may consider going back to the rural homelands where they used to live.

Local and global cultural interface

Among the many cultural roots of city formation in Korea, Buddhism and Confucianism, as seen in the history of Cheongju, can be identified as the most important cultural denominators. Values nurtured by Buddhism and Confucianism, now internalized and therefore no longer conscious, have provided the cultural and behavioural basis for daily life in the city. They provide a powerful leverage for developing a sustainable urban society. The most relevant part of the Buddhist way of living is frugality and philanthropy based on a strong moral ground. The important Confucian values include filial piety, moral emphasis over material well-being, living with nature, and concern with social harmony.[10] A careful analysis will quickly show that, among other elements, a frugal lifestyle and a concern for nature are what we need to be a sustainable society. Filial piety or family loyalty, usually connected with the extended family and caring for parents by their offspring, seems greatly to facilitate reduction of the societal burden of urban governance in terms of the aged and juvenile problems. The extreme commodification of human relationships that subordinates social and cultural institutions to the utility of markets tends to result in societal disorder. Another attribute of Buddhist and Confucian virtues is the emphasis on morals rather than material well-being. In addition, there is also emphasis on self-development and education.

Korean cities do not greatly deviate from being physical and spatial expressions of a Korean culture that has been largely influenced by Buddhism and Confucianism. Korean cities seem relatively egalitarian. Residential segregation by income, religion, and social status is hardly problematic and has never been a major social issue. As compared to Western cities, Korean cities are compact and characterized by mixed land use and temporal patterning. Urban neighbourhoods are still humane and convenient for living. Each section of urban residential blocks has various services, shops, and eateries. The central business district of Cheongju does not show any symptoms of decay or decline.

After an enchanted way of urban life which has featured unlimited low-density growth, centreless transportation networks, and segregation of land use by Euclidean zoning for more than half a century, Western cities, and especially American cities, are looking for an alternative vision of urban growth.[11] Key words of a new paradigm are compactness, mixed land use, urban growth boundaries, transit-oriented development, lively neighbourhoods, diversification, and inner-city gentrification, all of which are nothing new for Korean cities, nor for Japanese, Nepalese, and Malaysian cities. Most Asian cities have run the risk of blind imitation of alien urban paradigms. Now it is time for them to find their own paradigm, and to construct a new physical-spatial structure which is culturally embedded and sustainable.[12] One does not pretend to foretell what Korean cities culturally should be, although many attempts have been made in this regard. The present endeavour on culture and sustainability of cities must be the beginning of a long journey exploring a new urban cultural paradigm into the twenty-first century.

Globalization, flowing on the currents of new technologies, can place creativity at risk or offer new avenues for expression. Globalization can provide new energy to threatened traditions by offering renewed strength to cities. It can also give life to an increasingly borderless urban world that unites people through shared experience. Globalization, at the same time, can lead to the homogenization of cultures, which may undermine cultural diversity. The tension between cultural homogenization and heterogenization is the most controversial issue in the interpretation of cultural sustainability of cities over the world.[13]

Cultural homogenization points to the formation of a global consumer culture in the era of borderless cyber-society. Some have identified cultural homogenization as the process of cultural imperialism or (North) "Americanization" of the world. Some call it "the McWorld culture".[14] It is this culture that is most credibly subsumed under the categorization of "Westernization", since virtually all of it is of Western, and more specifically (North) American, provenance. Young people throughout the world dance to American music, wiggling their behinds in American jeans and wearing T-shirts with messages about American universities and other American icons of consumption. The global reach of American (consumer) cultural products provides large and complex repertories of images, narratives, and values to users and viewers around the world in which the world of commodities is profoundly mixed. Cheongju is not an exception in this vortex of globalization and commodification of culture.

There is an urgent need to take a closer look at the local level in order to understand the complex interaction between globalization and local responses. Take, for instance, cinema. Hollywood films have outpaced Korean ones in attracting audiences since the 1960s: they have accounted for seven or eight of the 10 top-grossing films in Cheongju each year, while no more than two local films have been successful each year for the past two decades. The remaining slots in the top 10 have usually been split between Hong Kong and European films. The cable TV system in Cheongju started in 1995; 29 channels owned by various private companies are currently operating. Among them five channels specializing in movies, documentaries, and cartoons currently have more than 50 per cent of their programmes supplied by major US networks and their Korean agents. CNN and NBC programmes account for a total of 29.4 per cent of news channel output.

American material cultural goods like films and TV programmes and American cultural and behavioural practices, along with the accompanying ideologies, have been significant vehicles for the spread of global popular culture. As modern Korea and Cheongju have never been completely insulated from globalizing forces, economic and political situations have always been intertwined with external powers – especially Japan before the Second World War and the USA after the war. Korean culture has been shaped through a series of borrowings from, adaptations, and interpretations of these two cultures. Over the last decade or so, Korean people have recognized the development of multiculturalism through diversified economic, cultural, and political connections with countries other than Japan and the USA. However, the two contradictory trends of global consciousness and nationalistic sentiments are on the rise.

This ambivalence is also seen in the changing cultural policy of Cheongju. Increasing foreign travel, a globalizing local economy, and the government's progressive globalization discourse have all contributed to the recent rise of cultural flows between Cheongju and the wider world. These rapid changes in Cheongju have, to an extent, resulted in waning consciousness among the residents of Cheongju about their local culture. Local sentiments, however, have also been enhanced by the very factors that contributed to the formation of global consciousness. The maintenance and cultivation of local identity have an increased rather than a diminished significance and role in contemporary Cheongju.

In this regard, Cheongju has organized two international events in order to uphold its image of itself as an international city and resurrect glorious historical legacies to identify itself as a cultural city. The first endeavour to this end was the International Craft Biennale in 1999 and 2001. As discussed earlier, Cheongju is the birthplace of the first movable metal printing technique. It intends to project this past into the future, promoting the image of traditional craftsmanship and eventually materializing this for economic revitalization. The biennale was not confined to metalwork alone, but also covered wood and lacquer works, glass and paper works, ceramics, and fibre works. This event drew half a million visitors from home and abroad. An international craft competition and invitational exhibition were organized concurrently. Immediate local impacts of the biennale may not be easily measured, but it has provided a venue for the citizens of Cheongju to acquaint themselves with trendy international tastes and global standards.

The second event was the International Printing and Publishing Expo in 2000. Along with the expo, the city has made great efforts to list *Jikji* as a world documentary heritage. It has also made efforts to reconstruct Heungdeok-sa Temple, where *Jikji* was first printed. Finally, the fifth meeting of the International Advisory Committee for the Memory of the World was held on 27–29 June 2001 in Cheongju. The meeting made recommendations to the director-general of UNESCO regarding the inclusion of *Jikji*. The city of Cheongju built the Early Printing Museum on the site of Heungdeok-sa Temple where *Jikji* was printed. The museum exhibits more than 800 items of old printing machinery and historical relics excavated from Heungdeok-sa Temple.

Unfortunately, the current owner of *Jikji* is the National Library of France. The city and national governments have made every effort to retrieve *Jikji*, but little progress has been made. Instead, it is suggested by UNESCO that Korea and France work together on the digitization of this book to make it widely accessible and have it translated into English and French with scholarly introductions.

Concluding remarks: A comparative view

As Professor van Ginkel succinctly pointed out in his keynote address at the initial stage of this research project, the purpose of the present study is to examine the role of culture in helping sustain life in our cities – expressed as culture in sustainability of cities, which has been developed as the research theme.[15] Returning to the key notions of culture, cities, and sustainability, these have been widely discussed above. The three concepts have rarely been brought into an integrated dimension, as has been done in this study. Four case study cities were selected to compare creative

Table 7.3 Population growth of case study cities

Cities \ Year	1980	1990	2000
Cheongju, Korea	252,985	455,148	582,758
Penang, Malaysia	248,200	219,376	229,400
Patan, Nepal	199,688	257,086	323,024
Kanazawa, Japan	417,684	441,911	453,008

urban transformation for culturally sensitive sustainable urban development. Before considering the case study of Cheongju, it would be useful to highlight some characteristics of the case study cities of Penang (Malaysia), Patan (Nepal), and Kanazawa (Japan), recognizing that they share many commonalities in term of size and historical legacies (Table 7.3).

As opposed to the other case study cities, which have been relatively slow in their population growth, Cheongju has grown twofold to threefold since 1980 (Table 7.3). The sharply growing population in Cheongju has been a great threat to its cultural identity and sustainability. In the last three decades it has also changed from being a "sleepy" administrative and educational city to become a vibrant industrial city. A quiet inner city has become a transportation hub as two expressways have been newly built to criss-cross Cheongju. A new international airport has just been opened to serve the central part of the country. Taking advantage of the opening of this new airport and the two arterial expressways, Cheongju is aspiring to be an inland distribution and logistics centre.

One must recognize the fact that cultural sustainability is strongly embedded in the sedentariness of a populace, and this is also the case for the economy in a city. The rapidity of urban transformation in terms of population and the economic base has uprooted local identity, but a new urban culture has yet to be created in Cheongju. Old and rich cultural heritage and local culture have been undermined by sweeping migration and globalization.

There are additional differences from the other case study cities. The city of Kanazawa has been successful in commodifying its cultural heritage. Penang and Patan, with their ethnic and religious heterogeneity, have resorted to cultural tourism and have become favourite destinations for cultural tourists. But Cheongju is not ready for cultural economic development and/or tourism. Cheongju has been trying to restore rich cultural remnants which were destroyed by wars or ruined by long periods of neglect. The rebuilding of Heungdeo-sa Temple where *Jikji* was first printed with movable metal type and the citizens' initiative for the restoration of the iron flagpole on the site of Yongdu-sa Temple are typical examples cited earlier in this chapter.

Religious belief has made many cultural footprints on the city as a whole and in the ways of life of the people. The common denominator that profoundly influenced cultural patterns in the four case study cities is Buddhism, although they have reflected this in their own unique ways and intertwined with other coexisting and rivalling religions such as Confucianism, Shintoism, Hinduism, Islam, and Christianity. The cultural legacies of Cheongju have been largely embodied in the philosophical-religious precepts of Buddhism and Confucianism. Cheongju and other Korean cities are very much in transition and struggling to find their own identity and a new paradigm for sustainable development.

Notes

1. OECD. 1996. *Innovative Policies for Sustainable Urban Development: The Ecological City*. Paris: OECD; Breheny, M. J. (ed.). 1992. *Sustainable Development and Urban Form*. London: Pion.
2. UNESCO. 1996. "The culture dimension of development", in *Involving Culture*. Paris: UNESCO, p. 8.
3. Cited in Yang, Byoung-E. 2001. "Sustainable development indicators and cultural indicators", in *Culture in Sustainability of Cities III*. Cheongju: Cheongju Cultural Promotion Foundation and IICRC, pp. 80–82.
4. Maclver, R. M. and C. H. Page. 1957. *Society: An Introductory Analysis*. London: Macmillan, p. 57.
5. Gravier, J. F. 1947. *Paris et le Desert francais*. Paris: Flammarion.
6. Massey, Doreen. 1993. "Questions of locality", *Geography*, Vol. 78, No. 2, pp. 142–144.
7. World Commission on Environment and Development (WCED). 1987. *Our Common Future*. New York and Oxford: Oxford University Press.
8. Rana, Ratna S. J. B. 2000. "Culture and sustainable development paradigm: Sharing experiences and building new perspectives", in *Culture in Sustainability of Cities I*. Kanazawa: IICRC, pp. 4–5.
9. Schumacher, E. F. 1973. *Small is Beautiful: Economics as if People Mattered*. New York: Harper and Row, p. 7.
10. Kim, Won Bae, Mike Douglass, Sang-Chuel Choe, and Kong Chong Ho (eds). 1997. *Culture and the City in East Asia*. Oxford: Oxford University Press.
11. Downs, Anthony. 1994. *New Visions for Metropolitan America*. Washington, DC: Brookings Institution, pp. 123–128.
12. Watanabe, Junichi. 1985. *A Study of Comparative Urban Planning*. Tokyo: Shiseido (in Japanese).
13. Appadurai, Arjun. 1990. "Disjuncture and difference in the global cultural economy", *Theory, Culture and Society*, Vol. 7, pp. 295–310.
14. Berger, Peter L. 2000. "Four faces of global culture", in P. O'Meara, H. Mehlinger, and M. Krain (eds) *Globalization and the Challenges of a New Century: A Reader*. Bloomington, IN: Indiana University Press, p. 423.
15. van Ginkel, Hans J. A. 2000. "Improving our urban tomorrows: Creative urban transformation", paper presented at International Conference on Culture in Sustainability of Cities, 18–19 January, Kanazawa, Japan.

8

Towards an urban cultural mode of production: A case study of Kanazawa, Japan, I

Masayuki Sasaki

Introduction: Background and framework to the study

The trend of globalization is progressing as we move into the twenty-first century, leading to the emergence of a few large cities with global functions in economics, politics, and culture. While these cities are at the apex of the global system, many other cities are integrated into this system and are being exposed to rapid financial and economic change brought on by "casino capitalism".[1] They seem to be on the verge of a crisis involving the deterioration of their healthy economic infrastructure and the loss of their unique cultures. Furthermore, environmental problems such as global warming and expansion of the ozone hole are becoming global in scale and assuming more seriousness in a growing trend towards urbanization across the globe – the creation of more and more mega-cities which inevitably lead to increased consumption of energy and a decrease in forests and agricultural land.

In this context, "creativity" and "sustainability" of cities are being examined as key concepts to offer solutions within the sustainable development paradigm in Europe, America, and Asia. Thus, for example, the European Creative Cities Research Group is analysing the experiences of cities trying to solve problems by bringing out latent social forces through the creative power of art/culture. They do this while keeping in mind the problems of how to find new urban development directions free from national government subsidies in a society faced with the decline of manufacturing industry, rising unemployment, and a welfare state system in danger.[2] Furthermore, over 150 cities in the EU have formed the Sustainable City Campaign, which attempts to strengthen efforts within the context of Local Agenda 21 – i.e. from the bottom up – in order to preserve the European/world environment. Stimulated by the movements in Europe, Japan has taken a similar path, researching creative cities and aiming at movements to realize sustainable cities.

If we go back far enough in the lineage of the creative city theory we arrive at the so-called founding fathers of cultural economics, namely John Ruskin and William Morris. Ruskin, who was active during Britain's Victorian period, resisted the utilitarian economics of the times and proposed art economics, which placed emphasis on creative human activities and receptiveness. According to him, all valuable goods, including artistic works, have both a functional and an artistic aspect which help to support the lives of consumers and increase their sense of humanity. That which brings out this intrinsic value is "work" – free, creative human activity – not "labour" forced upon one by another. He argued that this original, intrinsic value first became an effective value when it was met by a receptive consumer who could evaluate it. Morris, the successor to Ruskin's school of thought, criticized the mass production and consumption system put in place by large mechanized industries as leading to estrangement of labour and dehumanization of life. He went on to co-ordinate the Arts and Crafts movement, which aimed at "humanization of labour" and "art-ification of life", by reintroducing craft-like production based upon the creative activities of artisans (proposed by Ruskin). Subsequently, Geddes and Mumford began to apply Ruskin and Morris's thoughts to urban studies. Mumford in his *Culture of Cities* lambasted monetary economics that dominated the megalopolis, and proposed "cultural economics" which places emphasis on life and environment over anything else, emphasizing the "reconstitution of cities to fulfill human consumption and creative activities".[3]

Pursuing this line of development and looking at modern creative city research, one arrives at the American urban researcher Jacobs, the person who called those cities which were especially good at industrial innovation and improvisation "creative cities".[4] The abovementioned Creative City Research Group was influenced by her, and has defined creativity as something more than fantasy and imagination and placed it somewhere between intelligence and innovation – i.e. the concept that acts as a mediator between art/culture and industry/technology. At present the group is continuing with comparative research on cities, keeping in mind the question of what kind of role creative culture has in reconstructing urban economic infrastructure. It believes that cities which look at the creativity of artistic activities and try to have "free and creative cultural activities" and "cultural infrastructure" tend to embrace in-

Figure 8.1 The interlinkages between the various forms of sustainability

dustries which specialize in innovation, and are able to develop an administrative capacity to deal with difficult problems.

What is important for creative cities is not only the ability for creative problem-solving in the areas of economics, culture, organization, and finance, but also quick responses to change the existing system whenever change in one part affects another part. Aspects of creative problem-solving include people, creative technology, and environment (information and communications systems, variety in culture and art, education systems, stimulating environment, social safety, and freedom from riot and instability).

This chapter focuses on Kanazawa in Japan to explore how cities with cultural creativity can bring about sustainable development and contribute to the preservation of the global environment. Generally, if sustainability of a city is to be evaluated, the three elements of environmental sustainability, socio-cultural sustainability, and economic sustainability should be analysed (Figure 8.1). To discuss sustainability of a city's natural environment without considering urban economics would be purely utopian. Conversely, a city's economic development which leads to degradation of the environment would negatively affect the sustainability of the urban society.

Kanazawa has been chosen to elaborate the above through a case study of endogenous development. Kanazawa was selected because the city is not only developing its economy without harming but by preserving the natural environment, but also maintaining harmony between the local economy and culture.

Historical development of the city of Kanazawa

Kanazawa is a "human-scale" city with a population of 450,000. Roof tiles shine blackly on the rows of houses in the old city centre, giving a calm appearance. The local life and culture have spawned many traditional performing arts and crafts. Kanazawa also possesses a rich natural environment, including two clean rivers, the Sai and the Asano, as well as the surrounding mountains, covered with much greenery.

Historically, Kanazawa's roots can be found 500 years in the past when a religious autonomous government was established by followers of the

Ikkou sect of Buddhism. For the next 100 years this "country held by the peasants" prospered, and Kanazawa Gobou Temple was built as its centre. In 1583 Lord Toshiie Maeda began work on creating a town around Kanazawa Castle. By the middle of the seventeenth century the opulent *"hyakuman-goku* culture"[5] was established in Kaga province, which was the wealthiest province second only to the Edo Shogunate. The province gave up military resistance to concentrate instead on developing a peaceful administration and encouraging academia, crafts, and performing arts. Famous academics from all over the country were invited to pursue their literary activities, and the *sonkeikaku bunko* (library collection of the Maeda family) was created. In the seventeenth century *osaikusho* (lord's crafts workshops) were created and artisans from Kyoto were invited as instructors, which contributed to the cultivation of artisans in metalwork and gold lacquer work. Also, the lord of Kaga province was personally involved in *noh* (classic Japanese dance-drama) and the tea ceremony, and these were popularized among servants and the general population as a part of the culture of their everyday lives.

When the Shogunate fell and Japan opened to the West with the Meiji Restoration in 1868, Kaga province underwent rapid changes. With the fall of the warrior class the population of Kanazawa, which was ranked only after Tokyo, Osaka, and Kyoto at the time of the Meiji Restoration, rapidly declined from 130,000 to 80,000. In the 1890s Kanazawa set out on a new journey of industrialization, transformed from a "castle town" to "modern Kanazawa" by the textile industry, centred on *habutae* silk exports, and the textile machinery industry which supported it.

The promotion of crafts prior to the Meiji Restoration became the basis for the development of Kanazawa's mechanized industries. Kaga province had opened craft workshops and brought in many famous artisans from all over the country, paving the way for the development of crafts such as inlaid works, metal-casting, cabinet work, and "clockwork" crafts. With the Meiji Restoration these artisans lost the patronage of the Maeda family and their numbers declined, but some artisans opened new avenues such as the development of textile production.

A typical case is Yonejiro Tsuda, whose father, Kichinosuke Tsuda, was a master carpenter who designed the Oyama Shrine, one of the most famous of the Meiji-era architectural structures in Kanazawa and designated as an important cultural asset. In 1875 the elder Tsuda created the Kanazawa Thread Manufacturing Factory, modelled on the Tomioka Thread Manufacturing Factory in Gunma prefecture. His son Yonejiro developed the Tsuda-style loom 10 years later. As one can see from this example, the technical know-how of the Edo-era artisans was applied to modern industry.

More important in the context of the preservation, transmission, and development of know-how and techniques was the establishment of the Kanazawa Industrial Encouragement Research Institute (now known as the Industrial Research Institute of Ishikawa) in 1876, and the Kanazawa Technical High School in 1887. The former is said to be the first public research institute of its kind in Japan, and its goals were to preserve, foster, and develop the accumulated crafts knowledge in the region.

The latter was born from a citizens' movement to create an art school and was Japan's first technical high school, established by Kutani pottery instructor Benjiro Notomi. The goal of this school was to contribute to regional development through the modernization of traditional arts/crafts. It is a matter of interest that this started out as a technical school and not an art school. What needs attention is that this was Japan's first attempt at technical design education.

The Kanazawa Advanced Technical School (now Kanazawa University Department of Engineering) was created in 1920, and the Kanazawa City Technical School (now Kanazawa Municipal Technical High School) was established in 1924. The fact that various educational and research institutions are gathered in this regional city played a major role in the development of local institutional "thickness"[6] and the endogenous development of manufacturing industry through the development of human resources.

Coexistence of environment, culture, and economy: Endogenous development of Kanazawa

Many Japanese cities in the period of high growth that followed the Second World War became "economic branch cities" of Tokyo, in the process losing their original culture and independent economic infrastructure. However, Kanazawa has maintained its endogenous development through a balance of economy and culture, as illustrated in Figure 8.2. The following summarizes Kanazawa's characteristics as an endogenously developed city.

- Kanazawa does not have any head or branch offices of major corporations or large-scale factories. It has a group of sustainable and endogenously developing medium- and small-sized companies. It also has key factories with their head offices or decision-making departments within the region. This suggests that Kanazawa has a highly independent urban economy.
- Since the Meiji era, both textile and textile machinery industries have been developing as the two allied key industries. With these industries as the base, machine tools and food-related machine industries have

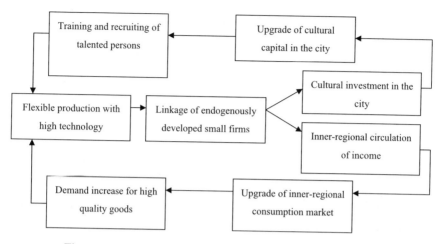

Figure 8.2 Urban cultural mode of production in Kanazawa

been growing since the Second World War, along with publishing/ printing, food, and apparel industries. Thus, as a local city with a population of only 450,000, Kanazawa has an urban economy with a diversified industrial base.

- As seen in the textile industry as a typical example, Kanazawa has a unique "industrial district system" with local trading companies in its centre with developed sales, distribution, and finance functions, in addition to manufacturing industry as the core.
- This endogenous development of Kanazawa's urban economy – through restriction of large-scale regional development and smoke-stack industries – has avoided drastic change in industrial as well as in urban structure. As a result, traditional industries, streets, and the natural environment are all well conserved to provide an enriching urban life.
- The urban economic structure described above increased added value through production inside the region, prevented profits produced in the region from flowing outwards, realized constant innovation in medium-sized enterprises, and developed the food and drink industry and various service industries. Furthermore, it brought about high-quality urban cultural agglomeration through increasing universities and colleges, vocational schools, and other academic institutions. In other words, the local cultural capital has been maintained through the local urban economic surplus.

Since 1985 rapid global restructuring has affected not only the economy of Kanazawa, but the whole of Japan. Those cities without sufficient endogenous developed economy – lacking decision-making entities and research and development institutions, and with only production capabilities – found themselves in competition with Asian newly industrialized economies (NIEs), with industrial activity based on mass-production factories dependent upon low wages. Due to this, economic activity became centred in Tokyo, a world city with its multinational corporations and financial institutions.

In the local regions there was extreme depopulation. Even in the economy of Kanazawa, the mass-production textile factories, vertically integrated by the textile production companies, faced hardship and many went bankrupt. On the other hand, the post-mass-production mechatronics industries and hi-tech industries, which dealt with many types of products in low quantities, developed. As stated previously, this was due to the existence of various research and development institutions and the preservation of craft production know-how, forming institutional thickness that was able to resist the rough waters of globalization.

Socio-cultural development of Kanazawa: The cultural policy and cultural creativity

As an endogenously developed creative city, Kanazawa has fostered its own unique industries; however, it can also be assessed by its unique and rich art and cultural development.

Next to Tokyo and Kyoto, Kanazawa stands out among regional cities in many areas, including traditional arts and crafts, performing arts, and literature. In the field of arts and crafts, Kazuya Takamitsu (human portraits), Gonroku Matsuda (gold lacquerware), Iraku Uozumi (gongs), Uzan Kimura (*Yuzen* silk dyeing), Kodo Himi (inlaid metalwork), Shogyo Oba (gold lacquerware), Naoji Terai (gold lacquerware), and others have been designated as living national treasures or members of the International Academy of Arts. There are also many artisans in the fields of ceramics, lacquerware, metalwork, dyeing, and wood and bamboo craft who are active on a national level.

For this, both the artisans who supported craft production and the citizens who had a high level of appreciation and included craft objects in their daily lives were indispensable. From the point of cultivating successors, the Kanazawa College of Arts and Ishikawa Prefectural Technical High School also played an important role. In actuality, many of the living national treasures were educated in these institutions and have gone on to become professors, cultivating new generations of successors.

In all of this, what characteristics can be seen in Kanazawa's cultural policies?

- Although Kanazawa has a population of only 450,000, it has established its own municipal College of Arts and has invited many famous artisans to serve as professors, contributing to the development of successors. As already mentioned, the citizens had petitioned for such an art school before the Second World War. In 1946 the school began as a junior college, the Kanazawa Art Technical School. At that time it had two faculties, the Art Faculty and the Craft Faculty. In 1955 it restarted as a university, offering four-year programmes. It again had two faculties: the Art Faculty and the Industrial Art Faculty; the latter included three specializations, namely commercial design, industrial design, and craft design, relating directly to modern industry.

- There are efforts to preserve cultural assets. In July 1949, a year before the establishment of the national Law for the Protection of Cultural Properties and six months after the destruction by fire of Horyuji Temple in Kyoto, the Regional Law for the Protection of Cultural Properties was passed. This marked the start of official promotion of culture in Kanazawa, which had been spared any real wartime damage, and its journey as a cultural city.

- In 1968 the Regional Law for the Preservation of the Traditional Environment of Kanazawa City was passed, which made efforts at preserving the traditional atmosphere of the city. During Japan's high-growth period the Law for the Preservation of Ancient Cities was passed, but only affected Nara, Kyoto, and Kamakura. Because of this, the unique traditional environment of Kanazawa was in danger of being destroyed. Kanazawa became the first city in the nation to pass such regional laws, and this was an epochal step in preserving the traditional environment of the city with the cooperation of local citizens. The first step was to preserve the traditional atmosphere in Kanazawa through protecting the natural environments of the two rivers (the Asano and Sai), Kenrokuen Garden and Honda Forest in the centre of the city, the temple districts of Tera-machi and Higashiyama, and the black roof tiles of private residences and the walls in the old *samurai* house district of Naga-machi. The law not only preserved buildings within the area designated as the traditional environment zone, but also offered financial support for restoring buildings outside of the zone that had been designated for preservation.

- In 1973, in commemoration of the 100th birthday of Kyoka Izumi, a literary giant from Kanazawa, the city established the Kyoka Izumi Literary Award and the Kanazawa Citizens' Literature Award, becoming the first regional city in Japan to sponsor a national literary award. The background to this award was an effort to resist the centralization of culture by getting many people to "recognize the customs and traditions of Kanazawa, which cultivated Kyoka literature", with the hope of strengthening the capacity of regional areas to serve as transmitters of culture.

In the late 1980s local governments, fearing the overemphasis on and development of culture in Tokyo, began efforts at promoting local culture and art. However, in most cases their efforts revolved around "hard" activities like the construction of large opera houses and symphony halls. The case of Kanazawa had the following characteristics.

- Priority was placed on "soft" activities cultivating Western culture as well, such as the formation of the Orchestra Ensemble Kanazawa. The orchestra was created in 1988 by Ishikawa prefecture and Kanazawa, with the cooperation of the famous Japanese conductor Hiroyuki Iwaki. This was the first professional chamber orchestra in Japan (a medium-sized group of 40). They play not only Mozart symphonies but also vigorously pursue modern music by composers including Toru Takemitsu and Toshiro Mayuzumi. They have raised their level to international standards.

- Emphasis was placed upon citizen participation in training and cultivation programmes. In 1989, in commemoration of the 100th anniversary of the establishment of modern Kanazawa, the Utatsuyama Craft Workshop was built and began recruiting interested students from the general public (five to eight students per class) for three-year training courses in ceramics, lacquerware, dyeing, metalwork, and glass crafts. This workshop helps to cultivate successors and pass on traditional techniques. The training courses are also open to local citizens. This workshop has been praised as carrying on the spirit of the traditional craft workshops in modern times.

- By controlling large-scale "hard" activities, Kanazawa has been able to preserve the traditional atmosphere and is determined to refine it. In April 1989, due to the growing bubble-economy trend of destroying old *samurai* houses and historical landmarks to make way for high-rise apartment complexes and office buildings, the city brought out the Regulations on City Views which stipulated standards in building heights, physical forms, colours, advertisements, etc. in line with the local region, making active efforts to harmonize them with the traditional environment. This movement developed into the Regional Law on Town Streets, the Regional Law for Preservation and Beautification of City Water, and the Regional Law for the Preservation of Slope Greenery.

Kanazawa's cultural policies certainly show enthusiasm about preserving traditional culture. However, there were criticisms of these policies and claims that they were culturally conservative. Clearly, a city culture that is too tied to tradition and lacks a critical spirit does not constitute a creative city. A city lacking the function to create culture will no doubt lose its ability to foster creative industries. On this point, the seeds of a new cultural movement are coming to bear fruits in Kanazawa.

The old warehouses of the spinning mills which are so symbolic of the past textile production area were reborn as the Kanazawa Citizens' Art Center. This art village, a creative space that can be used freely by citizens, consists of several workshops, namely drama, music, eco-life, and art, created by renovating the spinning mill warehouses, which serve as reminders of the heritage of modern industry. Adjacent to this is the Kanazawa Artisan School. This is an establishment for the preservation and transmission of Kanazawa's high-level artisan skills, and is available for 30–50-year-old artisans who already have basic skills. The training is offered for free. Kanazawa, which manages the art village, held talks with the representatives of the users and decided to make it open 24 hours a day, 365 days a year, to contribute to the creative activities of Kanazawa citizens.

In the case of the drama workshop, the Kanazawa Theatre People's Association formed in 1995 and decided how to use the facility. The opening drama festival began in October 1996, when local theatre groups ran a joint production of Shakespeare's *A Midsummer Night's Dream* for six months. Theatre groups performed a total of 64 shows, in which 14,507 people took to the stage and 21,129 citizens came to enjoy the performances. The effort was a great success. The art workshop saw some 24,000 people coming to see exhibitions of local artists; the music workshop saw over 15,000 users, mainly rock bands and students; and the eco-life workshop saw 18,000 people for a recycling fair and other activities. All in all, over 100,000 citizens visited the village in a little over half a year, and enjoyed events related to art, culture, and the environment from both a "producer's" and a "consumer's" point of view. In other words, this was a turning point for Kanazawa's cultural policies, which had been apt to lean more towards traditional culture and traditional performing arts. One can appraise this by saying that due to the active participation of the citizens, the new cultural infrastructure is turning into a creative art infrastructure.

Towards a cultural mode of production

In one light, Kanazawa's "cultural mode of production in an endogenous creative city" can be seen as a revival and reconstruction of the craft production that began in the Edo era, and can be placed in the historical progression from craft production to mass production to a cultural mode of production (new craft production). When the mass-production/mass-consumption system was placed in danger after the two oil shocks of the

1970s, a trajectory of a post-Fordist mode of production that emphasized culture began to gain more influence, making a sort of renaissance in Kanazawa's urban production system. It is interesting to note that in Kanazawa, *the craft production system of the traditional industries* became the base for the development of a post-Fordist cultural mode of production.

As we have already seen, the production system of the twentieth century was mass production, in which identical products were produced, distributed, and consumed in large numbers. This system, due to its ability to produce great quantities of products with the same quality, led to the realization of the "popular consumption society", and made possible an "industrial society" made up of large corporations (factories) and large cities. But by the end of the twentieth century it had run into a dead end with a number of critical difficulties.

The important factors here are loss of creativity and humanity in production due to the introduction of machinery as an accessory to producers, who became one part of a larger organization; and the producers, realizing they were the major players in effecting the trends that affected consumers, kept pursuing mass production, making flexible handling of the oil shocks and the collapse of the bubble difficult. Accordingly, what is expected of a system that can override the mass-production system is human-scale businesses/factories that can bring out the creativity of producers, flexible production of products with a high intrinsic cultural value that can keep up with changing markets, and customers with the ability to recognize genuine articles in the market and a high cultural standard to strengthen their life-planning abilities through their consumption activities. In other words, the "new cultural production" is a system in which cultural modes of production and consumption are unified.

Today, the keywords of "workshop-style business", "intelligent public", and "art-ification of daily life" are gaining currency. These emerging terminologies can be understood to articulate a new production system, challenging the older system. As a result of this development, there is an increasing interest in a new cultural production system that can replace mass production.

First of all, let us begin with the traditional industry renaissance. Kanazawa is second only to Kyoto in terms of distributing traditional crafts products from the past, and there are 26 verified traditional industries. There are over 800 offices related to these traditional industries with a total workforce of approximately 3,000. This covers 24 per cent of the total number of offices within the city and 8.2 per cent of the total workforce of Kanazawa, making it one of Kanazawa's key industries. Out of these, six have been designated by a national law concerning the promotion of traditional crafts industry, namely *Kutani* pottery, Kaga *Yuzen* silk dyeing, Kanazawa lacquerware, Kanazawa gold and silver leaf, Kanazawa

Buddhist altars, and Kaga embroidery. Let us take a specific look at Kaga *Yuzen* and gold and silver leaf.

Along with *Kyo-Yuzen* (Kyoto) and *Bingata* (Okinawa), Kaga *Yuzen* is one of Japan's famous silk-dyeing styles and has its roots in the unique Kaga plain silk-dyeing technique known as *Ume-zome* (literally "plum dyeing") developed about 500 years ago. Yuzensai Miyazaki was invited from Kyoto to Kanazawa, and he contributed to the establishment of Kaga *Yuzen* through adding *Yuzen*-style patterns to the Kaga dyeing techniques. It is quite different from the realistic plant and flower designs of *Kyo-Yuzen*. Kaga *Yuzen* does not have as much division of labour in its production process as *Kyo-Yuzen*, so it does not lend itself to mass production. On the other hand the process is consistent all the way through, so the artisan's originality can shine through.

The major characteristic is the flavour brought out by the *Yuzen-nagashi* (washing the finished product in flowing water). During the time that *Kyo-Yuzen* and others were advancing with their mass production, Kaga *Yuzen* established a craft production system known as the "artisan's signature system", placing high cultural value-added production on the tracks. Today there are 50 artisans with about 200 successors or assistants. The total sales in the late 1970s were 5–6 billion yen, in 1986 it was up to 15 billion yen, and in 1993 reached a record 18 billion yen (this has come down somewhat since the collapse of the bubble). In 1967 the Kaga Dyers' Promotion Association was formed, in which sellers and producers worked together to promote their wares. In 1970 the Kaga *Yuzen* Dyers' Union housing complex was built in Senkoji, Kanazawa, and the traditional *Yuzen-nagashi* is carried out in a human-made river within the complex.

Kanazawa gold and silver leaf gained popularity in the early eighteenth century when Kaga province invited leaf artisans from Kyoto to produce their wares. When Edo gold and silver leaf died out after the Meiji Restoration, Kanazawa became the only production area and holds a 99 per cent share of the entire leaf production in the nation. This can be attributed to the fact that Kanazawa's climate, temperature, and water quality are appropriate for the production of gold leaf, as well as to improvements in the machinery used in the production. Historically speaking, gold leaf was developed as an adjunct material for Buddhist altars and other religious articles such as gold folding screens, laquerware, ceramics, and other traditional crafts. However, with the changes in lifestyles in recent years, the gold leaf industry has worked out an arrangement with other traditional and modern industries and is now being used on prepaid telephone cards, interior decorative items, locally brewed *sake* and confectioneries, and even in cosmetics.

Kanazawa's original food industry, which supports the traditional food culture, is ranked alongside the traditional crafts. Kanazawa's refined *sake*, known as *Kaga no Kiku-hime* (the Chrysanthemum Princess of Kaga), has been famous since the Middle Ages, along with that of Tsurugi on the Tedori River. This is because the city was blessed with the necessary natural conditions (underground water flowing down from Mount Hakusan is considered good for making *sake*), superior techniques from the renowned artisan Mori Noto, and the "food culture of *hyakuman-goku*". The over 50 *sake* breweries that existed in the late 1890s had reduced to about 20 by the late 1930s. At present there are only six left in Kanazawa and two in Tsurugi, but there are some locally produced brands that are nationally popular.

Nakamura Brewery, at the forefront of the national "local *sake*" and "elegant *sake*" boom, is very active in its development of new products, bringing out many new, famous brands answering the varied needs of consumers. The company is also very involved in cultural activities. For instance, the former president of the brewery donated traditional arts and crafts to Kanazawa and established the Kanazawa Municipal Nakamura Commemorative Art Museum. The company is also moving into and taking advantage of the recent boom in locally brewed beer. Additionally, Yachiya Brewery, which used to make *sake* especially for the provincial lord, has in recent years begun to make order-made *sake* in small-lot production. The brewery also offers hands-on experience in *sake* making.

The beginnings of Ono *shoyu* (soy sauce) lie with the order of the lord of Kaga province. Just as with refined *sake*, the quality of water is vital. The Ono area was also considered perfect for shipping the products to marketplaces all over the country due to the proximity of Ono and Miyanokishi Harbour (now Kanaiwa Harbour), and it is said that Ono had 60 businesses at the end of the Edo era. Since then there have been many ups and downs and by the end of the Second World War there were 30 companies; this has now dwindled to 21. In 1970, 39 businesses formed a cooperative, building a joint factory near Kanaiwa Harbour. In 1982 a comprehensive reconstruction took place. The *shoyu* production yield has been maintained at fifth in nationwide terms and the market covers a fairly wide area, including Toyama, Fukui, Aichi, Gifu, Hokkaido, Tokyo, and Kyoto. The leader of the Ono *shoyu* group, Katsumi Yamamoto (president of Yamato Miso and Shoyu Company), is striving to preserve the traditional food culture and also put energy into the construction of the Ono Benkichi Clockwork Doll Museum, which is dedicated to Benkichi Ono, a famous artisan from the end of the Edo era. Katsumi Yamamoto serves as the chairman of the board of directors.

In Kanazawa, as in Kyoto, where traditional lessons in the tea ceremony, traditional Japanese dance, and traditional music were firmly rooted in the daily lives of the citizens, there are also many nationally popular brands of uniquely Kanazawa tastes in *wa-gashi* (Japanese confectioneries) and *tsukudani* (foods preserved by boiling down in soya).

The 360-year-old Morihachi company is one of Kanazawa's most famous makers of *wa-gashi*. Morihachi not only preserves traditional sweets preferred by the old Kaga provincial lord but also earnestly works on developing new products to suit changing lifestyles. Building a new factory in Senkoji, its dual strategy is to focus on both modern, sanitary, machine-produced sweets and hand-made sweets by confectionery artisans. In a city with many businesses over 100 years old, Tsukuda Foods is relatively young at only 40-odd years. It chose the famous Kanazawa food product *tsukudani* as its family business, combining the traditional techniques of artisans with its own unique freezing and wrapping systems. It has renewed the image of traditional *tsukudani* as a health food.

In 1983 the presidents of several local businesses, including Tsukuda Foods, formed the Association for Considering Old Businesses, Literature, and Romantic Town Buildings, which worked on turning the area around Kyoka Izumi's birthplace (around Morohachi Confectioners) into *Geijutsu no Mori* (literally, "art forest"). It is also involved in the "neighbourhood building" of the Higashiyama area around the Asano River, where many artisans and old businesses are found. The Asano River *Enyukai* was born from this and ranks with the annual Food Pier/Fair as a new traditional-style cultural event in Kanazawa.

In 1986, when a high-rise apartment complex was proposed to be built at the site of the event mentioned above using funds from Tokyo – an effect of the bubble economy – the association began the City Sights Trust movement in order to preserve the traditional city streets. With the help of Kanazawa citizens, this movement succeeded in stopping the apartment complex from going up. It is no overstatement to say that citizens are supporting Kanazawa's traditional culture through both their jobs and their volunteer activities. Another group, the Kanazawa Higashiyama Town Building Council, was formed to look into the rebuilding of old teahouses that were a part of the old civilian culture.

The accumulation of technical know-how brought about by the traditional craft production system lives on in Kanazawa's new urban industries. Without going into too much detail, let us take a quick look at the new urban industries in the hi-tech/hi-touch field. In the field of personal computer equipment, I. O. Data, famous throughout the country, has 325 employees (80 R&D, 25 planners), and started with capital of 1 million yen in 1976. At first the company was subcontracted by large computer manufacturers like NEC to produce computer equipment. Subsequently it changed its business activities when it created the textile work supervision system for local textile factories. With the popularity of personal computers, the company has also been involved in developing new memory technologies. The secret to its success was its ability to enter areas that large companies could not get into as it retained its artisan-like quality, and recently the company has been venturing into areas outside of memory equipment such as hard disks and modems.

Shibuya Industries (1,261 employees), which boasts the top national share in bottling, has become one of the core hi-tech businesses of Kanazawa. Originally it made distilling machines for Kanazawa's local *sake* brewer, Nakamura Brewery. It can be said to be a mechatronic industry forged by traditional industry.

In addition, makers of food-related machines, such as automatic *tofu*-making machine makers who work with local *tofu* and *sushi* shops, automatic deep-fryer makers, revolving *sushi* conveyor makers, etc., all hold top shares in the national market. They all offer a variety of products in small quantities, and are active as leaders in "craft production in the hi-tech era".

What is more, they are all aiming at computerized systems. For example, Takai Manufacturing (116 employees), which boasts a top share in the national automated *tofu*-making machine market, works with local computer manufacturer PFU and has succeeded in utilizing neuro-technology, which functions much like a human brain, in the boiling process. *Tofu*-making artisans claim this is one of the most difficult processes of their trade. These hi-tech machines with "an artisan's touch" may just be the salvation for the *tofu* industry, which is suffering from a lack of successors.

A new-wave boom in the apparel industry ushered in the revival of the textile industry. Local companies boasting a top share in the new field of "fashionable uniforms" emerged. Yagi Corporation (200 employees) was originally subcontracted to produce sports slacks. The president foresaw the future potential of fashion uniforms and entered into the fray with catalogue-based direct sales as his weapon.

Fukumitsuya (140 employees) stands at the top of the *sake* industry in Kanazawa, and is the top *sake* maker in both the Tokai and Hokuriku regions. Other *sake* makers such as Fushimi made television commercials and went the way of mass production and mass sales during the high-growth period, taking large chunks of the national *sake* market share. But decline in the quality of their products brought about a distaste for Japanese *sake* among consumers. In response to this, by keeping production in-house Fukumitsuya was able to maintain its product quality, and gained recognition for responding to the needs of customers with various new products. While advances in biotechnology and rising quality of new products are occurring throughout Japan, the nationally acclaimed endogenous event of the Food Pier/Fair Kanazawa was produced by the president of Fukumitsuya. The concept of the Food Pier/Fair Kanazawa is that of a combined gourmet festival and climate festival. While it is an effort to spread the local food culture, it also reinforces belief in the local "wind" and "earth". "Wind" represents the people who gather at the Food Pier/Fair from all over the country, while "earth" represents the local citizens and local businesses. One can see the influence of Kunio Yanagida's ethnology and Kazuko Tsurumi's sociology on the event.

The event was a success due to the ability of the various cultured and learned people gathered for the event in Kanazawa to disseminate information. This not only brought an increase in tourists during that season but also gave economic stimulus to Kanazawa, through providing a local identity to the local economy. Indeed, it was an event in which *culture led economic activity*.

Kanazawa International Design School opened in April 1992 as the Japan branch of Parsons School of Design in New York. This shows a will to cultivate new designers, which had been lacking in Kanazawa. The effort to create a place in the city centre in which new artisans can be supported as a form of cultural investment by businesses is believed to be the same as the so-called "Third Italy" efforts.

An "urban cultural accumulation" process that cultivates and establishes software and human resources to support hi-tech professionals as well as designers who create hi-touch products will also give birth to new industries and enterprises that produce high value-added goods and services. This formula for developing new industries based upon urban economic development through high-quality cultural accumulation can be termed the "urban cultural mode of production through cultural accumulation". The "cultural production system" that Kanazawa is aiming at is the following:

- production of high cultural value-added goods and services through an integration of artisan skills and feelings with hi-tech machinery in the production process
- recycling of income generated within the region, leading to new cultural expenditure and consumption through a close network of the endogenous industries in the region, from producers of daily goods to mechatronics/software/design industries.

Kanazawa: A creative and sustainable city – The main actors

The three main actors in Kanazawa's development as a creative and sustainable city are the business sector, the citizens, and the local government. This section explores how they conceive the issues and development directions of the city.

The Kanazawa Association of Corporate Executives' activities are playing a big role, and include preservation of town scenery and addressing urban transportation and environmental issues. These activities reflect an underlying ethos among business leaders of Kanazawa, which strives to harmonize the tense relationships between culture and economy, and Kanazawa's traditional culture and global material culture. One of the association's central activities has been the Kanazawa Creative City Conference, exploring the problems cities must overcome in the twenty-first century and appropriate urban models.

In comparison to the business sector, citizen movements related to the urban environment and urban culture (including movements opposing the construction of high-rise apartment complexes and dams that pose a threat to natural cultural properties) are unfortunately lagging behind. However, groups involved in the Ishikawa Environment Network have been learning from the experiences of Freiburg in Germany and have proposed limiting the use of private automobiles in the city centre.

In June 1995 Kanazawa's mayor, Tamotsu Yamade, proposed the Kanazawa World City Concept, which was accepted as a long-term plan in 1996. The basic theme is to strengthen local urban pride through developing Kanazawa's uniqueness, cultivated over 400 years as a city of peace. Specific contents include the introduction of high-level urban functions such as a wide-area transportation system (bullet trains, highways, and an international airport) and a high-level communications system, as well as a new transportation system for the revitalization of the stagnating urban centre; protecting Kanazawa's natural environment and history while fostering its traditional culture, creating an attractive city, the creation of new culture, and a future industrial system; and the establishment of a unique Kanazawa system as a welfare model city and creation of a good living environment for citizens through community revitalization.

In support of these goals, the International Conference of World Cities Renowned for Arts and Crafts has been held every other year since 1997. The aim is for Kanazawa to interact with other cities that place the same emphasis on crafts as a joint activity between art and industry, and to introduce new and creative ideas into Kanazawa's traditional crafts and city planning efforts. The 1997 conference included participants from Florence, Copenhagen, and Istanbul and the 1999 conference brought experts from Venice and Geneva.

Indicators of the creative and sustainable city

The above analysis presents the following elements of the creative and sustainable city.

Table 8.1 Guide to development indicators for the creative and sustainable city

Creative activity	• Growing number of artists, scientists, and crafts people • Acquisition of ISO14000, demonstrating the work environment
Urban life	• Amount of income and free time • Expenditure on cultural affairs and entertainment
Creative support infrastructure	• Quantity and quality of universities, technical schools, research institutions, theatres, libraries, and cultural institutions
Historical heritage, urban environment, and amenities	• Number and condition of cultural assets that are being preserved • Quality of air/water; traffic conditions
Balanced economy	• Transition of industrial structure, number of businesses (formed and closed), amount of shipments, retail sales, and net production within a city
Citizens' activities	• Non-profit organization activity • Participation of women in non-profit organizations
Public administration	• Financial situation (healthy and independent) • Policy-making ability

- Not only artists and scientists should expand their creative activities, but also workers and craftsmen should involve themselves with creative work. In order to realize this, it is necessary to encourage production of useful and culturally valuable goods and services and to improve the environment of factories and offices.
- Artistic activities should be encouraged in the lives of citizens. This requires sufficient income and free time, as well as high-quality consumer goods at reasonable prices. Also, culture/art such as performing arts should be priced low enough for general consumption and appreciation.
- Universities, technical schools, research institutes, theatres, libraries, and cultural institutions which support creative activities of science and art in a city need to function as the creative support infrastructure.
- A comprehensive environmental policy is crucial, as it preserves the historical heritage, protects a city's environment, and improves public amenities. This in turn enables citizens to enhance their creativity and sensitivity.
- A city needs a well-balanced economic base which supports sustainability and creativity.

- Public administration must be composed of creative urban policy and democratic management of urban issues in relation to public finance and industrial, cultural, and environmental policies.

The examination of Kanazawa as a case study of a "creative and sustainable city" offers a guide for indicators of cultural identification and development (Table 8.1).

Conclusion

Until now globalization has actually implied Americanization. Ill effects of globalization include the worsening of environmental problems and the decline of local cultures and industries. Such a situation seems to be closely connected with the American way of life and consumption. There are, however, alternatives. In the twenty-first century, in the move towards true globalization with harmony and moderation, we must come up with a *new production system model* that is global yet varied. Creative and sustainable cities will make possible this move towards a global yet varied social model, as opposed to a globally homogenized social model. These cities will be based on originality in industry and culture, and will aim at sustainable development while interacting with "universal world civilization". Such a network of creative cultural cities will usher in a new century of sustainable cities.

Notes

1. Sassen, Saskia. 1991. *The Global City. New York, London, Tokyo*. Princeton, NJ: Princeton University Press.
2. Landry, Charles. 2000. *The Creative City – A Toolkit for Urban Innovators*. London: Demos.
3. Mumford, Lewis. 1938. *The Culture of Cities*. New York: Harvest Books.
4. Jacobs, Jane. 1984. *Cities and the Wealth of Nations: Principles of Economic Life*. New York: Random House.
5. *Hyakuman-goku* literally means 1 million *koku* (one *koku* equals five bushels) of rice, a form of currency in feudal Japan.
6. See Amin, A. and N. Thrift. 1995. "Globalization, institutional 'thickness' and the local economy", in P. Healey, S. Cameron, S. Davoudi, S. Graham, and A. Madani-Pour (eds) *Managing Cities: The New Urban Context*. New York: John Wiley & Sons, pp. 91–107.

9

Sustainability in a traditional castle city: A case study of Kanazawa, Japan, II

Shigekazu Kusune

Introduction

In the era of globalization, the role of nation-states seems to be losing its meaning. Economic systems and production methods have been increasingly standardized. Metropolises of the world such as London, New York, Tokyo, Shanghai, Seoul, and so forth have very similar "urban-scapes" and skylines. English as a means of international communication is actively used in remote corners of the world, even in villages. Thus, language and cultural barriers seem to have been overcome. Multilateral institutions, regional commercial and military alliances, and multinational super-companies are so powerful and dominating that nation-states, in comparison, are powerless. Against this backdrop, the city in a nation, not the nation itself, will gain increasing importance in global settings.

Globalism, regionalism, and localism go hand in hand. Every city must compete with other cities over the availability of competent labourers as well as production sites. A city must be attractive for consumers and producers. It is not enough for a city just to offer employment possibilities to its residents, but it should also offer all the necessary amenities and make them accessible, and give residents reasons to be proud. A city as a local unit with character will gain importance and will be or become sustainable. A city which fails in this would not be sustainable. For this purpose, it is quite natural that each city should take its cultural values and heritage, its history and tradition, very seriously. To be attractive for the residents, *each city needs its own character and specialities, which should be derived from its own tradition and culture.* Just looking back to the past is not enough. It is equally important to make an investment for the future.

A city must adjust itself to new circumstances. It must be proactive and create new culture. Therefore, the second decisive factor for sustainability of a city is *creativity.* Culture can be understood with the metaphor of a living organism. Culture is a living, growing thing. It is born and it can die. It survives through time by being handed down from one generation to another.

The third factor is *cooperation between residents and the local government.* In democratic countries the government must account for expenditures on culture. It must be able to explain the necessity of investments and persuade taxpayers to give consent for these. Politicians should know exactly what the people (the voters) want. Their support is indispensable. In the long run, a policy that has the consent and support of the electorate will be adopted and carried out. In short, even for sustainability of cities with an emphasis on culture, cooperation between the residents and the local government is a *sine qua non.*

This chapter will examine the policies that govern Kanazawa based on the abovementioned three perspectives, and report the extent to which the city has adopted policies in order to maintain its character as an old castle city. It will also discuss how the local government cooperated with local actors and stakeholders for the same purpose.

The character of Kanazawa

In the Edo period (1603–1867) Kanazawa was the second largest castle town in Japan after Edo (now Tokyo). Around Kanazawa Castle there were huge *samurai* districts; outside the *samurai* districts were the merchant and manual worker districts. The castle town was known as "the Library of the Realm" because of the cultural policy of the Maedas (rulers of the area), which was a product of their tactical fight for survival. The Maedas were the second strongest family after the Tokugawas in the Edo period, and feared retaliation by the Tokugawas because they had once challenged these mightiest rulers of Japan. In order to show that they had no intention of challenging the Tokugawas again, the rulers in Kanazawa spent money on peaceful activities and culture. They invited many artists, poets, writers, philosophers, scholars, and so on to settle in their town, and Kanazawa developed into an eminent art and cultural city in Japan.

Kanazawa was and is still very famous for *noh* theatre, flower arranging, lacquerware, Kaga-Makie inlaid work, Ohi and Kutani pottery, gold-leaf work, Kaga *Yuzen* silk painting, *koto* (a long Japanese zither with 13 strings), *shamisen* (a three-stringed Japanese banjo), *utai* (chanting of *noh* texts), tea-ceremony schools, Kaga cooking, and education (e.g. the Meirin Kan, a school for *samurais* from the eighteenth century and forerunner of Kanazawa University).

Even today, this city as a castle city has not lost much of its cultural atmosphere. In alleys off the main streets one can hear even today *shamisen*, *koto*, *utai*, and so forth, and one may encounter a group of women in kimonos on their way to a tea ceremony or flower-arranging lessons. It is no wonder that many Japanese selected Kanazawa as one of the most popular cities in Japan in which they want to live (according to a survey published in a local newspaper in April 2001). The citizens of Kanazawa are very proud of their cultural heritage and history.

Measures undertaken by the local government

When one looks on the history of various measures taken by Kanazawa, it turns out that the notion of the city's sustainability and culture has grown. At first Kanazawa wanted to restore only culturally important spots which seemed to be useful for tourism. In 1964 the Ordinance of Restoration System for Earthen Walls, the Gate, etc. in a Samurai Residence Area (*Bukeyashikigunchiku no Dobei Mon nado no Shufukuseido*) was established. Then, in 1968, the Kanazawa City Traditional Environment Preservation and District Specification Ordinance (*Kanazawashi Dentokankyo Hozon Joreiseitei Kuikishitei*) was enacted. This regulation was the first local law of its kind in Japan, after the Law for Protection of Old Cities (*Kotohozonho*) such as Kyoto, Nara, and Kamakura was enforced. In 1970 the Restoration Assistance System for Earthen Walls of Buddhism Temples in Traditional Environmental Districts (*Dento Kankyo Chikunai Jiin Dobei Shufuku Hojoseido*) was established. In 1978 the Beauty and Culture Prize of Kanazawa City (*Kanazawa Toshi Bibunkasho*) was founded. In 1980 Kanazawa introduced the Establishment of Buddhist Temples and Gates Restoration Assistance System in Traditional Environmental Districts (*Dento Kankyo Chikunai Jiin Sanmon Shufuku Hojoseido*).

The *samurai* houses, the temples, and the *geisha* areas have become objects of protection. In 1982 the *geisha* areas were covered under the Ordinance for Additional Expansion of Traditional Environment Preservation District (*Dentokankyo Hozonkuiki no Tsuika Kakudai*). In 1984 the Former Kazoemachi Region Maintenance Plan (*Kazoemachi Ittaiseibi Keikaku*) was adopted to protect Kazoemachi, the teahouse district. However, at the end of the 1980s the course of Kanazawa's policy changed. The preservation of cultural objects moved away from tourist locations, and protection was not only given to the so-called "sightseeing spots" but also to culturally valuable "objects" like the living spaces of citizens. This change of policy was necessary because there was considerable depopulation in the old town. Motorization created a strong desire among citizens to escape from enclosed downtown spaces to build bigger houses in the suburbs. This decreased the number of people who lived in the traditional core area (about 860 ha) as well as the sales volume in the merchant districts (420 ha). However, various policies were taken to stop this negative trend, including financial assistance for redeveloping and re-settling in the urban area. These were only a beginning, and it is too early to say if these measures are sufficiently powerful to stop the negative trend.

Kanazawa took various measures in order to show how it used cultural values to revitalize the urban area. In 1989 the Ordinance Concerning Formation of Traditional Environment Preservation and Beautiful Landscape in Kanazawa City (the so-called Landscape Ordinance or *Keikan Jorei*) was enacted. The space to be protected was expanded with this ordinance from the original 422 ha to 599 ha. The height of the houses in this preservation area was regulated. In 1994 the Kanazawa City Komachinami Preservation Ordinance (*Kanazawashi Komachinami Hozonjorei*) was established, to which Mayor Yamade Tamotsu made a great contribution. The Japanese word *komachinami* means streets with rows of houses with a historical atmosphere. *Ko* in the word *komachinami* has two meanings, old and small. This regulation provides the city with a subsidy system and helped foster spontaneous activities by citizens (Table 9.1). At the time this chapter was written, 14 *samurai* streets and 27 manual-worker streets had received the assistance of the city government under this law.

In 1995 the Conception of World City (*Sekai Toshi Koso*) was approved by the city council. In 1996 the Kanazawa City Canals Maintenance Ordinance (*Kanazawashi Yosui Hozen Jorei*) was enacted. This ordinance, which was another achievement of Mayor Yamade Tamotsu, covered 41 km out of the total length of over 150 km of canals. The protected canals flow in the old core of the city: canals from the Edo period were used to protect Japanese wooden houses from fire and dispose of heavy snow in the winter seasons. To protect trees and forests the Kanazawa City's Green Slope Protection Ordinance (*Kanazawashi Shamenryokuchi Hozenjorei*), yet another achievement of Mayor Yamade, was enforced in 1997. The Kanazawa City's City Planning Master Plan (*Kanazawashi Toshikeikaku Master Plan*), which was established in 1998, provided the city with the House Construction and Recommendation Money System of Old Town (*Machinaka Jutakukensetsu Shoreikinsedo*).

Through this plan Kanazawa is now ready to pay 10–15 per cent of the

Table 9.1 Subsidies awarded under Kanazawa'a *komachinami* subsidy programme, 2000

Subsidy	Preservation zone	Preservation building	Building with preservation contract
Design cost	30% (max. ¥300,000)	30% (max. ¥300,000)	30% (max. ¥300,000)
Appearance of new buildings and repairs	70% (max. ¥2 mil.)		
Appearance		70% (max. ¥5 mil.)	70% (max. ¥7 mil.)
Restoration and maintenance of earthen walls	70% (max. ¥3 mil.)	70% (max. ¥3 mil.)	70% (max. ¥3 mil.)
Restoration and maintenance of wooden walls, hedges, etc.	70% (max. ¥1 mil.)	70% (max. ¥1 mil.)	70% (max. ¥1 mil.)
Restoration and maintenance of entrance	70% (max. ¥1.5 mil.)	70% (max. ¥1.5 mil.)	70% (max. ¥1.5 mil.)
Restoration and maintenance of lattice doors	90%	90%	90%
Firefighting equipment		90% (max. ¥3 mil.)	90% (max. ¥3 mil.)
Fireproof construction		90% (max. ¥3 mil.)	90% (max. ¥3 mil.)
Activities by preservation organizations	Yearly within ¥100,000	Yearly within ¥100,000	Yearly within ¥100,000

housing loan if citizens want to build a house in the old town and in the traditional Japanese style. The Traditional Building Restoration Support System (*Dentoteki Kenzobutsu Shufuku Shienseido*) of 1998 makes it possible to subsidize traditional house construction. Kanazawa has tried to bring people back from the suburbs into the main urban area. In Japan the Law Concerning United Promotion of Urban Maintenance, Urban Improvement and Activation of Commerce, etc. in Center Urban Area (*Chushin Shigaichi niokeru Shigaichi no Seibikaizen oyobi Shogyo tono Kasseika no Ippanteki Suishin nikansuru Horitsu*) was enforced on 3 June 1998. Based on this law, Kanazawa made the Basic Plan for Activation of Kanazawa City Core Urban Area (*Kanazawashi Chushin Shigaichi Kasseika Kihonkeikaku*) in 2000. This plan outlines the following basic policies.

- To build a town for pedestrians by using history, culture, and nature. Construction of pedestrian-friendly promenades and community parks to vitalize the city. Redevelopment of irrigation canals flowing through the city, and financial aid to restore traditional houses and build museums.
- To make a living environment which matches with the traditional environment. Financial aid (2–3 million yen) for construction of new houses in traditional style in the urban area and for restoration of traditional houses and preservation of traditional areas.
- To make an attractive commercial environment with consideration for the special conditions of commerce.
- To improve access in the general transportation system and its activation by promoting basic infrastructure.

In 2000 the Ordinance Concerning Promotion of City Planning through Citizens' Participation in Kanazawa City (*Kanazawashi niokeru Shiminsankaku niyoru Machizukuri no Suishin ni kansuru Jorei*, abbreviated as *Machizukuri Jorei*) was enacted. The regulation is of a "citizen participation" nature: in order to get an agreement, Kanazawa's government needs the consent of 80 per cent or more of the affected residents. Then it can regulate building usage, building coverage, ratio of building volume to lot size, site space, height of buildings, architectural style, fences, etc. in a voluntary contract between the residents and Kanazawa's municipal authorities. In this way it is possible to design an entire area. Such a case will be found in Yuwaku, a spa site in the suburbs of Kanazawa. Here one can speak not of preservation, but of creation or recreation of the culture.

The Ordinance Concerning Promotion of Green City Planning in Kanazawa City (*Kanazawashi niokeru Midori no Machizukuri no Suishin nikansuru Jorei*) states: "You have to try your best to grow trees, flowers, etc. and to plant trees in the site, which is used for an office, a store, a factory or the other kinds of bureau. Kanazawa City will buy lots and estates and make from them pocket parks and playgrounds and community squares." In 2003 in Hirosaka, on a site where an elementary school and a junior high school attached to Kanazawa University were located, they will give way to a complex consisting of a museum for modern art and a pavilion for art exchange.

Various sections of local government are taking part in Kanazawa's approach: of these the Green and Flower Section (*Midori to Hana no Ka*), City Planning Section (*Toshikeikaku Ka*), Streetscape Section (*Machinami Taisaku Ka*), Planning and Coordination Section (*Kikaku Chosei Ka*), Canals and Streets Maintenance Section (*Yosui Michisuji Seibi Ka*), Commercial Promotion Section (*Shogyo Shinko Ka*), and Sightseeing Section (*Kanko Ka*) are noteworthy.

It is now clear how culture and the traditions in Kanazawa have heavily influenced the administration of the city. The castle character of Kanazawa and its cultural heritage without doubt decide the direction of civic planning. Kanazawa is using cultural heritage for the reproduction, redevelopment, and long-term sustainability of the city.

Participation of citizens

As the Ordinance Concerning Promotion of City Planning through Citizens' Participation in Kanazawa shows, participation and cooperation of the citizens are very important for the sustainability of the city. A city could give certain incentives to shape the city's development in the form of consultation and financial assistance, but if there is no echo from the citizens' side it is almost impossible to make public policy in the appropriate way. In this sense one can consider the case of Owaricho, a traditional and prestigious merchant district in Kanazawa. The next section will present the history of the Owaricho district.

History of Owaricho

The Buddhist priest Rennyo of the militant Ikko sect constructed the religious headquarters at Oyama-Gobo, which later became Kanazawa Castle. Older Kanazawa residents still use the name Oyama to refer to the castle. At the same location there was already a marketplace named Kubo-ichi (Kubo market), which later developed into Owaricho. In 1580 the feudal lord Sakuma Morimasa drove the Ikko sect from the fortress, and following his death in 1583 the castle was occupied by a new ruler, Maeda Toshiie. During the next 400 years Kanazawa experienced neither war damage nor natural disaster, and under the rule of the Maedas developed into one of the most prosperous cities in Japan. As cities at that time depended upon powerful merchants and tradesmen, the castle had a famous adjoining merchant district, known as Owaricho.

The Owaricho merchant district was located at Otemon, the main entrance of Kanazawa Castle. Only selected and élite merchants were permitted to live there, and they were called Arako-shu (Arako group) after the Arako district of Owari (now Nagoya) from which they came. The district name Owaricho comes from the Owari: people who followed the Maeda family from Arako/Owari and settled in Owaricho in front of the castle. This was quite significant, because usually only reliable subjects were allowed to live in such areas. The Maeda clan clearly thought that they could rely only on those people whom they had known for a long time. This was quite natural in the Warring States period, when betrayal and surprise attacks were everyday happenings. This location close to the castle may be symbolic of the close relationship between the merchants and the Maedas. Because the *samurais* were not involved in commerce, merchants who supported *samurais* were needed. The *samurais* obtained rice and other goods as their salary, and they needed merchants who could cash these. When the Maedas needed money, these merchants were ready to lend to them. They enjoyed political affiliation to the family and a high reputation as Owaricho merchants: other merchants dreamed of being able one day to live in Owaricho and open their shops there.

Even though the first generation of Arako merchants were gradually taken over by newcomers, the new merchants had the same self-consciousness, prestige, and close relationship with the Maedas as their predecessors. Owaricho, at the front door of the castle, was a route for the Daimyo Procession (*daimyo* means feudal lord) during the Edo period. The Daimyo Procession, a pilgrim trip to Edo (now Tokyo), cost huge amounts of money and was compulsory: the Tokugawa family, rulers of all Japan, used it to prove the loyalty of various lords. It was a duty for lords to show their power and wealth on the way to Edo and they took care about the appearance of the main streets used by the procession, especially in their home towns. In Kanazawa this meant Owaricho, the most prestigious and magnificent street in the city – this is demonstrated by the fact that the streets in this area are laid out in a grid pattern, an exception in Kanazawa because the other streets were planned as a labyrinth for defensive purposes.

The Owaricho district flourished through the Edo period, and at the beginning of the nineteenth century Kanazawa was the fourth largest city in Japan after Edo, Osaka, and Kyoto. The prosperity continued even after the Meiji Restoration. After the establishment of prefectures in place of feudal domains, the Seventh Infantry Division and the divisional headquarters of the Japanese army moved into Kanazawa Castle. The merchant district of Owaricho profited from the castle through business with the army, so the district had to be enlarged: new streets came to Owaricho, such as Shinmachi and Imamachi. Hashibacho, a corner of Owaricho, was the greatest amusement centre in Hokuriku (Ishikawa, Toyama, and Fukui prefectures). Even in the Meiji (1868–1912), Taisho (1912–1926), and the beginning of the Showa (1926–1989) periods, Owaricho embodied the dream of merchants in Hokuriku. Owners of shops at Owaricho were conscious of this historical value and prestige.

After the Second World War the military was banned from the castle and Kanazawa University, established in 1949, became its new tenant/occupant. Even though the university could not financially substitute the role of the Maedas or the military, as one can easily imagine, and there was no direct relationship any more between the castle and the Owaricho merchants, the castle did not lose its symbolic value for the Owaricho merchants and also for ordinary citizens of Kanazawa: at the least, some powerful and prestigious institutions were still located there. Meanwhile Katamachi/Korinbo, another merchant district, succeeded in modernization and advanced to become the business centre of Kanazawa after the Second World War. Owaricho lost its position as the centre of Kanazawa's commerce. Then something happened that might have given the final blow and put an end to the tradition of Owaricho merchants: Kanazawa University moved from the castle to the suburbs in 1989. The castle lost its symbolic ruler, and a vacuum was generated. Kanazawa is now reconstructing the castle buildings according to an old plan from the Edo period to fill this vacuum. Kanazawa was and still is a castle town which has been growing with the castle. Now the former centre of power, politics, finance, and learning is a park, and Owaricho seems to have a bleak future. People speak self-deprecatingly that Owaricho is *owari*: *owari* in Japanese means "end" or "hopeless", implying that Owaricho is a district without any hope.

Some merchants who could see no future prospects moved from the once-prestigious district. However, the so-called hard-core merchants, who were very conscious of their tradition and history, decided to stay there and opened the Chomin Bunkakan (Pavilion for Merchants' and Ordinary Citizens' Culture) in Owaricho in 1986, subsidized by Kanazawa's local government. They gather in a group named Wakatekai, a society established in 1980 for younger-generation merchants who have shops in Owaricho. They have begun to study their own history and go back to their roots, Owari in Nagoya. Kanazawa has acknowledged their activity, and the Shinise Koryukan (Exchange Hall for Long-established Stores) was established in 1996 in order to inform visitors and tourists of Owaricho's history.

This citizens' initiative is also subsidized by Kanazawa. The exchange hall, once an optician's shop on the Owaricho shopping street, is actually a romantic-looking house from the Taisho period (1912–1926). Both the pavilion and the exchange hall are managed by the Owaricho Shopping Centre Promotion Union (Owaricho Shotengai Shinko Kumiai). Younger members of the union belong to the Wakatekai. Three years before the opening of the hall, in 1993, the Wakatekai opened two mini-museums. At the corner of their shops, tiny museums were constructed which are lit up even at night to draw the attention of passers-by. These museums are not an advertisement for the shops; in fact the museums should have no direct relation with the business of the concerned shops. What they want to show is the spirit of the shop. Tools and goods displayed in these museums help recall the past. The shop owners reorganize their shops to construct a mini-museum, and half of the construction cost, with a maximum of 2.5 million yen, is subsidized by the Kanazawa city government. At present there are 10 mini-museums, and the Wakatekai has published 26 booklets to explain the history of Owaricho.

The Owaricho merchants have a "mercantile spirit". As mentioned above, they were affiliated to the lords who promoted the local culture. The Owaricho merchants were supposed to invest money and time in culture and divided their wealth in three areas: land, money, and the arts. They learned *noh*, the tea ceremony, *utai* (Japanese opera), and *mai* (Japanese dance), and invited scholars and poets. They were and are the bearers of Japanese culture. This district will be enriched by another museum in the near future: a "museum for sounds", meaning "library of music". Kanazawa does not want Owaricho to lose its cultural atmosphere or significance. This is only possible when its citizens take the first step, motivated by a strong feeling of cultural heritage like the Owaricho merchants.

Conclusion

Culture exists in a constant state of change. If we do nothing, it will disappear quickly. Thus, if the policies that governed Kanazawa had remained the same from the 1960s and if it had not widened its scope to include not only tourist spots but also ordinary citizens' living areas, the distinctive landscape and atmosphere of Kanazawa would not have been the same. If nothing had been done against motorization and depopulation of old town centres, Kanazawa would be like a city in the USA: big houses in the suburbs, while urban centres appear deserted and without life.

If we carefully consider the implications of environmental degradation, extinction of fossil energy, and a rapidly ageing society, it would be very careless to take a course of expansion. Kanazawa has developed a number of good policies. These have contributed to investments to acquire uninhabited houses in order to reconstruct them so that they may be reused or transform their premises into "pocket parks", police offices, and/or spaces where citizens come together in order to build community spirit and maintain the city's pride as a castle city (i.e. maintaining its old character). There are some initiatives developed and managed by citizens or through cooperation between the municipal government and local stakeholders.

Some cultural indicators for sustainable urban development in the case of Kanazawa would be the pride of citizens in their own history and culture; the castle town character; citizens' initiatives; social mobilization; cultural emphasis in the city planning policy; and concrete and spiritual support for this policy from voters.

Preservation of the past culture alone is not enough. A city must continuously produce new culture and new cultural icons to engage the young and old alike. It is needless to say that harmony between economic prosperity and tradition is very important. In this sense, creativity is critical and must also be one of the cultural indicators. One cannot say that Kanazawa has done enough. In the author's opinion, much still remains to be done. In the centre of the city there are numerous car-parks which were once residences that should have been protected. Over time the character of Kanazawa as a castle town has certainly been damaged. Kanazawa is unlikely to cease the construction of wide streets through the old town. Thus, according to the construction plan of the city, even the main street of historical Owaricho will be widened. What will happen to the traditional wooden shops that house mini-museums? Kanazawa has not succeeded in constructing the spacious pedestrian zones which are so common in European countries and which certainly contribute to sustainability. But, irrespective of some shortcomings faced by Kanazawa, it, along with a few other Japanese cities, has the best preconditions to be a model of using culture in its sustainability as a city.

10

Common themes and differences: Approaches to culture in sustainability of cities

M. Nadarajah

Some common concerns

There are a number of common areas and concerns in the case studies, though the depth and scope are different. The discussion on governance issues and the importance of citizens' initiatives in the struggle for a sustainable city come across strongly in all the studies. This concern is critical in many other areas that are being explored in this volume, such as "Who decides on cultural indicators for a locality – the expert or the citizen?"

Another important concern that has been explored in the case studies is the nature of the present form of unsustainable urbanization, its West/American-centredness, its consequences, and the urgent need for an alternative/Asian form of urbanization. While this is strongly stated in Choe's study, it figures indirectly in the other studies. As the next section will show, the alternative form of urbanization that is being suggested places importance on culture in sustainability of cities.

Yet another concern that figures subtly in the studies is the recognition of the impact of globalization on urbanization. In all cases there is recognition of the danger of the homogenizing tendency of globalization that, for instance, produces the same skyline across Asia and the world. However, there is also a desire to engage actively with it. Sasaki, for instance, suggests that we develop a cultural production system that is universal in form but varied locally. Nadarajah suggests "sustainable enlightened localism" where engagement with globalization is more creative and unfolds in terms of "glocalism".

186

Table 10.1 Four approaches to drawing on culture for sustainable urbanization

City	Country	Mode of engagement with culture
Patan	Nepal (South Asia)	Internal cultural transformation
Penang	Malaysia (South-East Asia)	Multi-culturalism and enlightened localism
Cheongju	Korea (East Asia)	Urban cultural identity
Kanazawa	Japan (East Asia)	Cultural mode of production

Last, an important and critical dilemma has been captured by all the case studies. This pertains to culture and economics. The major threat to culture and a culture orientation in urban theory and planning is the market or the market discourse. The homogenizing power of the market, now immensely enlarged by globalization, threatens local cultures and multicultural expression. While there is a need to pay attention to the economic viability of cities, there is also an equally important drive to sustain some sort of distinctiveness and cultural identity for cities. Though it is not elaborately addressed here, there is a need to overcome this dilemma.

Different modes of engagement with culture

The four case studies covering Patan, Penang, Cheongju, and Kanazawa (PPCK) present four approaches to harnessing the power of culture in the struggle for sustainable urbanization (Table 10.1).

For the purpose of capturing the differences between the studies and making a meaningful comparison, the contributors' approaches can be explored in terms of the "mode of engagement" with culture. This examination is critical, as it is the basis for the proposal to make culture the primary principle to influence urban planning in order to counter the purely technical and market-driven approaches. To elaborate, if we take culture from the "urban cultural identity approach" then that will become the central basis for planning the urban area/city.

Internal cultural transformation approach

In discussing Patan, Tiwari draws attention to the historical specificity and pervasive religious basis of urbanization. In capturing the changes that culture underwent in this urban area, he specifically draws attention to the transformational aspects of culture and how these will eventually contribute to the sustainability of Patan.

Tiwari identifies eight – mostly religious – cultural activities that contributed to sustainable urbanism in Patan. Take, for instance, his discussion on the Rato Matsyendranath festival, which is an activity related to a religious festival but which contributed to the maintenance of waterworks necessary for the city.

Tiwari makes the following critical observation.

The way cultural processes achieve sustainability is ... through striking a balanced dialogical existence between nature (resources and waste assimilation), economic pursuits (resource capitalization and waste generation), and social relationships (essential ordering of competition for resources and waste disassociation, i.e. separation of waste into its "components"). While we can see that balanced cultural processes were designed, developed, and practised in the past to support sustainability, a culture able to put the three elements together in the present-day context is only now being sought through international ethical norms and standards.

He goes on to observe that:

Whereas in the past culture and cultural practices seemed to have been used to cause appropriate community behaviour towards sustaining ecology, environment, and social relationships over longer periods of time, current practices relate to creative exploitation of cultural practices as resources by themselves and aim at immediate economic gains at the individual, community, and institutional levels ... Providing for the needs of the citizen in town may be a matter of economic investment, but its sustenance needs to be approached through culture-building processes and should maintain continuity with past cultural mechanisms. Internally guided regeneration and not externally supported revival should be the basis for creative use and management of historic environments.

The multiculturalism and enlightened localism approach

Nadarajah attempts to identify and recover the various discourses on sustainable development/urbanization in Penang. He identifies the governance, market, conservation, human rights, and culturalist discourses. An active engagement with culture unfolds as a central concern only in the culturalist discourse, although it is touched upon by both the governance and conservationist discourses. In examining this discourse and engaging with culture creatively, Nadarajah suggests an organized sensitivity to eight principles covering the symbolic universe, wholeness, development, democracy, circularity, diversity (biological and cultural), localism, and spatialization. An integration of these principles highlights localism and the cultural repertoire that defines it. The culturalist discourse eventually gives prominence to multicultural diversity and enlightened localism.

Table 10.2 Most desirable policy options for the development of Cheongju

	No.	%
Strengthen economic base by high-tech industries	85	27.0
Expansion and improvement of urban infrastructure	95	30.2
Creation of urban identity by cultural development	126	40.0
Other	9	2.8

These become pathways for not only an active engagement with culture but also the strategy of sustainable urbanization.

The urban cultural identity approach

Choe's study of Cheongju provides yet another approach to engaging with culture in order that it contributes to sustainable urbanization. Choe approaches the reality of cultural identity through his case study, and takes that as the trajectory to engage with culture and urbanization. An examination of one question in his survey (Q5 in Table 7.1) is revealing. In response to the question "What is the most desirable policy option for the development of Cheongju in preparing for the twenty-first century?", 40 per cent of people thought that creation of urban identity by cultural development was the most important (Table 10.2).

In addressing culture, the aim must be built around specific urban cultural identity. Thus the urban cultural system, covering cultural administration and intermediaries, consumers, cultural infrastructure, and producers, must combine to provide a distinctive cultural identity. But this by itself is not effective in the realization of culturally sensitive sustainable urbanization. As Choe observes, "Culture when articulated as a mere abstract concept would not explain sustainable urban development. But it will have strong explanatory power when it is permeated into other sectoral and functional concepts like governance, economy, environment, spatio-physical structure, and societal systems." Thus, to realize sustainable urbanization, culture, and the identities it produces, must intimately influence such areas as governance, economy, environment, spatio-physical, and societal systems.

The cultural mode of production approach

In his discussion on Kanazawa, Sasaki argues for the encouragement of "the production of goods and services that are not only utilitarian but also artistic". There needs to be an "art-ification of daily life". He observes that in the twenty-first century, "in the move towards true globalization with harmony and moderation, we must come up with a *new pro-*

duction system model that is global yet varied. What will make this move towards a global yet varied social model, as opposed to a globally homogenized social model, possible are creative and sustainable cities. These cities will be based on originality in industry and culture, and will aim at sustainable development ..." Sasaki's contribution, a discussion on the new "cultural mode of production", marks the fourth approach to engaging with culture in the struggle for sustainable urbanization.

Conclusion

This section of the book is long not because of the pages it covers to capture the case studies, but really because of its importance to the Kanazawa Initiative, which is a collective and considered attempt to counter the mainstream and traditional concerns and approaches to urban studies and planning and to make a clear case for culture in sustainability of cities. It is an attempt to capture the critical importance and central role of culture in contributing to urban theory and planning, in particular to sustainable urbanization, in an age when sustainable development has come to mean the survival of humanity, today and tomorrow.

The case studies essentially looked at the mode of engagement with culture in order to draw its creativity to inform urban planning. The four modes of engagement also give us four alternative approaches, in addition to discussions raised in Chapter 2 by Rana and Piracha. In a way they are independent approaches, but one can also consider them as part of an integrated approach to culturally sensitive sustainable urban planning. The Kanazawa Initiative seeks to elaborate and articulate these views, and present them as pathways to sustainable urbanization. Of course, these approaches need more attention and development into a consistent framework.

Part III

Culture in sustainability of cities II

11

Approaches to cultural indicators

Sang-Chuel Choe, Peter J. Marcotullio, and Awais L. Piracha

Introduction

Culture is increasingly being recognized as the key to sustainable economic and social development. Sir Peter Hall, in his book *Cities in Civilization*, has mentioned that culture, technology, and order will bring the "coming golden urban age".[1] This highlights the recent prominence that culture is receiving in research circles as a tool for urban development. Incorporation of culture and cultural heritage in planning and development frameworks, however, depends upon how cities identify, assess, clarify, and prioritize issues, and build consensus for and mobilize the active participation of the various actors and stakeholders. Cultural indicators can help in this process to assist cities to incorporate cultural aspects into overall and sectoral development policies and strategies.

The Kanazawa Resolutions (KR) recognized the significance of culture in the sustainability of cities and the need to develop indicators for the same. The resolutions point out that the majority of the world's people will soon live in urbanized societies. Rapid urbanization was among the most significant transformations of human settlements in the last century. This trend is expected to continue at an even faster pace, especially in the developing countries of Asia and Africa, during the current century. The KR further recognize increased social exclusion of the poor, intensifying the problem of poverty and diminishing equity. The other consequence of the fast pace of urbanization is unsustainable resource use and environmental degradation with growing – and sometime acute – impacts on

193

human and economic health. Then there is a danger that cities are also losing their distinctive cultures and becoming engulfed in a homogenization process that is both global and cultural. In this context, culturally informed city governance with participation of citizens is the way forward for making cities sustainable. The resolutions envisioned development of *cultural indicators* as one of the mechanisms that could help in achieving the goal of making cities socially, ecologically, and economically sustainable.

The positive role that culture can play for two subthemes of sustainable development, namely economy and the environment, is being actively investigated. International institutions are investigating how to utilize culture for improving economies. Amartya Sen's work[2] on culture and development has provided these organizations with intellectual input in their pursuit. At the local level, cities are exploring ways and means of utilizing culture for enhancing their economies. At the environmental end the role of culture is again actively being investigated. Milton[3] discusses the ways in which culture/urban culture is linked with the environment/ urban ecology, and shows us how an understanding of culture can throw light on the way environmental issues are perceived and interpreted, both by local communities and within the contemporary global arena. Fischer and Hajer[4] provide us with a discussion on socio-cultural dimensions of the environmental debate.

While there is agreement that culture as a tool for sustainable development is getting more attention, the subject is complex and open to a broad array of interpretations. Opinions can roughly be divided into the two elaborated below.

One opinion is that culture can and should be used for sustainable development (of cities), and that empirical research needs to be done to this end. The holders of this opinion also feel that urban cultural indicators are for the use of the policy-makers. The second opinion is that it is the sustainability of the culture which has to be sought. People holding this opinion also think that the indicators have to be for civil society.

Whether there should be one, two, or several sets of indicators is another issue that often comes up in debate on culture in the sustainability of cities. Separate sets of cultural indicators could be developed depending on the scale (neighbourhood/city), cities at different stages of socio-economic development and connectivity with the global system, target audience (policy-makers/researchers/civil society activists), and rationality (subjective/objective).

The authors of this chapter feel that both lines of thinking have merits and they are not necessarily contradictory. The debate in this chapter thus tries to accommodate both points of views. The chapter is a synthesis of the debate on indicators carried out in the workshops of the Culture in Sustainability of Cities project in a series of three international conferences – particularly the third held in Cheongju, Korea (2001) – as well as the authors' own thoughts on the topic.

The chapter starts with a comprehensive overview on the construction of indicators for quantifying the role of culture in the sustainability of cities. The second section elaborates on the need for developing cultural indicators as well as highlighting the challenges in constructing such indicators. It presents accounts of some pioneer systems of cultural indicators/statistics practised in some countries. It also presents the recent work of international development agencies on cultural indicators of human development/well-being. And lastly, the second section discusses urban culture and urban indicators. The third section elaborates on a new research agenda for cultural indicators for sustainable urban development in Asia. The research agenda highlights the importance of distinguishing between indicators for policy-makers and for conceptual research, as well as between production and consumption of culture. The section then embarks upon a framework for international research. The fourth and last section presents conclusions on the role of culture in the sustainability of cities and the creation of indicators for the same.

Culture and cultural indicators

According to the KR, culture should be viewed as a way of life and a way of living together in dialogical coexistence, creatively adjusting to changes or encouraging them. There are a number of other definitions of culture that are, in essence, quite similar to this definition.

According to Tylor,[5] culture is "knowledge, belief, art, moral, laws, custom, and any other capabilities and habits acquired by man as a member of the society". In contrast to this *way of life* definition of culture, there is another notion of culture that focuses only on intellectual and aesthetic achievements. Culture in its narrow sense can be considered, in the words of the *Oxford English Dictionary*, as "the art and other manifestations of the achievement of the human intellect regarded collectively".

A good definition of culture is that in the *World Cultural Report*,[6] where culture is defined as *the ways of living as individuals and ways of living together*. This broad definition of culture includes the narrow understanding of culture as *arts and other activities involving human intellect*. Culture, defined broadly, goes well beyond the usual understanding of *literature, art, music, and so forth* to encompass everything that makes up a *way of life*. This anthropological sense of culture refers to the way people live together, interact, compete, and cooperate.

Culture plays an important role in sustaining a strong sense of local/ national identity and stimulating economic growth and prosperity. Cultural policies and programmes are capable of wielding considerable social and economic influence. In Garonna's words, "As in the case of 'Green GDP', we now have every hope of creating a 'Golden GDP' that will take the full account of culture and its impacts on development and society."[7]

According to Garonna, the complexity and uncertainty of decision-making, particularly in art and culture, calls for more solid infrastructures of information and a more informed and rational approach, with less irrational exuberance. A solid basis is therefore essential for the proper evaluation of the effectiveness of cultural policies and programmes, recognizing that indicators are needed to stimulate policy dialogue. While there is need for a clear definition of culture to make cultural indicators sensitive, they will help convince not only academics and civil society organizations but also politicians, policy-makers, and the media.

Garonna also points to four outstanding reasons for the widespread popularity of indicators. Firstly, clear and policy-relevant indicators based on sound, comparable, and credible statistics are needed for peer pressure, reviews, and benchmarking that can be a very powerful policy tool to stimulate reform and guide behaviour. Secondly, to increase investment in culture, more transparency is needed in cultural markets and institutions. Cultural indicators can help manage risk, allocate resources and time efficiently, focus commitment, and invest capital. Thirdly, indicators can help improve accountability of public policies for culture. And we need governments to be made more accountable for their actions in the field of culture and arts, as this is an essential precondition for greater and swifter public support for culture. Fourthly, for international dialogue exchanging and communicating cultural experiences and assets on a global scale, high-quality statistics and indicators that can be compared and contrasted on the international level are absolutely essential.

Tolila[8] argues that culture and statistics do not match well, but there are certain questions that we need to answer. What share of wealth is devoted by a society to what it defines as its culture? What are the cultural products of that society, and how are they devised and disseminated? How much employment do these sectors provide? What is their contribution to national/local wealth? These are some of the issues where statistics are needed not only for cultural development but also for potentially fruitful dialogue.

The objective should be to develop a full-fledged international system of statistical information on culture through which policy performance at the local level can be understood, measured, and assessed against perfor-mance in other localities. In addition, policy performance at the national level can be compared among countries and across different regions.

It follows from this argument that cities/localities should be the starting points of collecting statistics on culture. Cities should then, according to an internationally recognized framework, compute their cultural indica-tors to be used as policy aids and pass on information to the national level. The national level should use this information for national policy guidance and then pass it on to the international level/UNESCO. UNESCO would like to reinforce the notion that cultural indicators are a tool for policy dialogue and guidance, and that their creation should therefore be encouraged.

However, it should be recognized that local communities have unique conditions and circumstances which may require them to develop indica-tors in a participatory manner. This means that national governments and international organizations should not dictate what indicators commu-nities ought to develop. These institutions can provide a loose framework for indicator development, but the final decision and selection of indica-tors have to rest with the communities themselves. This argument has been strongly reflected in the KR.

Challenges in constructing cultural indicators

Research on cultural indicators is still in its infancy. Fukuda-Parr[9] argues that indicators are a tool of policy dialogue and are not the same thing as statistical data. They should contain evaluative and not merely descrip-tive information. She further argues that no single indicator/index can capture the complex reality of culture. Probably a set of indices will have to be deduced from the cultural statistics.

Laya[10] identifies various difficulties in the quantitative monitoring of culture and the arts. The available data are of varying quality and focus largely on revenue and income, volume of activity, and cultural literacy survey results. One difficulty is the definition of the variables to be mea-sured. Another challenge arises because a significant part of cultural activity is in the non-monetary and/or informal economy sector. Qualita-tive differences in artistic outputs raise the problem of how to cope with variations in the quality and type of cultural work.

Garonna[11] points to three main challenges in the field of cultural sta-tistics and indicators. The first concerns the establishment of a complete system of cultural statistics and indicators that would be integrated and comprehensive. This means linking and networking many sources of data. Secondly, statistical information and transparency are needed in order to generate trust and "social capital". The third challenge concerns measurement issues. The difficulties with indicators arise from conceptual inadequacy. Unfortunately, theoretical concepts have not yet been translated into operational ones for standard statistical measurements of outputs, assets, and welfare.

No indicators can be expected to make sense without a clear conceptual framework. As stimulators of policy debate, they should be developed in such a way as to provide objective data on positive or negative trends. The following questions might be asked. What precisely is the reality to be measured? What is culture, and how can it be defined as an aspect of sustainable development of cities? How should we evaluate progress in culture and sustainable development of cities?

Cultural statistics/indicators in some selected countries

France created its Ministry of Culture over 40 years ago, and was also the first country to come up with a cultural policy and cultural strategy. According to Tolila,[12] the Ministry of Culture was conscious from the outset of the need for statistical data so that political action could be taken properly. In 1963 the Department of Statistical and Prospective Studies (DEP) was set up for this purpose. Since then DEP has been collecting cultural information to fulfil the needs of public policy in cultural customs, funding and employment in the cultural sector, etc. The experience with DEP shows that statistics are truly the most reliable agents for culture's development.

Canada has a national Cultural Statistics Program housed in Statistics Canada, the national statistical agency. The Cultural Statistics Program has traditionally attempted to respond to the information needs of those who identify themselves with the culture sector. Efforts have also been made in tracking government spending in culture, vetting the size and characteristics of the labour force in the sector, and gauging demand for cultural goods and services.

The Leadership Group on Cultural Statistics of the European Union (LEG) was set up by Eurostat and is led by the Italian National Institute of Statistics (Istat) with the participation of the statistical offices and ministries of culture of several European countries. LEG has made considerable efforts, achieving significant results in revising and updating the classification of cultural activities.

The Philippines has a development plan for culture and the arts. The objectives of cultural development are national unity as well as encouraging artistic expression and public appreciation and patronage of artistic and cultural activities. The plan envisages and encourages various activities in the spheres of cultural heritage, artistic expression, and cultural dissemination.

In the USA several states compile statistics on crimes, divorces, school dropouts, etc., and these are widely available on official state websites. The statistics are then termed "cultural indicators". William J. Bennett has been doing comprehensive work on these kinds of indicators.[13] In his *Index of Leading Cultural Indicators* he takes up six main themes of crime, family, education, youth behaviour, popular culture and religion, and civic participation. Clearly, terming these indicators as "cultural" is misleading; "social indicators" would be a more suitable terminology.

The political dimension of cultural indicators

The political implications of indicators in general and cultural indicators in particular are of utmost importance. The political agenda behind the construction of indicators needs to be addressed, as it is one critical factor influencing such an activity. One of the critical discussions in the Kanazawa Initiative was how to get people's (civil society's) involvement in contributing to sustainable development of cities/sustainable urbanization and its governance.

It was highlighted in the KR that cities need creative transformation in order to solve the problems they face. The challenge to cities will be to tap the wealth that has remained hidden in their rich cultures and their adaptive creativity. Though economic imperatives traditionally predominated development strategies, there is now recognition of the need to use culture to influence and guide development. While development has traditionally been conceived and carried out by local authorities, central governments, and private enterprises, it is the people's direct contribution, through participatory processes, to development that is the primary instrument to bring about culturally informed creative urban transformation and development. Strong partnerships that involve the equitable allocation of responsibilities to civil society and the private sector and seek their active participation and ownership of new initiatives, under the democratic and collective leadership of local authorities supported by central governments and NGOs representing different constituencies, hold the key to sustainability and sustainable city governance.

In summary, culture is difficult to grasp through an economic understanding. Cultural indicators have to be for communities and for civil society. Indicators will therefore have to be for different levels, i.e. national and community. International agencies have something at/for the national level, but there is nothing at the local level and that is where research needs to be done.

The work of international organizations on culture and development

In the past 10 years a big debate has been floated by international organizations on the use of culture as a tool of development. The main world institutions working on this theme are UNESCO and the World Bank.

UNESCO's cultural indicators of human development/well-being

UNESCO considers culture as both the context for development and the missing factor in policies for development.[14] UNESCO promoted the establishment of the World Commission on Culture and Development (WCCD) in December 1992. In 1995 the WCCD presented its well-known report, *Our Creative Diversity*, to the General Conference of UNESCO and the General Assembly of the United Nations.[15] In this report the commission recommended that an "annual Report on Culture and Development be published as an independent statement addressed to policy makers and other interested parties".

Following the recommendations of the WCCD, UNESCO in collaboration with the UN Research Institute for Social Development (UNRISD) started preparation for the publication of the *World Cultural Report*. A joint UNRISD-UNESCO series of occasional papers on culture and development marked the first step in facilitating and catalysing an international debate on culture and development. The main thrust of UNRISD-UNESCO research was a discussion on development of cultural indicators of human development or well-being.

Utilizing the background research of the UNRISD, UNESCO published its first *World Cultural Report* in 1998 with the main theme of "culture, creativity, and markets".[16] As this theme clearly indicates, it tried to explain how culture could be a tool for (sustainable) development. It is set in the new context of economic interdependence, global creativity, the changing role of states, and the rise of new communication and information technologies. The report discusses building cultural indicators and presents statistical tables and cultural indicators.

A good basis for cultural indicators is Amartya Sen's concept of "functionings" – the "doings" and "beings" that people value.[17] Cultural indicators are then defined as those indicators of human development which seek to measure intellectual, aesthetic, and political functionings, but not the physical functionings such as life expectancy, adequate nourishment, etc. These cultural indicators deal with culture defined in its broader sense.

For developing cultural indicators, UNESCO identified three areas of study: global ethics, cultural vitality, and cultural diversity. Recently UNESCO has identified three further issues, namely participation in creative activity, access to culture, and repositioning cultures (conviviality). It is important to note that the first three refer to development outcomes while the latter three refer to development as a process; the former relate to the vision of culture as the end of development and the latter to culture as the social basis of development.

To hammer its point home, UNESCO organized an intergovernmental conference on cultural policies for development in Stockholm in March–April 1998. This conference called on governments to "make more human and financial resources available for cultural development".

In the year 2000 UNESCO issued its second *World Cultural Report*.[18] The theme this time was "cultural diversity, conflict, and pluralism". This report discusses, among other things, new media and cultural knowledge, and national and international practices of measuring culture; it also presents statistical tables and cultural indicators. UNESCO made an attempt to broaden the country coverage and increase the subject depth of the indicators.

In essence, UNESCO has done a lot of good groundwork in initiating debate on the issue of culture and development and developing broad indicators for the same. But as UNESCO itself highlights, it is just a beginning; researchers can use this work as a starting point for more focused study of their own. They can enhance these indicators for their own specific objectives and regional interests.

The World Bank and economics of culture for sustainable development

The World Bank has a slightly different way of looking at the issue of culture and development. In his foreword to the World Bank's report *Culture and Development at the Millennium: The Challenge and the Response*, president Wolfensohn stated: "Along with protecting the heritage of the past we must foster and promote living culture in all its many forms. Recent economic analyses have consistently shown that this makes economic sense as well."[19] The same report highlights that the World Bank would like to see extensive research in the area of economic justification of investment in culture, recognizing its intrinsic value, its public goods character, and the positive externalities it brings. The Bank has identified environmental economics as a tool that could be refined and used for this purpose. It has also identified some research partners, like the Getty Conservation Institute, and would like to see more partnerships as well as independent research initiatives in this direction.

The September 1998 World Bank conference, Culture in Sustainable Development: Investing in Cultural and Natural Endowments, held in Washington and co-sponsored by UNESCO, was to assert the Bank's recognition of the tangible and intangible value of culture in sustainable development. Later, in October 1999, the government of Italy and the

World Bank, in cooperation with UNESCO, convened a conference in Florence, Italy, to address the importance of financing, resources, and the economics of culture in sustainable development.

According to the World Bank,[20] it is working on projects that advance financing for preserving and enhancing cultural assets within client countries as components of, or as stand-alone, development projects. The objective is to provide new opportunities for poor communities to grow out of poverty, encourage local-level development, conserve and generate revenues from existing physical assets, strengthen social capital, expand opportunities for education, and provide and/or improve attention to cultural aspects of infrastructure.

In the World Bank's view there is a critical need to focus on analysis and assessments that can relate culture and sustainable development. Culture in sustainable development is ultimately about the need to advance development in ways that allow human groups to live together better, without losing their identity and sense of community, and without betraying their heritage, while improving the quality of life.

Urban culture and urban indicators

Urban culture

Famously, Lewis Mumford did one of the first and most comprehensive studies on culture and cities.[21] He romanticized small, quiet, garden-like cities, reflecting his belief that modern-day crowded metropolises give rise to misery. He did not believe in the popular mass culture that is a hallmark of the major cities of the world. People have since been writing on different aspects of the culture of cities or culture in cities.

Frank Roost took up the issue of culture in cities by arguing that, in the name of culture and city-centre revitalization, multinationals (those in the entertainment/mass-culture business) are using city centres as extensions of their theme parks.[22] These multinationals are interested in international/global cities that receive millions of tourists, and have no respect for diversity or marginalized groups. Roost came up with detailed accounts of how this happened in New York's Times Square and Berlin's Potsdamer Platz.

Choe argues that while East Asian cities have been largely devoid of cultural identity, the collapse of socialism and rise of globalization have reinstated the search for cultural identity.[23] Choe talks of virtues and vices of Asian cities in a cultural sense, and believes that Asians will soon look for their own urban process. While Confucianism views urbanism as evil and nature as good, it has positive aspects like care for the elderly and an emphasis on virtue over wealth. While in Western cities diversity between neighbourhoods is greater than diversity within neighbourhoods, rich and poor are not separated in Asian cities. Cities may look like jungles, but there are advantages in the mix. Services are available close to living places, and mixed living, leisure, and work is energy conservative.

The arguments presented above indicate that large arrays of issues are discussed under the rubric of the culture of/in cities. This chapter is mostly concerned with the aspects of culture on which policy recommendations can be made.

Urban indicators

A number of institutions are currently engaged in development of urban indicators. Often the objective is to come up with a comparison of the quality of life in different cities. For instance, *Asiaweek* ranks Asian cities using a set of eight indicators and publishes an annual report entitled *The Best Cities in Asia*. These indicators make no mention of culture, and cannot help much in policy debates on how culture can help in the sustainability of cities.

The UN Centre for Human Settlements (HABITAT) compiles databases and indictors on cities under its Global Urban Observatory (GUO) programme.[24] The GUO was established in response to a decision of the UN Commission on Human Settlements, which called for a mechanism to monitor global progress in implementing the Habitat Agenda and monitor and evaluate global urban conditions and trends. The GUO focuses on building local capacity to select, collect, manage, and apply indicators and statistics in policy analysis. The flagship GUO products are urban indicators, statistics, and city profiles. Urban indicators are regularly collected in a sample of cities in 20 key areas at the city level. A very important product from the UNCHS is the report entitled *The State of the World's Cities, 2001.*[25] All these efforts by the UNCHS in compiling and synthesizing urban statistics and indicators are laudable, but they do not give much prominence to culture.

Another initiative in development of urban indicators is that of the Asian Development Bank. The ADB has done comprehensive background work to come up with a set of 13 comprehensive urban indicators as part of its efforts in compiling its *Cities Data Book.*[26] A study is being undertaken by the ADB in 18 cities, aimed at initiating the development of a source of useful, timely, and comparative information on urban conditions and trends in the Asia Pacific region. It is also aimed at establishing a network among cities for exchanging good practices. The World Bank also keeps what it calls urban indicators, but these are actually basic statistics on urbanization.[27]

As mentioned earlier, while these initiatives put forward by international organizations are valuable, there is a need to develop cultural indicators for communities and civil society through participatory mechanisms. There is a clear need to cater for the poor, minorities, women, the elderly, and other disadvantaged groups in formulating indicators. International organizations should encourage such locality-based initiatives in addition to developing indicators of their own.

Cultural indicators for sustainable urban development in Asia: Sketching a research agenda

Spurred by the increasing realization that culture matters to sustainable development, researchers across the world and from different organizations are exploring the ways in which socio-cultural activities have impacted on cities and, in turn, how contemporary urban development has impacted on social systems and cultural traditions. The work in this area is, however, very new, particularly in terms of urban or local area studies, and therefore there are few guidelines within which to formulate policies. A research agenda that can identify what local policy-makers need to know in terms of both the impact of culture on the local economy and the changes within the local economy and how they impact on the region's traditional culture would be extremely valuable, particularly in relation to sustainable development of cities or sustainable urbanization. This section attempts to develop a broad framework for this ambitious agenda.

Conceptual research in developing indicators

A general definition of indicators has been provided by the World Bank, as "performance measures that aggregate information into a usable form".[28] That is, indicators are more than mere measures of conditions: they are aggregates of statistical data that are usable for a particular client. With this definition, composites such as GDP or the HDI (Human Development Index) are considered indicators, while the number of newspapers per 1,000 people is merely statistics. Statistics are important, as they help researchers identify driving forces or outcomes. Indicators, on the other hand, are more useful to policy-makers as they are for evaluation purposes. The difference between the two types of statistical information is largely an issue of evaluative information and descriptive information.

Much of the indicator work has produced information for economists and social scientists, largely in the form of statistical data. In general, indicators should stimulate policy dialogue among a variety of actors and participants.[29] Researchers, including those from NGOs and other civil society institutions, can also employ indicators to understand conditions and trends, evaluate policies, and predict future scenarios given different governmental interventions. This perspective argues that the most effective role for indicator usage is among those groups attempting to evaluate policy: decision-makers, the media, and activists.

This distinction is important, as observers have noticed that a problem which has arisen from the use of indicators is the confusion related to their meaning. A variety of "sustainable" indicators have been constructed for cities, regions, and administrative units around the world.[30] Despite the enormous amount of data produced, this information has often been of limited use. This failure can be attributed to the failure of the indicator developers to distinguish between "statistics" and "indicators" and to articulate clearly the indicator client. The most important of the clients as stakeholders for indicators are communities and policy-makers.

In failing to understand this point, the sustainable indicator experiment has failed to demonstrate the positive impacts of new policies and practices, creating public confusion and weakening the sustainable development agenda.[31] Thus in the development of cultural indicators both civil society and public policy orientation efforts are needed.

Production and consumption of culture

In this section, discussion on "production of culture" and "consumption of culture" is mostly in line with the economic discourse. However, it should be highlighted that overemphasis on the economic discourse and quantification is only one aspect of the field of culture or cultural indicators. In this context, the discussion earlier referring to Fukuda-Parr[32] and Laya[33] is of relevance. In their writing both researchers have drawn attention to difficulties in quantifying culture and stressed the need for the indicators to be evaluating not mere statistics.

As discussed above, UNESCO identified six areas of focus for cultural indicators, namely global ethics, cultural vitality, cultural diversity, participation in creative activity, access to culture, and repositioning cultures (conviviality).[34] Global ethics is associated with a core set of international standards of human rights. Cultural vitality is a composite measure of various statistics, including literacy, media content, popular arts and crafts, preservation of cultural heritage, and others. Cultural diversity includes access, participation, and equity, with special attention to minorities.

Among the last three indicators, participation in creative activity includes measures on the equitable participation of all people in cultural expression. Access to culture includes the ability for all groups to participate in creative activities. Lastly, conviviality concerns measures of diversity and respect for cultures. Further, UNESCO urges that future work should identify whether these indicators can indeed be quantified.

While this work is important, there are obvious disagreements over the meaning of these indicators. Further, they seem to touch more upon political and social issues than upon economic ones. Rather than this distinction, however, the present authors argue that another possible way to divide cultural indicators is simply by separating the production of culture and the consumption of culture, both of which are important aspects of urban environments. The production of culture can include the work of cultural industries (fashion, music, art, dance, etc.) and the creation of public spaces and physical images of a city (production of images). Cultural consumption, on the other hand, connotes spending on cultural goods and services. These measurements are interrelated, as the growth of cultural consumption (of art, food, fashion, music, and tourism) fuels the city's symbolic economy and therefore enhances its visible ability to produce both symbols and space.[35]

In terms of the importance of cultural production, a city's image as a centre of cultural innovation includes an ample number and type of restaurants, *avant garde* performances, and architectural design. Those involved in producing these cultural assets compete for tourist dollars and financial investment. While the result is symbolic, there are definite material roots. For example, the symbolic economy recycles real estate as it does designer clothes. Visual display matters in American and European cities today, because the sites of delectation establish the identities of places. These spaces and their interrelated symbols must be produced.[36]

Further, it is important to track the trends in consumption and production of culture within cities. In the USA, for example, as cities and societies place greater emphasis on visualization, the Disney Company and art museums play more prominent roles in defining public culture (processes of negotiating images that are accepted by large numbers of people). Cultural industries and cultural institutions have stepped into the vacuum left by government, with considerable impact. Understanding these trends, therefore, is extremely important for urban managers.

Cities are also the centres of consumption. It is no secret that consumption levels are higher in urban areas than in rural ones. Urban lifestyles are significantly different from rural lifestyles. An important component to add to this type of indicator is not just the monetary value of cultural items consumed but also the public and non-monetarized cultural aspects of cities (historic buildings, parks, etc.) that are used by citizens. Cultural consumption indicators should also include these components.

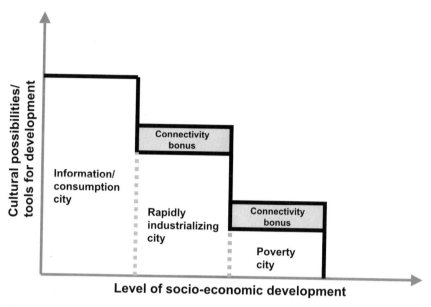

Figure 11.1 Cultural possibilities/tools for development of cities at different socio-economic development levels

Framework for research

No indicators can be expected to make sense without a clear conceptual framework within which they are put to effect. The "functional city system" concept, which describes a hierarchy of interdependent cities, although limited in scope, provides for an interesting way to make a distinction among the economic aspects of cities and a way in which to examine their different social and environmental conditions.[37]

This concept could be extended to include urban cultural consumption and production. The overarching perspective would include the idea that both income and levels of connectivity (i.e. articulation to the global socio-political and economy system) are related, in some form, to these processes. One broad hypothesis might be that both the number and types of cultural tools that can be used as urban development strategies increase with both income and connectivity to the regional city system (Figure 11.1).

One simple way of understanding the cultural production/consumption differences between cities within a region is to compare daily circulation of newspapers (Table 11.1[38]). As expected there are differences in both the numbers of newspapers in circulation per 1,000 people in the different countries within a region as well as differences in the annual rate of

Table 11.1 Cultural activities and trends: Newspaper statistics

	Newspaper circulation (per 1,000 people)	1980–1998 rate of annual change
Japan	577	0.1
South Korea	394	3.6
Hong Kong	714	0.5
Singapore	286	−0.3
Indonesia	15	2.6
Malaysia	59	3.8
Thailand	57	7.0
Philippines	41	2.7
China	34	0.3
Mexico	97	−1.3
Argentina	62	−4.5
Brazil	46	0.1

Source: UNESCO, 2000, Part Seven, Statistical tables and culture indicators, pp. 292–295.

change. Among these data, further interesting questions can be formulated. For example, why are there more newspapers per 1,000 people circulated in Hong Kong than in Japan, given that Hong Kong's per capita income is lower than that of Japan? Could this difference be related to the connectivity of Hong Kong? Further, there seem to be significant differences between both the numbers and the rates of change in Asian NIEs and those of South America. Why?

The thesis that cultural tools for development vary with income is supported by World Bank research[39] suggesting that culture could be a tool in development and by UNESCO[40] putting into place efforts at identifying "cultural indicators" of development. While attention to the importance of culture in development and the compilation of indicators is vital, the current work groups cities and applies indicators in such as way as to obscure the growing complexity and divergence of urban centres. It suggests that all cities, from both the North and the South, are growing more alike rather than, in the cultural context, hybridizing.

One of the reasons why we might expect these dynamics is that as cities increase in wealth the publics become more mobile and diverse, impacting on traditional institutions and making them less relevant as mechanisms of expressing identity. For example, in the USA the public sector was the traditional producer of large spaces in urban environments. Significant public spaces of the late-nineteenth and early-twentieth centuries – such as Central Park, the Broadway theatre district, and the top of the

Empire State Building – have now been joined by Disney World, Bryant Park, and the entertainment-based retail shops of Sony Plaza.[41]

A further important issue is the role of globalization in development and its impact on urban culture. As Kris Olds suggests, globalization flows, or increasing connectivity, are highly implicated in the production of spaces within a region.[42] For example, those in Vancouver and Shanghai have been generated by networks that span the Pacific Ocean. He views these networks as "extended social relations" that span distances and vary in density and connectivity, but are concentrated in cities. The importance of connectivity and flows of finance and expertise is an extremely important factor in producing urban space and therefore urban culture. Understanding these trends and bringing the globalization debate from "ethereal space" down to the urban pavement will require a thorough understanding of these extended social relations in the production of urban culture.

In terms of consumption, "few expressions of globalization are so visible, widespread and pervasive as the world proliferation of internationally traded consumer brands, the global ascendancy of popular cultural icons and artefacts, and the simultaneous communication of events by satellite broadcasts to hundreds of millions of people at a time on all continents".[43] The unparalleled transfer of cultural images and forms around the globe is perceived as one of the most important and sometimes disturbing aspects of contemporary development. Some have heralded this as the homogenization of the world under the auspices of American popular culture or Western consumerism in general.

These advocates and critics point out the media's role in the transference of a type of "culture" is not merely transitory or immediate, but that its impact signals the emergence of a new conjuncture, a transformation of the nature, form, and prospects of human communities.

While this is true – i.e. while there is no doubt that media, particularly those associated with the global conglomerates, are associated with changes in patterns of behaviour – the authors argue that the impact has not *only* been one of homogenization. Rather, and in cases such as Japan, a new form of culture has been generated, a cultural hybrid, which has been both the same as and different from its progenitor. Rather than simply signalling a movement towards convergence of culture and sameness, globalization also generates new forms and new distinct types of behaviour.

Understanding the dynamics between globalization and urban cultural consumption will require much new research. The authors argue that a better understanding of these issues requires both policy and research on cultural urban indicators.

Discussion and conclusions

The discussions in the workshops in the Culture in Sustainability of Cities project pointed to two different but not necessarily mutually exclusive discourses. While one group of researchers is very enthusiastic about economics of culture, use of culture as a tool for development, and standard methodologies and international research on this topic, the other group points to the importance of locality-based indicators, participation of communities and civil society in production of indicators, the qualitative nature of culture, and use of culture for the social ends of equality. These two discourses are both important, and are neither contradictory nor mutually exclusive. Both need further research.

The second discourse, locality/community-specific cultural indicator development, needs more attention, as very little work has been done in this direction yet. International organizations and national governments have already done a number of studies in the more standard, quantitative, and national/international-level indicator development discourse. The dearth of research on locality/community-based cultural indicator development has been reflected in this chapter as well, in which there seems to be an overemphasis on the international/national-level indicator development efforts. That has not been the intention of the authors, and is merely an outcome of the shortage of literature in the locality/community-based cultural indicator development field.

Culture is the fourth important dimension of sustainable development (the other three being economy, environment, and social sustainability). Before embarking on development of the indicators for culture in the sustainability of cities, it is important to note the ways in which cities, culture, and sustainability are linked in a situation of mega-trends of globalization, urbanization, deepening environmental crises, localization, and homogenization. In addition, a discussion is imminent on the threats and opportunities of the related issues of cultural economy, urban form and structure, environmental sustainability, and governance of urban cultural regimes. The major challenges in this endeavour are to distinguish between cultural sustainability and a culture of sustainability, the national and the local culture, and the high culture and the popular culture.

Extensive research work is being done in relating culture to development and the environment. The cultural indicators of development have been developed and are being refined. A number of institutions are working on indicators for urban areas, but most of these so-called urban indicators are actually statistics on various aspects of cities. All these are good efforts, but they are fragmented and limited when one considers the issue of measuring the role culture plays in sustainable development of cities. In order to develop cultural indicators of sustainable city development, a close look at the above efforts will have to be made in order to develop a conceptual framework.

The third part of this chapter attempted to sketch the broad outlines of a framework/research agenda for the cultural indicators to examine the sustainability of cities in the Asia Pacific. The argument suggests that indicators, as aggregate performance measures, should be targeted at either decision-makers or researchers. For city managers these indicators can be best used if they are divided into those that measure cultural production and those that measure cultural consumption. For researchers, when applying the concept of indicators to the measurement of urban sustainability, income and connectivity to the global system can provide an overarching framework within which cities can be categorized. In this schema, it is expected that the number and type of cultural tools or possibilities to use culture for sustainability change with these factors.

In the field of cultural indicators, UNESCO plays a very important role. At the national level, countries like France, Italy, and the Republic of Korea have interesting systems of cultural indicators. A different argument from that narrated above is that culture is difficult to grasp through an economic understanding. UNESCO has something at the national level, but there is nothing at the local level – and that is where research needs to be done.

Some general recommendations can be extracted from the debate on culture in sustainability of cities.

- There is a need to have more case studies in addition to the conceptual discussion.
- It is essential to have a dialogue with local people to identify the future research agenda.
- The idea of "self-cultivation" is fine, but "self-expression" should not be neglected. When it comes to culture, people should not be passive; they should actively participate.
- Culture and conservation are important, but one should remember that cities have to have diversity and provide their citizens with choices.
- There is a need to agree on a common definition of sustainability as the first step. The definition of sustainability coined by Scott Campbell of Rutgers University highlights the three elements of green cities, growing cities, and just cities.[44] Perhaps one can change this triangle into a rectangle by adding a fourth corner of cultural cities.
- The methodology of developing indicators is of utmost importance. One way can be to develop a multiple of indicators, although this path is prone to the problems of what to include and how much weight to give to each of the included elements.

Notes

1. Hall, Peter. 1998. *Cities in Civilization: Culture, Innovation and Urban Order*. London: Weidenfeld and Nicolson.
2. Sen, Amartya. 1999. *Development as Freedom*. New York: Alfred A. Knopf; Global Development Network. 2000. "Amartya Sen's keynote address on culture and development", paper presented at Beyond Economics: Second Annual GDN Conference, Tokyo, December.
3. Milton, K. 1996. *Environment and Cultural Theory: Exploring the Role of Anthropology in Environmental Discourse*. London: Routledge.
4. Fischer, F. and M. A. Hajer. 1999. *Living with Nature: Environmental Politics and Cultural Discourse*. Oxford: Oxford University Press.
5. Tylor, E. B. 1871. *Primitive Culture*. London: J. Murray. Quoted in Pattanaik, Prasanta K. 1997. "Cultural indicators of well-being: Some conceptual issues", Occasional Paper Series on Culture and Development, No. 2. Geneva and Paris: UNRISD/UNESCO.
6. UNESCO, 1998. *World Cultural Report: Culture, Creativity and Markets*. Paris: UNESCO.
7. Garrona, P. 2000. "Towards an international system of cultural statistics and indicators: The Italian experience", in *World Cultural Report: Cultural Diversity, Conflict and Pluralism*. Paris: UNESCO.
8. Tolila, P. 2000. "Culture and its statistics: A glance at French experience", in *World Cultural Report: Cultural Diversity, Conflict and Pluralism*. Paris: UNESCO.
9. Fukuda-Parr, S. 2000. "In search of indicators of culture and development: Review of progress and proposals for next steps", paper presented at Global Forum 2000: Second Global Forum on Human Development, Rio de Janeiro, Brazil, 9–10 October.
10. Laya, J. C. 2000. "The Philippines approach to cultural statistics", in *World Cultural Report: Cultural Diversity, Conflict and Pluralism*. Paris: UNESCO.
11. Garonna, note 7 above.
12. Tolila, note 8 above.
13. Bennett, William J. 1999. *The Index of Leading Cultural Indicators: American Society at the End of the 20th Century*. New York: Broadway Books.
14. UNESCO, note 6 above.
15. World Commission on Culture and Development. 1995. *Our Creative Diversity*. Paris: UNESCO.
16. UNESCO, note 6 above.
17. Sen, Amartya. 1998. "Culture, freedom and independence", in *World Cultural Report: Culture, Creativity and Markets*. Paris: UNESCO.
18. UNESCO. 2000. *World Cultural Report: Cultural Diversity, Conflict and Pluralism*. Paris: UNESCO.
19. World Bank. 1998. *Culture and Development at the Millennium: The Challenge and Response*. Washington, DC: World Bank.
20. World Bank. 2000. *Culture Counts: Financing, Resources, and the Economics of Culture in Sustainable Development*, proceedings of conference held in October 1999 in Florence, Italy. Washington, DC: World Bank.
21. Mumford, Lewis. 1997. *The Culture of Cities*. London: Routledge/Thoemmes Press.
22. Roost, Frank. 1998. "Recreating the city as entertainment center: The media industry's role in transforming Potsdamer Platz and Times Square", *Journal of Urban Technology*, Vol. 5, No. 3, pp. 1–21.
23. Choe, Sang-Chuel. 1998. "A search for a cultural paradigm of urbanization in East Asia", in Hemalata C. Dandekar (ed.) *City, Space and Globalization*. Ann Arbor, MI: College of Architecture and Urban Planning, University of Michigan.

24. UNCHS. 2001. *Global Urban Observatory and Statistics: Better Information for Better Cities*, available at www.unchs.org/guo/.
25. UNCHS. 2001. *The State of the World's Cities, 2001*. Nairobi: UNCHS.
26. ADB. 2000. *Cities Data Book: Urban Indicators for Managing Cities*, available at http://coldfusion.pacificgroup.com/adbcdb/index.cfm.
27. World Bank. 2001. *East Asia and the Pacific: Urban Indicators*, available at http://wbln0018.worldbank.org/External/Urban/UrbanDev.nsf/East+Asia+&+Pacific/C8A6D2CD108282FB85256937006B0664?OpenDocument.
28. J. O'Connor, cited in Rogers, P., K. Jalal, B. Lohani, G. Owens, C. Yu, C. Dufournaud, and J. Bi. 1997. *Measuring Environmental Quality in Asia*. Cambridge, MA: Harvard University/Asian Development Bank.
29. Fukuda-Parr, note 9 above.
30. For a discussion and examples of sustainable indicators for developing world cities see, for example, Sustainable Seattle. 1998. *Indicators of Sustainable Community*. Seattle: Sustainable Seattle; Ravetz, Joe. 2000. *Cityregion 2020: Integrated Planning for a Sustainable Environment*. London: Earthscan; Brugmann, Jeb. 1997. "Is there method in our measurement?", *Local Environment*, Vol. 2, No. 1, pp. 59–72; Rogers, P., K. Jalal, B. Lohani, G. Owens, C. Yu, C. Dufournaud, and J. Bi. 1997. *Measuring Environmental Quality in Asia*. Cambridge, MA: Harvard University/Asian Development Bank.
31. Brugmann, *ibid*.
32. Fukuda-Parr, note 9 above.
33. Laya, note 10 above.
34. UNESCO, note 6 above.
35. Zukin, Sharon. 1995. *Cultures of Cities*. Cambridge, MA: Blackwell Publishers.
36. *Ibid*.
37. Lo, Fu-Chen, and Peter J. Marcotullio. 2001. "Globalization, world city formation, the functional city system, and urban sustainability in the Asia-Pacific region", in Asfaw Kumssa and Terry G. McGee (eds) *Globalization and the New Regional Development; New Regional Development Paradigms; Vol. 1*. Westport, CT: Greenwood Press, pp. 91–128.
38. UNESCO, note 18 above, pp. 292–295.
39. World Bank, note 19 above; World Bank, note 20 above.
40. UNESCO, note 6 above; UNESCO, note 18 above.
41. Zukin, note 35 above.
42. Olds, Kris. 2001. *Globalization and Urban Change: Capital, Culture, and Pacific Rim Mega-projects*. Oxford: Oxford University Press.
43. Held, D., A. McGrew, D. Goldblatt, and J. Perraton. 1999. *Global Transformations: Politics, Economics and Culture*. Stanford: Stanford University Press, p. 327.
44. Campbell, Scott. 1996. "Green cities, growing cities, just cities? Urban planning and the contradictions of sustainable development", *Journal of the American Planning Association*, Vol. 62, No. 3, pp. 296–312.

12

Voices II

Byoung-E. Yang: Sustainable development indicators and cultural indicators

Byoung-E. Yang is a professor in the Graduate School of Environmental Studies, Seoul National University, South Korea.
Indicators are an essential component in the overall assessment of progress towards sustainable development. Desirable indicators are variables that summarize and make phenomena of interest perceptible, and quantify, measure, and communicate relevant information. The major functions of indicators are to assess conditions and trends, compare across places and situations, assess conditions and trends in relation to goals and targets, provide early warning information, and anticipate future conditions and trends.

There are other universal requirements or desirable properties of indicators.
- The values of the indicators must be measurable.
- Data must either be already available or should be obtainable.
- The methodology for data gathering, data processing, and construction of indicators must be clear, transparent, and standardized.
- Means for building and monitoring the indicators should be available.
- The indicators or sets of indicators should be cost-effective.
- Political acceptability at the appropriate level must be fostered. Indicators that are not acceptable by decision-makers are unlikely to influence decisions.

- Participation of, and support by, the public in the use of indicators is highly desirable.

Cultural indicators should be developed with consideration of the abovementioned functions and requirements. A set of cultural indictors can be devised within the conceptual framework of seven key dimensions: cultural identity, cultural diversity, participation in cultural activity, sustainable cultural policy, perceptions of sustainable development and a sustainable way of life, cultural creativity, and cultural heritage.

- *Cultural identity* can be measured with indicators such as traditional cultural activity, traditional folk festivals, local music, paintings, sculpture, and handicrafts, and voluntary organizations for cultural activities.
- *Cultural diversity* is of fundamental value. What is most conducive to human development is a flourishing, interactive diversity in which people of different cultures are able to communicate their values, beliefs, and traditions to one another in an atmosphere of mutual respect and learning. The indicators to measure cultural diversity include the means of communication, varieties of cultures, diversities of cultural spaces, linguistic abilities of the people, and literacy.
- *Participation in cultural activity.* There are three categories of people who engage in cultural activities: those who do it as a profession, e.g. painters, poets, and performances artists; those who engage in such activity only on a part-time basis, as a secondary source of income; and those who engage in cultural activity as leisure. Participation can thus be measured by indicators such as the number of people who engage in cultural activities by category and the rate of participation of various groups, including minority groups, in cultural activities.
- *Sustainable cultural policy.* Indicators to measure sustainable cultural policy are institutions that support cultural activities, policy that encourages creative cultural expressions, policy that accelerates participation in cultural activities, and policy that preserves the various cultural heritages.
- *Perceptions of sustainable development and a sustainable way of life* can be measured by indicators such as participation in waste recycling, population stabilization, preservation of natural environment, and use of solar energy.
- *Cultural creativity* is difficult to identify as a distinct measurable phenomenon. Much of the data that we need do not exist. The categories of cultural creativity indicators based on currently available data are expenditures on cultural products and activities; creation of new products; and number of people directly involved in creative activity.
- *Cultural heritage.* The most visible element of cultural heritage is the tangible heritage, comprising immovables such as monuments, build-

ings, archaeological sites, and historic complexes; natural elements such as trees, caves, lakes, and mountains; and movables, including artworks of every kind, objects of archaeological importance, and those representing skills. To these must be added the intangible heritage comprising intellectual heritage. The number of cultural assets protected by the law and expenditures on rehabilitation of cultural heritage items are potential indicators for measuring cultural heritage.

Sang-Chuel Choe: Cultural indicators for the sustainability of cities

Sang-Chuel Choe is professor of urban and regional planning in the Graduate School of Environmental Studies, Seoul National University, South Korea.

Table 12.1 UNESCO's cultural indicators of development

Indicators of cultural freedom	• Integrity of self • Non-discrimination • Freedom of thought and expression • Right of self-determination
Indicators of cultural creativity	• Expenditure on cultural products and activity (publication of books) • Creation of new products (consumption of cultural goods and services) • Number of people directly involved in creative activity (professional, part-time, amateur)
Indicators of cultural dialogue	• Literacy and educational attainment (literacy rate, mean years of schooling) • Means of communication (newspapers, telephone, TV, and computers) • Diversity and dialogue (linguistic abilities in another language)

Source: UNESCO. 1998. *World Culture Report: Culture, Creativity and Markets.* Paris: UNESCO.

Young-Chool Choi and Hyoung-Kee Kang: In search of cultural indicators for the city of Cheongju (Korea)

Young-Chool Choi and Hyoung-Kee Kang are on the staff of Chungbuk National University, South Korea.

Table 12.2 Suggested cultural welfare indicators (South Korea)

Categories	Subcategories	Indices
Cultural development supportive indicators	• Organization and manpower	• Government organization and officials
	• Funds and charities	• Total amount and annuity
	• Programme development	• International and local festivals
	• Facilities	• Performance/event/ exhibition space
	• Citizens' participation	• Membership enrolment, NGOs, performance troupes
Cultural finance indicators	• Budgetary appropriation	• Total amount, % of total budget
	• Cultural finance index	• Per capita cultural expenditure
Cultural welfare and infrastructure indicators	• Performance facilities	• Total number of seats per 1,000 persons
	• Movie theatres	• Same as above
	• Exhibition halls	• Total number of halls per 100,000 persons
	• Public libraries	• Same as above
	• Cultural facilities for youth	• Same as above
	• Local art institutions and conservatoires	• Total number

Source: Korea Cultural Policy Institute. 1996. *A Research on the Development of Regional Cultural Welfare Indicators.*

Cultural indicators

This research defines a cultural indicator as "a reference by which the level of local culture and local government cultural policies can be measured". In this research, cultural indicators include not only cultural resources (including facilities, events, industries, budgets, and people who contribute to culture and art) but also the quality of cultural life for citizens. In other words, the research evaluates cultural policies according to their success in developing local areas through culture over a given period of time. The cultural indicators constructed in this research consequently differ in some respects from the indicators used in other studies. However, in accordance with the selection criteria for "cultural local government of the year", the cultural indicators employed here still give greater weight to the resources, administration, budget, and policy of

Table 12.3 Sustainable urban development indicators (Seoul, Korea)

Categories	Subcategories	Indices
Environmental quality indicators	• Air • Water • Ecosystem	• SO_x, NO_x, O3, TSP • BOD (surface water, drinking water), sewerage discharge • Land cover, acidity of rainfall, number of species
Resource use efficiency indicators	• Resource use • Transportation • Living pattern	• Water, electricity, oil consumption, waste recycling • Trip generation, mass transportation usage, traffic accident rate, roadside noise • Population density, housing parks, building permits
Social equity indicators	• Culture • Welfare	• Registered cultural assets, number of libraries and cultural centres • Crime rate, female workforce participation, teacher/student ratio, number of medical doctors, welfare facilities

Source: LG Research Institute for Environment and Safety. 2001. "A study on the sustainable development indicators of Seoul" (in Korean).

local government than to the cultural activities and demands of local residents ...

The cultural indicators suggested in the research are explained as follows.

Area 1: Willingness to develop local culture

Sub-areas: Cultural development plan, finance, organization, and manpower.
Indicators:
• whether or not a cultural development plan exists
• contents of plan
• size of fund for local culture and art improvement
• ratio of cultural budget to total budget
• status of cultural administration within city organization
• composition of committee for local culture and art improvement, and its operation
• number of local government employees involved in cultural administration
• whether or not training programmes for local government employees involved in cultural administration exist.

Area 2: Distribution of local cultural spaces

Sub-areas: Performance and exhibition facilities, public libraries, cultural centres, cinemas.

Indicators:

- number of performance halls having more than 300 seats
- number of seats in all performance halls
- area of performance halls
- number of public performance halls
- number of private performance halls
- number of galleries
- number of possessions in each museum
- number of exhibition halls, both public and private
- number of libraries, and numbers of seats, books, and visitors in each library
- number of local cultural centres, their floor area, and seating capacity
- number of cinemas.

Area 3: Operation of local cultural facilities

Sub-areas: Management of local cultural centres, management of city centres.

Indicators:

- frequency of use of local cultural facilities
- organization, manpower, marketing, and finance of local cultural facilities
- number of cultural lectures
- cultural information service
- number of performances, and of participants in each performance.

Area 4: Events of culture and art, and festivals

Sub-areas: Performance events, exhibitions, literature events, culture and art festivals.

Indicators:

- number of performances conducted by the private sector
- number of international cultural exchange programmes
- number of local-government-supported performances
- finance composition
- marketing activities such as publicity or public relations by volunteers
- nature of festivals (international or national)
- extent of private sector's cooperation.

Area 5: Size of culture and art organizations and their activities

Sub-areas: Public culture and art organizations, private performance organizations.
Indicators:
• number of public performance organizations
• working days of public performance organizations
• number of private performance organizations.

Area 6: Cultural spaces projects

Sub-area: Street culture.
Indicators:
• existence or non-existence of street culture
• existence or non-existence of municipal ordinance regarding local street culture.

Area 7: Management of local culture information

Sub-areas: Guidance pamphlets for cultural events and festivals, culture maps, culture calendar, computer network for culture information.
Indicators:
• number and kind of guidance pamphlets and their contents
• existence or non-existence of culture map and culture calendar
• operation or non-operation of computer network for culture information.

Area 8: Education in culture, art, and society

Sub-areas: Local government, public culture and art centres, public libraries, public museums, local cultural centres.
Indicators:
• contents of programmes
• number of participants in programmes provided by, respectively, local government, public culture and art centres, public libraries, public museums, and local cultural centres.

Area 9: Local cultural industries

Sub-areas: Publishing, music disks, video sale and rental industries.
Indicator:
• number of business people engaged in publishing, music disks, and video sale and rental industries.

Area 10: Relationships between local enterprises and culture and art

Sub-areas: Seminars on the role of local enterprises for culture, support of local enterprises for culture and art.

Indicators:
- whether or not seminars take place
- amount of support for local cultural enterprises.

Cultural indicators employed to select "cultural local government of the year"

The indicators employed to select "cultural local government of the year" are as follows.

Area 1: Investment in culture

Sub-area: Budget for culture.
Indicator:
- ratio of cultural budget to total local government budget.

Area 2: Fundraising for cultural projects

Sub-areas: Local culture and art improvement fund.
Indicators:
- ratio of raised funds to total amount of budget
- amount of funds raised per head.

Area 3: Cultural facilities and spaces

Sub-areas: Public performance and exhibition facilities, public libraries.
Indicators:
- number of public performance facilities provided by local government and their seating capacity
- number of galleries and their seating capacity
- number of public libraries and population per library.

Area 4: Cultural and art events

Sub-areas: Local culture and art festivals, cultural and artistic events, cultural policy projects.
Indicators:
- new projects, marketing, and size of festivals
- economic impact of cultural and artistic events
- extent of public-private partnerships
- number of local-government-supported performances
- local-government-supported performances taking place in foreign countries
- novelty of festivals
- local government's positiveness.

Area 5: Cultural development plan

Sub-areas: Comprehensive cultural development plan, declaration of cultural improvement, fund establishment for improving local culture and art, status of cultural administration within city organization.
Indicators:
- existence or non-existence of cultural development plan
- publication of comprehensive report
- whether or not the cultural indicators are included in local government development indicators
- whether or not a fund for culture and art is established
- whether or not the municipal ordinance for fund-establishment is enacted
- whether or not the cultural administration organization has the status of a department.

Area 6: Management of local culture centre

Sub-areas: Performance and exhibition halls, days of performances and exhibitions, cultural education programmes.
Indicators:
- existence or non-existence of performance and exhibition halls
- days of performance and exhibitions
- number of programmes offered to local residents
- number of participants in performances and exhibitions.

Area 7: Effective management of public cultural facilities

Sub-areas: Use of public cultural facilities, degree of specialization within public cultural facilities.
Indicators:
- work rate of public culture facilities
- whether the posts involved in performances are dependent on public cultural facilities or not.

Area 8: Public culture and art organizations

Sub-areas: Size of the organization, activities of the organization.
Indicators:
- number of performance organizations
- annual working rate of performance organizations.

13

Conclusion

M. Nadarajah

A narrative ordering for "culture in sustainability of cities"

This volume captures but one voice among the many that inform us on urbanization in general and sustainable urbanization in particular. However, the voice articulated here is directed at addressing urban crisis in Asia through examining culture in sustainability of cities, an articulation which, while growing, is in the minority. Sustainable urbanization or sustainability of cities has been discussed largely from a techno-economic, market-driven point of view. While an exercise of this type – which includes contributions of experts from various disciplinary and subdisciplinary areas and numerous cultural contexts – will necessarily have contradictions, ruptures, and multilevel or directional possibilities, the volume as a whole offers a narrative that articulates the agenda of culture in sustainability of cities and elaborates the heart of the Kanazawa Initiative. The "narrative order" broadly includes the following elements.

- The dominant form of urbanization based on and influenced by the Euro-American experience is today leading to an urban crisis in Asia. The urbanization strategies are far too techno-economic and market-driven. Asians, and planet Earth, cannot sustain or survive on lifestyles and urban orientation established, for instance, by the Americans.
- A greater sense of the relationship between globalization, regionalization, and localization is needed in making sense of sustainability of cities.
- Alternative (Asian) forms of being and urbanization are required that work within the concerns of sustainability.

- A form of sustainable urbanization could be based on active local culture and take account of issues like cultural identity, value creation, population increase, popular citizen participation, and inequitable distribution.
- Coherent and sophisticated theoretical frameworks are needed that emphasize the primacy of culture, i.e. a cultural theory of sustainable urbanization and city development.
- Case studies of cities and their modes of engagement with culture will build a case for culture in the sustainability of cities, and also for its creative adaptation and/or development.
- Research enquiries into local cultures are needed, identifying the wisdom and alternatives they offer. This will include exploration of the modes of engagement with cultures within city-scapes.
- Cultural indicators are required that can both qualitatively and quantitatively "measure" culture in sustainability of cities (to realize the Kanazawa Initiative politically and practically).
- Comprehensive policy intervention is needed to realize an alternative, and more sustainable, urbanization – a policy that must necessarily incorporate cultural sensitivity, democratic governance, and citizen action.
- Revitalizing, planning, and/or building sustainable cities vibrant with local culture(s) is paramount.

These elements are important in that they offer a plausible "storyline", or a narrative ordering, sufficient to expand the imagination, concretize institutional structures, and broaden the support for the cause of culture in sustainability of cities. While narrative ordering is a necessary step to build a perspective,[1] there are certainly some key issues that need to be addressed in subsequent research, policy intervention, and development of the Kanazawa Initiative. These issues provide productive tensions and ruptures, and therefore the potential of multiple sustainable futures.

Some critical issues

Culture

The discussion on culture throughout this volume has not addressed the definition of culture adequately given the concern of many of the contributors. While it is given a working definition in the Kanazawa Initiative document, it is an unresolved issue. Thus, most of the contributors are working with only an implicit understanding of what culture is, not an explicitly agreed-upon definition of culture. Perhaps this is practical and useful to begin with, but it can gloss over a number of critical tensions.

First, the present debates on culture – with reference to ethno-cultures or cultures of locality based on such cultures – raise a query on an essentialist view of it. As the argument goes, there is no essence as such and culture is primarily creative, dynamic, and constantly changing. This needs to be resolved if we want to defend a culturally sensitive sustainable urbanization strategy that suggests the distinctiveness of local culture(s), based as it were on ethno-cultures (e.g. Japanese, Korean, Nepali, or "Malaysian"). In this context, it is also important to understand the numerous ways in which cities organize their mode of engagement with culture.

Second, there is a need for a proper understanding of cultural hybridity, to avoid its present misuse and make greater sense of the creativity and transactional capability of (local) cultures. Hybridity should not, for instance, become a rationale for a careless view of local cultures, which may result in the disappearance of cultural practices that could have been revitalized or reinvented.

Third, there is a need to have a proper understanding of the creativity and adaptability of cultures and their dynamic nature, or else the Kanazawa Initiative will be guilty of what Dix calls the "pacemaker view of culture", i.e. "preserving what is really dead, giving it an extended life".[2] Culture has the power to adapt and direct – it can play both passive and active roles.

Fourth, there is a need to be sensitive to internal differentiation of (local) cultures, suggesting heterogeneity. For instance, differential codes exist according to social classes or gender affiliation.[3] This needs to figure in the construction of culture; otherwise the definition of culture would essentially constitute a hegemonic intervention of the powerful, of the élite.

Fifth, as one read the various case studies, a position is implied that orients our understanding of the relationship between culture and sustainability against the backdrop of a social setting (a locality, a nation, etc.). The implied position is that a "cultural theory of sustainable urbanization" is possible and can be applicable only to closed societies – closed economically and culturally. Only in a situation of closedness can a cul-

Table 13.1 Relationship between culture, society, and sustainability

Culture in sustainability of cities	Supportive/achievable	Resistant/challenge
Type of city	Cultural (long history)	Functional (recent)
Nature of culture (in society)	Closed (opaque boundaries)	Open (porous)

ture be preserved and develop endogenously. If it is an open cultural space, globalization will overwhelm local culture(s) and present a serious obstacle to any effort to consolidate, strengthen, or reinvent and develop local culture(s) in the service of sustainable urbanization. With this possible trajectory, we need to re-examine the relationship between culture and sustainability of cities (Table 13.1).

Theoretical framework

A critical aspect of the contributions to this volume is a theoretical framework to offer culture primacy in order that sustainability of cities can be theoretically imagined and practically achieved. The first international conference called upon the paper contributors to present a theoretical framework that places culture as central to sustainability of cities. Some of these have been taken for consideration by Ratna Rana in Chapter 2, while others can be seen in the case studies by Sasaki, Choe, Nadarajah, and Tiwari. A close examination shows that the deliberations have a number of productive trajectories.

A coherent cultural theory of a sustainable city or of sustainable urbanization has yet to be articulated. But this volume certainly presents a rich crop of starting points and "sensitizing" concepts that can be developed to form a number of coherent cultural theories of a sustainable city or urbanization, depending on the ontological and epistemological positions held by researchers and their cultural locations. The sensitizing concepts offer a productive debate on the cultural theory of sustainable urbanization. They also indicate that the Kanazawa Initiative needs to be taken further in this direction, i.e. from sensitizing/descriptive conceptual schemes to analytical ones.[4]

Culture and economic growth

Throughout this volume there exists a tension between the need to protect and develop local culture and the need to make a city viable economically. In the case studies there are examples of what economic growth has done to local cultures and communities. Also, while there is clear recognition of the fact that some aspects of globalization are advantageous, there is also a fear that a purely market-driven, corporate globalization will seek to promote economic growth aggressively, supported by a "standardized" global culture, and in the process destroy or marginalize what is local.

The economic case for city formation and planning is so great that every other discourse is subordinated to it. Heritage, cultural practices, and local communities among others suffer as a result of the imperialist market and economic growth discourse. An important contribution to this issue is addressed by, for instance, David Throsby (see Chapter 3), who questions among others the notion of value and extends it in a fruitful direction that can help provide the primacy culture needs conceptually.

Cultural indicators

All exercises to promote a cultural perspective on a city and its sustainability would mean nothing if we do not make sense what "indicates" (local) culture and its contribution – present or potential – to sustainability. We certainly need indicators to promote culture in sustainability of cities. This is one of the recommendations of the Kanazawa Initiative. But how do we go about developing or applying cultural indicators? Are indicators going to be qualitative or quantitative, or both? Are they going to be standard methodologies for international comparison and development or are they going to be locality-based and specific (a distinction presented by Choe, Marcotullio, and Piracha in Chapter 11)? Are indicators going to be developed by experts or by the community in a locality, or both? Indicators are seen as neutral, objective tools for measurement. But are they? Or is their use really a reflection of a political stance?

Nadarajah has tried to provide this relationship in his proposal for a "sustainable enlightened localism". But the deliberations on cultural indicators really need far more attention than was possible here. The questions raised above need to be examined carefully. Further examination of some of the contributions to the third international conference (Chapter 12), an intense deliberation on cultural indicators, suggests many concerns and tensions. Tiwari, for instance, sensitizes us to the question of time in deciding indicators, since we cannot discuss sustainability nor achieve sustainable urbanization in the short term or in one generation. In fact, the temporal aspects of sustainability need greater attention. Another aspect is "inventorying". Creating an inventory of cultural "objects" (material, practical, and symbolic) in a city is one of the recommendations of the Kanazawa Initiative. While this has been implied in the lists of cultural indicators presented by a number of contributors, the active uses of inventorying and mapping[5] have not been addressed directly by them and need attention.

Governance

Another key issue is (democratic) governance, a critical recommendation of the Kanazawa Initiative and integral to the effort to articulate culture in sustainability of cities. The case studies have certainly brought to the fore the importance and effectiveness of citizens' action to protect local culture. While this is something addressed in all the case studies, a coherent theoretical stand is yet to be stated explicitly or developed. In addition, its implication for the process of urban policy formulation and its contribution to post-Euclidian planning strategy, like for instance what is referred to as radical (or empowerment) planning, need to be addressed.[6] This concern expands our understanding of sustainability from economic, environmental, and cultural sustainability to political sustainability. It also forces us to expand the sustainable modes of engagement with cultures within city-scapes.

Among the issues that need to be addressed in this context are those pertaining to the powerless and marginalized, for instance the poor, women, and the disabled. There is also a need to work out effective strategies for fruitful dialogue between stakeholders. While the issue of women has not really been addressed, the concerns for the poor in terms of governance have been addressed to some extent by Paul Taylor in Chapter 3. This concern highlights issues of equity and equality, today and tomorrow (intergenerational).

Certainly, governance requires further attention. All the issues in relation to governance will make this volume less attractive to policy-makers and politicians.

The above critical issues need to be addressed more elaborately to build a strong case for culture in sustainability of cities. They offer a number of analytical schemes to understand culture in sustainability of cities, research possibilities for urban studies and planning, and potential policy alternatives.

Conclusion: The Kanazawa Initiative and the future of (Asian) cities

We come to the end of our journey in understanding and addressing the urban crisis and unsustainable urbanization in Asia. What is the implication of the Kanazawa Initiative for the future of cities and/or urbanization? To make some sense of this, we have to place the text of the Kanazawa Resolutions in the universe of alternative texts presented in the Introduction, i.e. texts of resolutions such that passed in Calcutta in 1995 on architecture and cities, or the text on urban "cultural individuality" passed in Yokohama in 1996. What is the use of all these resolutions of concerned citizens? A careful examination shows the critical importance of local culture in these texts. They articulate, directly or indirectly, and quite consistently, culture in sustainability of cities. In this sense, the Kanazawa Initiative is not alone in its resolutions or recommendations. It is a part of an evolving concern for the importance and centrality of culture in social life *and* sustainability of cities. Perhaps it is with the Kanazawa Initiative that we see a consistent attempt to develop a *cultural theory of sustainable city/urbanization*, complete with a political praxis. But it is still a distant reality.

To conclude, the proposal of the Kanazawa Initiative for the sustainability of (Asian) cities can be concretized in terms of a definite theory and practice of sustainable urbanization. Such a theory would contribute to a better understanding of culture, its specificity, cultural identity, and endogenous notions of sustainability; globalization and its relationship to local cultural specificities and sustainability; the non-material culture and its relation to economic value creation; the nature of economic development (not growth); formulation of sensitive cultural indicators; and governance and policies for a sustainable mode of engagement with culture within cities. This would further mean the separate and integrated development of a theory of culture and localism; a theory of globalization; a theory of value (going beyond the economic and the material); a "theory of practice" of indicators development; and a "theory of practice" of governance. These would all contribute to building a "cultural theory of sustainable urbanization". This opens a massive intellectual enterprise with long-term practical implications. The full articulation and development of these areas would certainly constitute what may be called the "Kanazawa School of Sustainable Urbanization".

Notes

1. "Another way to put this [narrative thought] would be to say that human beings perceive any current action within a large temporal envelope, and within that envelope they perceive any given action, not as a response to the immediate circumstances or current mental state of an interlocutor or of oneself, but as part of an unfolding story." See Carrithers, Michael. 1992. *Why Humans Have Cultures: Explaining Anthropology and Social Diversity*. Oxford: Oxford University Press, p. 82.
2. Personal discussion with Professor Dix, Professor Emeritus, Liverpool University, UK, during the third international conference on Culture in Sustainability of Cities, held in Cheongju, South Korea, 2001.
3. This is something that came out quite strongly during the discussion on the paper presented by Professor Joyce Zemans of York University, Canada, entitled "The role of arts and culture in revitalizing urban centres". This was a presentation made during the first international conference on Culture in Sustainability of Cities, held in Kanazawa, Japan, 2000.
4. See Turner, Jonathan H. 1987. *The Structure of Sociological Theory*. Jaipur: Rawat Publications, pp. 21–28.
5. Suggested by Salma of Penang Heritage Trust. Mapping allows us to record not only what exists but where it exists and its status.
6. See Douglass, Mike and John Friedman (eds). 1998. *Cities for Citizens: Planning and the Rise of Civil Society in a Global Age*. Singapore: John Wiley & Sons.

Appendix I

List of selected organizations working on sustainable urbanization issues (with a web presence)

Mega-Cities Project
www.megacitiesproject.org/about.asp

The Mega-Cities Project is a transnational non-profit network of community, academic, government, business, and media leaders dedicated to sharing innovative solutions to urban problems. The aim is to make cities more socially just, ecologically sustainable, politically participatory, and economically vital. Its mission is to create new knowledge; to shorten the lag time between successful urban innovations and their implementation; and to prepare the next generation of urban leaders for the complex challenges ahead.

Organization of World Heritage Cities
www.ovpm.org/

Heritage is the memory and legacy of the world. It is also the key to tolerance and understanding between peoples. The Organization of World Heritage Cities was founded in September 1993 in Fez, Morocco. As of December 2001 the organization was made up of 198 cities, included on the UNESCO World Heritage List, in which there are inhabited sites. Of the member cities, seven are located in Africa, 35 in Latin America, 20 in Asia and the Pacific, 117 in Europe and North America, and 19 in the Arab states.

Kathmandu Valley Preservation Trust
www.asianart.com/kvpt/

The purpose of the Kathmandu Valley Preservation Trust is to safeguard the extraordinary and threatened architectural heritage of Nepal. With seven UNESCO World Heritage Sites in a tiny area, the Kathmandu Valley boasts a concentration of monuments and townscapes of an importance almost unmatched in the world. The unique syncretism of Hindu and Buddhist cultures which gave rise to these monuments survives today in Nepal, making their protection, repair, and maintenance as "living monuments" all the more compelling.

Asia and West Pacific Network for Urban Conservation
www.awpnuc.org/

The Asia and West Pacific Network for Urban Conservation was formed for the purpose of exchanging cultural information and technical expertise in the area of urban conservation. The member countries share much in common in terms of cultural heritage, building technology, and urban forms as well as contemporary urban problems and challenges. As a unique cultural organization that links East Asia, South Asia, South-East Asia, Australia, and the Pacific, the network plays a significant role in heritage conservation in the region. The members are predominantly urban conservation advocates, professionals, and practitioners who are actively involved in international networks and/or projects outside their home countries. The network was formed in 1991 at a seminar in Penang on Urban Conservation and Public Participation supported by the UN Centre for Regional Development of Nagoya, Japan. Since then, affiliated organizations have taken turns to host the annual symposium. At each symposium, two or more organizations "bid" to host the next symposium.

International Centre for Sustainable Cities
www.icsc.ca/about_icsc.html

Founded in 1993 as a partnership between three levels of government, the private sector, and civil society organizations, the ICSC is governed by a board of directors from private, public, and civil sectors. It also has an international panel of advisers comprised of eminent persons.

Supporting the Philippines Clean Cities Project
www.cleancities.net/

The project aims to reduce city resource supply and waste management costs; improve the economic efficiency of companies and households; create new jobs from recycling wastes; and improve the environment and public health.

The Bremen Initiative
www.bremen-initiative.de/index.html

The Bremen Initiative is a global platform for all local business-municipality partnership programmes and projects aiming at sustainable development. As a campaign, its goal is to affect awareness, influence legislation, and be a catalyst in developing new solutions based on best practices.

The Sustainable Cities Project
http://europa.eu.int/comm/environment/urban/home_en.htm

This project is the urban dimension of the European Community's Fifth Environmental Action Programme: "Towards Sustainability".

Asia-Pacific City Summit
www.city.fukuoka.jp/asiasummit/english/

The Asia Pacific region is drawing global attention for its remarkable economic growth. This rapid economic expansion has, however, also aggravated urban problems associated with a massive influx of new residents. In response to this social situation, the Asia-Pacific City Summit has been held every other year since 1994 as a forum where leaders of the Asia Pacific region can get together and exchange opinions in a candid manner. The purpose of the summit is to promote friendship and mutual cooperation in this region towards solution of urban problems and network-building for further development of Asian cities.

Sustainable Cities Research Institute
http://sustainable-cities.org.uk/

The Sustainable Cities Research Institute at Northumbria University aims to develop and promote sustainable approaches to urban living. It is an applied research and consultancy organization committed to informing policy-making and the public; enhancing community involvement; developing innovatory approaches in research and policy implementation; and delivering the principles of sustainable development through working closely with local, national, and international organizations.

Asian Network of Major Cities 21
www.chijihon.metro.tokyo.jp/asianet/indexe.htm

The major cities of Asia are close geographically, have close cooperative ties in economic relationships, and share many common cultural characteristics. The network aims to deepen these social and economic bonds and cooperation, and to make a significant contribution to the prosperity and development of Asia in the twenty-first century.

CityNet
www.citynet-ap.org/

CityNet's vision is to act as a focal point and facilitator in the Asia Pacific region. It puts this vision into practice by promoting the exchange of expertise and experiences among various stakeholders, particularly local authorities and NGOs, and expanding bilateral relationships into a multilateral network. CityNet aims for members' self-reliant development, and endeavours to make cities in the Asia Pacific region "people friendly": environmentally friendly, socially just, economically productive, participatorily managed, and culturally vibrant.

The Urban Governance Initiative (TUGI)
www.tugi.org/

Towns and cities within Asia and the Pacific are home to more than 1.3 billion people, with urban populations growing rapidly throughout the region. Cities attract economic investment and provide a wide range of jobs and means for a better quality of life. In fact, the high rate of urbanization has created a number of significant impacts on the development and management of cities. Among the challenges that cities face are the negotiation of competing demands for infrastructure, land scarcity and security of tenure, balancing employment and the pace of industrialization, transportation and its effect on the urban environment, employment and job creation, urban conflict and communal violence intensified by issues of access to resources, and the limited funds available to local governments to address these issues. This programme aims to meet the situational demands of towns and cities in the Asia Pacific region for innovative approaches, institutional reforms, and capacity-building efforts that support participatory, transparent, accountable, and equitable urban governance. The programme will do so by enhancing its role as a regional cooperation hub that promotes better urban governance through supporting institutional capacity-building, providing policy advice, training, and support services, enabling innovations on tools and methodologies for urban governance, and ensuring information-sharing and networking on all of the above within and between cities in Asia and the Pacific. The governing structure of the project includes a programme steering committee and an international advisory panel on urban governance. The project secretariat is based in Kuala Lumpur, Malaysia, and is supported by the principal project representative in UNDP Malaysia and the regional bureau for Asia and the Pacific.

The Penang Heritage Trust
www.pht.org.my/

The Penang Heritage Trust is a registered, tax-exempt, non-governmental organization based in Penang. Its objective is to promote the conservation of Penang's heritage, and to foster cultural education about the history and heritage of Penang.

The International Council for Local Environmental Initiatives
www.iclei.org/

The ICLEI is an international association of local governments implementing sustainable development. Its mission is to build and serve a worldwide movement of local governments to achieve tangible improvements in global environmental and sustainable development conditions through cumulative local actions.

UN-HABITAT
www.unhabitat.org/

The mission of UN-HABITAT is to promote sustainable urbanization through policy formulation, institutional reform, capacity-building, technical cooperation, and advocacy, and to monitor and improve the state of human settlements worldwide.

The Sustainable Cities Initiative: Putting the City at the Centre of Public-Private Infrastructure Investment
www.nrtee-trnee.ca/eng/programs/ArchivedPrograms/Sustainable_Cities/intropage.htm

Canada has the potential to be a world leader in the provision of environmentally sound infrastructure in developing countries. Few commercial, environmental, and political opportunities are as significant. Strengthening and developing Canada's competency in urban-based public-private infrastructure will lead to a global competitive advantage while contributing to a more sustainable planet.

The Learning for Sustainable Cities Project
www.dep.org.uk/cities/indexmain.htm

The Learning for Sustainable Cities project aimed to help young people explore the concept of sustainable cities and communities, and to identify opportunities for them to be involved in positive change. The project ran from January 2001 to December 2003. The project produced a common core of teaching resources and case studies which may be augmented to be more country-specific in each case. It also developed training programmes for teachers to be able to use the methodology and materials effectively. Materials and information are available on the website

Sustainable Seattle
www.sustainableseattle.org/

Founded in 1991, Sustainable Seattle is an award-winning non-profit organization dedicated to enhancing the long-term quality of life both locally and internationally. Sustainable Seattle achieves its mission through awareness – creating opportunities to learn about sustainable living principles and practices; assessment – developing tools to monitor community progress towards long-term sustainability; and action – fostering dialogue among diverse constituencies and their development of local models.

The Sustainable Penang Initiative
www.seri.com.my/spi/

The Sustainable Penang Initiative is organized by the Socio-economic and Environmental Research Institute in Penang. The project is supported by the Canadian International Development Agency through the Canada-ASEAN Governance Innovations Network Program, which is coordinated by the Institute on Governance. The Sustainable Penang Initiative is also supported by the UN Development Programme and the UN Economic and Social Commission for Asia and the Pacific.

Asian Coalition for Housing Rights
www.achr.net/

The Asian Coalition for Housing Rights is a regional network of grassroots community organizations, NGOs, and professionals actively involved with urban poor development processes in Asian cities.

Sustainable Cities Framework: Best Practices
www.blpnet.org/learning/learning06.htm

The framework has been designed to model the manner in which healthy and successful cities evolve. In stark contrast to many other projects on sustainable cities, which usually address those factors which inhibit the development of cities, the framework identifies those criteria which a city must achieve in order to be healthy, successful, and, ultimately, sustainable. For this framework, a city is taken to be the built environment and the resident population considered as a combined whole and functioning as a coherent (living) system (analogous to, yet different from, other living systems such as ecosystems and organisms).

Sustainable Cities: Environmentally Sustainable Urban Development
www.rec.org/REC/Programs/SustainableCities/

This information module is the result of the joint work of five leading organizations, located all across the world, in the field of sustainable development. The focus of this online module is urban sustainability, which is highlighted both from a general (global) and from a more focused (local, regional) context.

Local Sustainability: European Good Practice Information Service
http://www3.iclei.org/egpis/index.htm

The Local Sustainability project has been conceived and developed as a service of many partners, disseminating and making accessible the good practice experiences of European cities, towns, counties, and their associations, national and regional governments, research and educational institutions, and directorate generals of the European Commission.

The SUSTRAN Network
www.geocities.com/sustrannet/

The Sustainable Transport Action Network for Asia and the Pacific (the SUSTRAN Network) was launched in 1995 and has established contact with several hundred individuals and organizations around the region and beyond. So far, SUSTRAN has active participants in Malaysia, India, Pakistan, the Philippines, Korea, Japan, Australia, Singapore, Sri Lanka, and Thailand. It also has active partner organizations in North America, Europe, Latin America, and Africa.

Index